THE LIMITS *of*
INTERNATIONAL LAW

JACK L. GOLDSMITH

AND

ERIC A. POSNER

THE LIMITS *of* INTERNATIONAL LAW

OXFORD
UNIVERSITY PRESS

OXFORD
UNIVERSITY PRESS

Oxford New York
Auckland Bangkok Buenos Aires Cape Town Chennai
Dar es Salaam Delhi Hong Kong Istanbul Karachi Kolkata
Kuala Lumpur Madrid Melbourne Mexico City Mumbai Nairobi
São Paulo Shanghai Taipei Tokyo Toronto

Copyright © 2005 by Oxford University Press, Inc.

Published by Oxford University Press, Inc.
198 Madison Avenue, New York, New York 10016

www.oup.com

First issued as an Oxford University Press paperback, 2007

Oxford is a registered trademark of Oxford University Press

Library of Congress Cataloging-in-Publication Data
Goldsmith, Jack L.
The limits of international law / Jack L. Goldsmith, Eric A. Posner.
p. cm.

ISBN: 978-0-19-531417-5

1. International law—Philosophy. 2. International law—Moral and ethical aspects.
I. Posner, Eric A. II. Title.
KZ3160.P67A38 2005
341'.01—dc22   2004008190

Printed in the United States of America
on acid-free paper

FOR LESLIE AND EMLYN

CONTENTS

THE LIMITS *of*
INTERNATIONAL LAW

INTRODUCTION

International law has long been burdened with the charge that it is not really law. This misleading claim is premised on some undeniable but misunderstood facts about international law: that it lacks a centralized or effective legislature, executive, or judiciary; that it favors powerful over weak states; that it often simply mirrors extant international behavior; and that it is sometimes violated with impunity. International law scholarship, dominated for decades by an improbable combination of doctrinalism and idealism, has done little to account for these characteristics of international law. And it has made little progress in explaining how international law works in practice: how it originates and changes; how it affects behavior among very differently endowed states; when and why states act consistently with it; and why it plays such an important role in the rhetoric of international relations.

This book seeks to answer these and many other related questions. It seeks to explain how international law works by integrating the study of international law with the realities of international politics. Our theory gives pride of place to two elements of international politics usually neglected or discounted by international law scholars: state power and state interest. And it uses a methodological tool infrequently used in international law scholarship, rational choice theory, to analyze these factors. Put briefly, our theory is that international law emerges from states acting rationally to maximize their interests, given their perceptions of the interests of other states and the distribution of state power. We are not the first to invoke the idea of state interest to explain the rules of international law (Oppenheim 1912). But too often this idea is invoked in a vague and conclusory fashion. Our aim is to integrate the notion of state interest with simple rational choice models in order to

3

offer a comprehensive theory of international law. We also draw normative lessons from our analysis.

This introduction discusses the assumptions of our analysis, sketches our theory in very general terms, and locates our position among the various schools of international law and international relations scholarship.

Assumptions

The assumption that states act rationally to further their interests is not self-evident. All components of this assumption—that the state is the relevant agent, that a state has an identifiable interest, and that states act rationally to further these interests—are open to question. Nonetheless, we believe state-centered rational choice theory, used properly, is a valuable method for understanding international law. What follows is a brief discussion of our use of the concepts of state, state interest, and rationality. Further detail is provided in subsequent chapters.

State

The existence of a state depends on the psychology of its citizens. If all U.S. citizens stopped believing that the United States was a state, and instead began to believe that they were citizens of Indiana or Texas or some other subunit, then the United States would cease to exist and numerous new states would come into existence. (This is in effect what happened when the Soviet Union and Yugoslavia disintegrated in the 1990s.) Moreover, "the state" is an abstraction. Although the identity of the state is intuitively clear, the distinction between the state and the influences on it sometimes blurs. Relatedly, the state itself does not act except in a metaphorical sense. Individual leaders negotiate treaties and decide whether to comply with or breach them. Because the existence of a state and state action ultimately depend on individuals' beliefs and actions, one could reject the assumption that states have agency and insist that any theory about the behavior of states must have microfoundations in a theory of individual choice.

Despite these considerations, we give the state the starring role in our drama. The main reason for doing so is that international law addresses itself to states and, for the most part, not to individuals or other entities such as governments. NAFTA did not confer international legal obligations on President Clinton or the Clinton administration, but rather on the United States. The United States remains bound by these obligations until a future government withdraws the United States from the treaty. Moreover, although states are collectivities, they arrange themselves to act like agents, just as corporations do. Corporations are generally easier to understand than states. Corporate interests—to make money for the shareholders, subject to agency costs resulting from the delegation of authority to individuals who run the firm—are (usually) easier to identify. And it is easier to assume that corporate obligations remain in force despite the turnover of managers, directors, and shareholders because the obligations are enforced by domestic courts regardless of who happens to be in control of the corporation. Still, state interests can be identified (as we explain later), and through various domestic institutions states can and do maintain their corporate identity. Both ordinary language and history suggest that states have agency and thus can be said to make decisions and act on the basis of identifiable goals.

The placement of the state at the center of analysis necessarily limits the scope of analysis. We do not discuss, except in passing, difficult and important topics at the margins of international law about how states form and disintegrate. Many scholars view European Union integration as a possible model for a more ambitious public international law. Although the EU project is in some respects constituted by international law, we think it is more usefully viewed as an example of multistate unification akin to pre-twentieth-century unification efforts in the United States (which, during its Articles of Confederation period, was viewed by some as a federation governed by international law), Germany, and Italy. In any event, we offer no theory of state unification or integration. Nor (except briefly in chapter 4's analysis of human rights) do we have much to say about the opposite claim that the state is losing power downward to smaller state units (for example, the disintegration of the Soviet Union and the former Yugoslavia), to substate units (for example, the devolution movements throughout Europe), and to multinational corporations and transnational NGOs.

State Interest

By state interest, we mean the state's preferences about outcomes. State interests are not always easy to determine, because the state subsumes many institutions and individuals that obviously do not share identical preferences about outcomes. Nonetheless, a state—especially one with well-ordered political institutions—can make coherent decisions based upon identifiable preferences, or interests, and it is natural and common to explain state action on the international plane in terms of the primary goal or goals the state seeks to achieve.

We generally identify state interests in connection with particular legal regimes by looking, based on many types of evidence, to the preferences of the state's political leadership. This assumption is a simplification and is far from perfect. But it is parsimonious, and it is appropriate because a state's political leadership, influenced by numerous inputs, determines state actions related to international law. In some contexts in the book—for example, in explaining the significance of the ratification process for treaties, or in analyzing the domestic interest groups that affect a state's international trade policy—we will depart from this simplifying assumption and consider how various domestic groups and institutions influence the political leadership's decisions related to international law.

We avoid strong assumptions about the content of state interests and assume that they can vary by context. This distinguishes our work from the work of some realists, who assume that a state's interests are limited to security and (perhaps) wealth. Our relative agnosticism about the content of state interests has led some critics of our previous work to argue that we can adjust state interests as necessary to fit the conclusions we want to reach. It is true that the power of our explanations depends on the accuracy of our identification of state interests, and that state interests are in some contexts difficult to identify or controversial. We have tried to identify as objectively as possible state leaders' preferences in connection with particular legal regimes; we leave it to our critics to determine whether we have succeeded.

The concept of state interest used in this book must not be confused with the policy that promotes state welfare. In every state, certain individuals or groups—elites, corporations, the military, relatives of dictators—have disproportionate influence on leaders' conduct of state policy. Even in democratic states, the institutions that translate individual preferences into particular policies are always imperfect, potentially derailed by corruption, incompetence, or purposeful hurdles (like separation of powers), and sometimes captured by interest groups. The inevitable presence of these distorting mechanisms means that the "state interest" as we use the term is not necessarily, or even usually, the policy that would maximize the public good within the state. Any descriptive theory of international law must account for the agency slack of domestic politics, and we do so primarily by focusing on what leaders maximize (see Krasner 1999). One consequence of this approach is that our use of the term "state interest" is merely descriptive of leaders' perceived preferences and is morally neutral. To take an extreme example, when we analyze a leader's interest in committing human rights abuses, we refer only to what the leader perceives as the best policy to maintain his or her authority; we do not suggest that human rights abuses are ever morally justifiable.

Rational Choice

It is uncontroversial that state action on the international plane has a large instrumental component. Rational choice theory provides useful models for understanding instrumental behavior. Political scientists' use of rational choice tools has brought considerable insight to many aspects of international relations and has opened many fruitful research agendas. We believe rational choice can shed similar light on international law.

Our theory of international law assumes that states act rationally to maximize their interests. This assumption incorporates standard premises of rational choice theory: the preferences about outcomes embedded in the state interest are consistent, complete, and transitive. But we do not claim that the axioms of rational choice accurately represent the decision-making process of a "state" in all its complexity, or that rational choice theory can provide the basis for fine-grained predictions about international behavior. Rather, we use rational choice theory pragmatically as a tool to organize our ideas and intuitions and to clarify assumptions. No theory predicts all phenomena with perfect accuracy. And we do not deny that states sometimes act irrationally because their leaders make mistakes, because of institutional failures, and so forth. Our claim is only that our assumptions lead to better and more nuanced explanations of state behavior related to international law than other theories do.

There is a massive literature critical of rational choice theory, three components of which we address here. First, a word on collective rationality. As understood by economics, rationality is primarily an attribute of individuals, and even then only as an approximation. The term's application to collectivities such as corporations, governments, and states must be performed with care. For some of the reasons mentioned earlier, social choice theory casts doubt on the claim that collectivities can have coherent preferences. But if this critique were taken seriously, any explanation of international law, or, for that matter, even domestic law, would be suspect. Cycling is probably most prevalent not in states but in pre- or nonstates, that is, in aggregations of people who cannot develop stable institutions. As explained earlier, when states exist, people have adopted institutions that ensure that governments choose generally consistent policies over time—policies that at a broad level can be said to reflect the state's interest as we understand the term.

Another challenge to rational choice theory comes from cognitive psychologists, who have shown that individuals make cognitive errors, sometimes systematically. We do not deny the empirical claims of this literature. History is full of examples of state leaders committing errors while acting on the international stage, and it is conceivable that these errors can be traced to the standard list of cognitive biases (McDermott 1998). The problem is that the cognitive psychology literature has not yet produced a comprehensive theory of human (or state) behavior that can guide research in international law and relations (Levy 1997). Such a theory might well result in a more refined understanding of international law and relations. But it might not; individual cognitive errors might have few if any macro effects on international relations. Economic theory has produced valuable insights based on its simplifying assumptions of rationality. Our theory should be judged not on the ontological accuracy of its methodological assumptions, but on the extent to which it sheds light on problems of international law.

Finally, there is the constructivist challenge from international relations scholarship (Wendt 1999). To the extent that constructivism shares similarities with traditional international law scholarship—for example, its commitment to noninstrumental explanations of state behavior—we address its claims throughout the book. Here we address its critique of state preferences. As is usual (but not necessary) in rational choice theory, we take state interests at any particular time to be an unexplained given. Constructivists challenge this assumption. They seek to show that the preferences of individuals, and therefore state interests, can be influenced by international law and institutions. To the extent this is true, it would call into question our theory's ability to explain international law in terms of state interests. We doubt it is true to any important degree, but we cannot prove the point. On the other hand, constructivists have not shown that international law transforms individual and state interests. The relevant question is whether the endogenization of the state's interest, assuming it could be done in a coherent fashion, would lead to a more powerful understanding of how states behave with respect to international law. We provide our theory in the pages that follow, and we leave it to critics to decide whether constructivism provides a better theory of international law.

There is a related point. We consistently exclude one preference from the state's interest calculation: a preference for complying with international law. Some citizens, perhaps many, want their states to comply with international law, and leaders, especially in liberal democracies that tend to reflect citizen preferences, might act on this basis. A rational choice theory could incorporate this preference into the state's utility function. Nonetheless, for two reasons we reject a preference for complying with international law as a basis for state interests and state action on the international plane.

First, even on the assumption that citizens and leaders have a preference for international law compliance, preferences for this good must be compared to preferences for other goods. State preferences for compliance with international law will thus depend on what citizens and leaders are willing to pay in terms of the other things that they care about, such as security or economic growth. We think that citizens and leaders care about these latter goods more intensely than they do about international law compliance; that preferences for international law compliance tend to depend on whether such compliance will bring security, economic growth, and related goods; and that citizens and leaders are willing to forgo international law compliance when such compliance comes at the cost of these other goods. If we are correct about this—and the limited polling data are consistent with our view (Chicago Council on Foreign Relations 2002, 19)—compliance with international law will vary predictably with the price of other goods, the wealth of the state, and other relevant parameters.

Ultimately, the extent to which citizens and leaders have a preference for compliance with international law is an empirical question that we do not purport to resolve in this book. But there is a second, methodological reason why we exclude a preference for complying with international law from the state's interest calculation. It is unenlightening to explain international law compliance in terms of a preference for complying with international law. Such an assumption says nothing interesting about when and why states act consistently with international law and provides no basis for understanding variation in, and violation of, international law. A successful theory of international law must show why states comply with international law rather than assuming that they have a preference for doing so.

A related methodological point is that a theory's explanatory power depends, at least in part, on its falsifiability. Some critics of our earlier work have claimed that our theory is not falsifiable. We disagree. While we do not make fine-grained predictions, throughout the book we make claims—for example, that international law does not shift power or wealth from powerful to weak states, and that states cannot solve large-scale collective action problems through customary international law—that empirical evidence could contradict. These predictive claims are not as precise as, say, those made by sophisticated economic analyses. But that level of methodological sophistication is not our aim here. Our aim is, rather, to give a simple but plausible descriptive account for the various features of international law (including many that have been ignored) in terms of something other than a state's propensity to comply with international law.

Theory

With these preliminaries in mind, we now provide a skeleton of our theory of international law. We put flesh on these bones in subsequent chapters.

Consider two states, A and B. At time 1, the two states have certain capacities and interests. The capacities include military forces, economic institutions, natural resources, and human capital. The interests are determined by leaders who take account in some way of the preferences of citizens and groups. At time 1, the states divide available resources in some stable fashion. They divide territory along a border, and they divide collective goods such as airwaves, fisheries, and mineral deposits in ways that might or might not prevent overexploitation.

At time 2, as a result of a shock, the time 1 status quo becomes unstable. In the simplest case, A's power increases (for any number of reasons) relative to B's, and state A demands a greater share of resources from state B. In the past, this demand might have been for territory or tribute. In the modern world, A will often demand something less tangible, such as access to markets, greater protection for intellectual property, military assistance, base rights, foreign aid, or diplomatic assistance. State A might also threaten to close its own markets, violate B's intellectual property rights, reduce the military assistance or foreign aid it had been rendering B, cut back on diplomatic assistance to B, and so forth. Any of these might happen because A had provided these benefits to B in return for benefits that it no longer wants or needs.

If A and B had perfect information about each other (if, that is, each knew the other's interests and capacities completely), and if transaction costs were zero, their relations would adjust smoothly and quickly to the shock, and at time 3 there would be a new division of resources: a new border, new diplomatic activities, a new level of military assistance in one direction or the other, a new level of foreign aid, or new trade patterns. In the real world of transaction costs and imperfect information, their adjustments will be slow and suboptimal. There might be significant conflict, including war, as the states learn about one another and bluff and bargain over the new order, exaggerating their strengths and concealing their weaknesses. Eventually, the situation between the two states will stabilize.

The relations between the two states at any time can be described as a set of rules. But here care must be used, for several very different things might be going on. Consider a border between A and B. The border is a rule that delineates the territory of each state, where it is understood that neither state can send individuals or objects across the border without the permission of the other state. Territorial borders are generally thought to be constituted and governed by international law. Assume that states A and B respect the border. Our theory of international law posits that one of four things might explain this behavioral regularity.

First, it is possible that neither of the two states has an interest in projecting power across the border. State A does not seek resources in state B's territory and would not seek them even if B were unable to resist encroachment. A is barely able to control its own territory and wants to have nothing to do with B's. State B has the same attitude to state A. When a pattern of behavior—here, not violating the border—results from each state acting in its self-interest without any regard to the action of the other state, we call it a *coincidence of interest.*

There is a second possible explanation for the border. State A might be indifferent between one border and another border deeper in what is now state B's territory. The additional territory might benefit state A, but it would also bring with it costs. The main concern for the states is to clarify the point at which state A's control ends and state B's begins, so that the two states can plan accordingly and avoid conflict. State B has the same set of interests and capacities. Once the two states settle on a border, neither violates the border because if either did, conflict would result. This state of affairs is called *coordination.* In cases of coordination, states receive higher payoffs if they engage in identical or symmetrical actions than if they do not. A classic coordination game from domestic life is driving: all parties do better if they coordinate on driving on the right, or driving on the left, than if they choose different actions.

A third possible explanation for the border is *cooperation.* States A and B would each benefit by having some of the other's territory, all things being equal. But each knows that if it tried to obtain more territory, the other state would resist, and a costly breakdown in relations, and possibly war, would result, making both states worse off. Thus, the states agree (implicitly or explicitly) on a border that reflects their interests and capacities, and the border is maintained by mutual threats to retaliate if the other state violates the border. In such cases of cooperation, states reciprocally refrain from activities (here, invasion or incursion) that would otherwise be in their immediate self-interest in order to reap larger medium- or long-term benefits.

The final possibility is *coercion.* State A is satisfied with the existing border, but state B seeks to expand its territory at A's expense. If B is sufficiently powerful, it can dictate the new border. Because state A is weaker and state B benefits from the extra territory whether or not state A resists, state A yields (either before or after military conflict) and a new border is created. Other states might or might not object: they also might benefit from the new border or be powerless to resist it. Coercion results when a powerful state (or coalition of states with convergent interests) forces weaker states to engage in acts that are contrary to their interests (defined independently of the coercion).

This book argues that some combination of these four models explains the state behaviors associated with international law. These models do not exhaust the possibilities of international interaction. But they provide a simple and useful framework for evaluating a range of international legal regimes. As we explain throughout the book, each model has different characteristics that make it more or less stable and effective, depending on the circumstances. Taken together, however, the four models offer a different explanation for the state behaviors associated with international law than the explanation usually offered in international law scholarship. The usual view is that international law is a check on state interests, causing a state to behave in a way contrary to its interests. In our view, the causal relationship between international law and state interests runs in the opposite direction. International law emerges from states' pursuit of self-interested policies on the international stage. International law is, in this sense, *endogenous* to state interests. It is not a check on state self-interest; it is a product of state self-interest. This does not mean, as critics of our earlier work have suggested, that we think that international law is irrelevant or unimportant or in some sense unreal. As we will explain, international law, especially treaties, can play an important role in helping states achieve mutually beneficial outcomes by clarifying what counts as cooperation or coordination in interstate interactions. But under our theory, international law does not pull states toward compliance contrary to their interests, and the possibilities for what international law can achieve are limited by the configurations of state interests and the distribution of state power.

The bulk of the book is devoted to applying this framework to various regimes of international law. The argument unfolds in three parts. Part 1 analyzes customary international law. We are skeptical of the traditional claim that customary international law reflects universal behavioral regularities. And, we argue, the actual patterns of state behavior associated with customary international law reflect either coincidence of interest or *bilateral* cooperation, coercion, or coordination. We bolster these arguments with case studies of four areas of customary international law.

Part 2 analyzes treaties, the second form of international law. The main puzzle here is: Why do states use treaties instead of customary international law? We offer two general answers. First, treaties—which result from self-conscious negotiation and bargaining, and which are almost always embodied in written form that reduces ambiguity—are more effective than customary international law at specifying what counts as cooperation or coordination. Second, the institutions associated with treaties, including domestic ratification processes and the default rules of treaty interpretation, can provide valuable information that improves cooperation and coordination between states. In addition, part 2 explains how nonlegal agreements relate to legalized agreements; what multilateral treaties accomplish and why their efficacy tends to depend on the logic of bilateral monitoring and enforcement; and the relative roles of retaliation and reputation in treaty compliance. We support our arguments with case studies of international human rights treaties and trade treaties.

Part 3 addresses several external challenges to our theory of international law. Some scholars claim that the pervasive use of international legal rhetoric demonstrates the efficacy of international law that cannot be explained in instrumental terms. We argue that this claim is wrong and show why it would be rational for states to talk to each other in the language of international law even if they were not motivated by a desire to comply with it. Another challenge to our thesis comes from those who claim that, even if states comply with international law only when it is in their interest to do so, they nonetheless have a moral obligation to comply with it against their interest. We argue, to the contrary, that states have no such moral obligation. We also address a related challenge from cosmopolitan theory, which argues that states have a duty in crafting international law to act on the basis of global rather than state welfare. Such duties cannot, we think, be reconciled with cosmopolitans' commitment to liberal democracy, a form of government that is designed to ensure that foreign policy, including engagement with international law, serves the interests of citizens, and that almost always produces a self-interested foreign policy.

International Law Scholarship

Most scholarship on international law has been written by law professors. Although these scholars have proposed many different theories, most of them share an assumption that we reject: that states comply with international law for noninstrumental reasons. Doctrinally, this assumption is reflected in the international law rules of *opinio juris* (the "sense of legal obligation" that makes customary international law binding) and *pacta sunt servanda* (the rule that treaties must be obeyed). Theoretically, the assumption is expressed in various ways, but they all reduce to the idea that a state is drawn toward compliance with international law because compliance is the morally right or legitimate thing to do. Mainstream international law scholarship does not deny that states have interests and try to pursue them. But it claims that international law puts a significant brake on the pursuit of these interests.

Many international law scholars do not question the assumption that states follow international law for noninstrumental reasons. For them, the premise is enough to justify their research agenda, which is that of doctrinalism: identifying the "black letter law" of international law in any given domain, independent of actual behaviors. Other scholars seek to explain the conditions under which international law "exerts a pull toward compliance," that is, exercises normative influence on state behavior (Franck 1990, 24–25). Brierly (1963) says states obey international law because they have consented to it. Franck (1990, 24) says they do so because international law rules came into existence through a legitimate (transparent, fair, inclusive) process. Koh (1997, 2603) says that international law becomes part of a state's "internal value set." This theorizing often fuels, and is overtaken by, normative speculation about improving international law.

In our view, this research agenda is unfruitful. The assumption of a tendency toward compliance has little if any explanatory value. The narrower view—that states are pulled to comply with international law because it reflects morally valid procedures, or consent, or internal value sets—is not supported by the evidence, as we show in subsequent chapters. Noninstrumental accounts of international law also mask many different reasons why states act consistently with international law, and result in an impoverished theory of compliance. Finally, the theories do not provide good explanations for the many important features of international law unrelated to compliance, including variation and change in international law.

There is a more sophisticated international law literature in the international relations subfield of political science. The methodological commitments of international relations theorists in political science are different from those of most international lawyers. Positive analysis is the hallmark of international relations literature; international relations scholars seek primarily to explain, rather than prescribe, international behaviors. For this reason, among others, international relations scholars take theoretical, methodological, and empirical issues more seriously than international lawyers do, and they draw more generously on economics, sociology, and history.

Until recently, international relations theorists did not study international law as a category apart from the institutions embodied by international law. The dominant American theory of international relations—realism—treated international law as inconsequential or as outside its research agenda (Mearsheimer 2001; Waltz 1979). (A major exception is Hans Morgenthau 1948a.) Other political science theories, such as the English School's theory of international society (Bull 1977), were more optimistic about international cooperation but did not focus on international law as a distinctive institution.

A different strand of international relations theory—institutionalism—uses the tools of rational choice theory to understand international relations. This tradition dates back at least as far as Schelling's (1963) work. Institutionalism's major contribution was to show how states could productively cooperate in the absence of a centralized lawmaker or law enforcer (Keohane 1984; Snidal 1985; Oye 1986). The object of institutionalist analysis was the "regime," a term defined in the literature as "sets of implicit or explicit principles, norms, rules, and decision-making procedures around which actors' expectations converge in a given area of international relations" (Krasner 1983, 2). The original institutionalism movement did not focus on international law as a category distinct from international politics.

In recent years, political scientists have begun to study international law in its own right (Goldstein et al. 2000). A related development is a growing interest among some international law scholars in the tools of international relations theory (Slaughter, Tulumello, and Wood 1998; Burley 1993; Setear 1996; Abbott 1989). There is also a small but growing rational choice literature in international law being developed by economists and lawyers influenced by economics (Dunhoff and Trachtman 1999; Setear 1996; Sykes 1991; Guzman 2002a; Stephan 1996; Posner 2003; Sykes 2004 is a survey).

Our approach falls closer to the political science international relations tradition, and in particular to institutionalism, than to the mainstream international law scholarship tradition. But, as will become clear, our views differ from international relations institutionalism, from the newer international relations "legalization" movement, and from other rational choice approaches to international law in several respects. Ours is a comprehensive analysis of international law. The greatest overlap between extant international relations and rational choice international law scholarship and our book comes in part 2, on treaties. But international relations scholarship has ignored customary international law (the topic of part 1) altogether, and it has said relatively little about the normative issues discussed in part 3. In addition, we are more skeptical about the role of international law in advancing international cooperation than most (but not all) international relations institutionalists and most rational choice–minded lawyers. And our methodological assumptions are more consistently instrumental than those found in this literature, which frequently mixes instrumental and noninstrumental explanations (Abbott et al. 2000). Finally, unlike the political scientists, whose focus remains the realm of international politics, we are interested primarily in the nuts and bolts of international law.

PART 1 ⚏

CUSTOMARY
INTERNATIONAL LAW

Political scientists and some international lawyers maintain that the late twentieth century witnessed two novel and related trends: the "legalization" of international relations (Goldstein et al. 2000, 386) and the rise of multilateral institutions (Abbott and Snidal 1998; Koremenos et al. 2001). This view assumes that international law consists primarily of formal international organizations made by multilateral treaty, such as the United Nations, the World Trade Organization, the Law of the Sea regime, and the European Union.

This view betrays a lack of historical perspective. For there is another form of international law besides treaties: customary international law. Customary international law is usually defined as the customary practices that states follow from a sense of legal obligation. It has the same legal force under international law as treaties. Customary international law has always regulated important elements of international relations and has always been multilateral in the sense of purporting to bind all or almost all states.

Despite the rise of multilateral treaties and organizations, customary international law remains an important component of international law and an important object of study for international lawyers. Many of the foundational principles of international law (such as territorial sovereignty, sovereign equality, and even, at bottom, *pacta sunt servanda*) are still governed by customary international law. Even in areas where treaties have proliferated (such as the laws of treaty interpretation, the laws of war, and human rights), customary international law plays an important role. It provides interpretive presumptions, it extends treaty norms to nonsignatories, and it influences efforts to expand treaty regimes. For these reasons, no comprehensive theory of international law can ignore it.

And yet, we have a poor understanding of customary international law. Political scientists have said practically nothing about customary international law, much less about how it relates to treaties. (Indeed, a flaw in political science legalization theories is the implicit assumption that international law is coextensive with treaties.) International lawyers, by contrast, have proposed many theories about customary international law. But as we explain in the pages that follow, these theories are acknowledged failures.

CHAPTER 1

A THEORY OF CUSTOMARY
INTERNATIONAL LAW

Customary international law is typically defined as the general and consistent practices of states that they follow from a sense of legal obligation (*Restatement* 1987, § 102[2]). This definition contains two elements: there must be a widespread and uniform practice of states, and states must engage in the practice out of a sense of legal obligation. This second requirement, often referred to as *opinio juris*, is the central concept of customary international law. Because *opinio juris* refers to the reason a state acts in accordance with a behavioral regularity, it is often described as the "psychological" element of customary international law (Brownlie 1960, 7–9; D'Amato 1971, 47–55, 66–73). *Opinio juris* is what distinguishes a state act done out of interest or comity from one that a state performs because it is required to do so by law. Courts and scholars say that a long-standing practice among states "ripens" or "hardens" into customary international law when it becomes accepted by states as legally binding (*The Paquete Habana* 1900, 686).

This standard account of customary international law suffers from well-known difficulties (D'Amato 1971; Fidler 1996). There is little agreement about what type of state action counts as state practice. Policy statements, legislation, and diplomatic correspondence are the least controversial sources. Treaties, especially multilateral treaties, but also bilateral ones, are often used as evidence of customary international law, but in an inconsistent way. The writings of jurists are a common but tendentious source of customary international law. Even more controversially, United Nations General Assembly resolutions and other nonbinding statements and resolutions by multilateral bodies are often viewed as evidence of customary international law. Those who study and use customary international law—courts, arbitrators, diplomats, politicians, scholars—invoke these sources selectively.

There is similar disagreement about how widespread and uniform state practice must be. In theory, the practice is supposed to be general in the sense that all or almost all of the states of the world engage in it. But it is practically impossible to determine whether 190 or so states of the world engage in a particular practice. Thus, customary international law is usually based on a highly selective survey of state practice that includes only major powers and interested states (Wolfke 1964, 81–82; Charney 1993, 537). Increasingly, courts and scholars ignore the state practice requirement altogether (Bradley and Goldsmith 1997b, 839–40). For example, they refer to a customary international law prohibition on torture at the same time that they acknowledge that many states of the world torture their citizens (*Filartiga* 1980, 882). It is thus unclear when, and to what degree, the state practice requirement must be satisfied.

The *opinio juris* requirement raises more problems. Courts and scholars sometimes infer it from the existence of a widespread behavioral regularity (Brownlie 1960, 7). But this makes *opinio juris* redundant with the state practice requirement, which, by assumption, is insufficient by itself to establish customary international law. To avoid this problem, courts and scholars sometimes require independent evidence of *opinio juris,* such as a statement by a high-level government official, ratification of a treaty that contains a norm similar to the customary international law in question, or an attitude of approval toward a General Assembly resolution (Brownlie 1960, 7–9). The appropriate conditions for the use of such evidence are unsettled.

In addition, there is no convincing explanation of the process by which a voluntary behavioral regularity transforms itself into a binding legal obligation. *Opinio juris* is described as the psychological component of customary international law because it refers to an attitude that states have toward a behavioral regularity. The idea of *opinio juris* is mysterious because the legal obligation is created by a state's belief in the existence of the legal obligation. *Opinio juris* is really a conclusion about a practice's status as international law; it does not explain *how* a widespread and uniform practice becomes law.

These conceptual problems with customary international law are the subject of an enormous literature that endlessly debates definitional issues, the relative significance of practice and *opinio juris,* and other conceptual matters internal to the traditional account. Although our theory has implications for many of these issues, they are not the focus of the analysis. Instead, we focus on two sets of issues that are rarely discussed in the international law literature but that are fundamental to understanding customary international law.

First are the unarticulated assumptions that underlie the traditional conception of customary international law. Despite the many disagreements within the traditional paradigm, the parties to this debate assume that customary international law is *unitary, universal,* and *exogenous.* Customary international law is unitary in the sense that all the behaviors it describes have an identical logical form. Customary international law is universal in the sense that its obligations bind all states except those that "persistently object" during the development of the customary international law rule (*Restatement* 1987, § 102, comment d). And customary international law is exogenous in the sense that it represents an external force that influences state actions. Our theory of customary international law challenges each of these assumptions.

The second set of issues concerns the traditional paradigm's inability to explain international behavior. The traditional paradigm does not explain how customary international law emerges from disorder, or how it changes over time (see D'Amato 1971, 4). For example, as we discuss in chapter 2, the customary international law rule governing a state's jurisdiction over its coastal seas changed from a cannon-shot rule to a three-mile rule to a twelve-mile rule with many qualifications. On the traditional account, the process of change is illegal, because some states must initiate a departure from the prior regularity that they were bound to follow as a matter of law. More broadly, the traditional account cannot explain why customary international law changes in response to shifts in the relative power of states, advances in technology, and other exogenous forces.

The traditional account also cannot explain the fact that states frequently change their views about the content of customary international law, often during very short periods of time. Nor, relatedly, can it explain why domestic courts and politicians almost always apply a conception of customary international law that is in the state's best interest. In addition, it does not explain why states sometimes say that they will abide by particular customary international laws and then violate their promise.

Finally, the traditional account does not explain why states comply with customary international law. Some believe that *opinio juris* is the reason for compliance, but the "sense of legal obligation" is what requires explaining and cannot itself be the explanation. Others say that consent is the reason, but as many have noted, this position begs the question of why states abide by the international rules to which they have consented (Brierly 1963, 51–54). A prominent theory in the natural law tradition contends that states abide by customary international law because "they perceive the rule and its institutional penumbra to have a high degree of legitimacy," where legitimacy is understood as "a property of a rule or rule-making institution which itself exerts a pull toward compliance on those addressed normatively because those addressed believe that the rule or institution has come into being and operates in accordance with generally accepted principles of right process" (Franck 1990, 24–25). Another theory argues that "repeated compliance [with international law] gradually becomes habitual obedience" as international law "penetrates into a domestic legal system, thus becoming part of that nation's internal value set" (Koh 1997, 2603). Yet another theory, while nodding to the idea of self-interested state behavior, explains international law compliance mainly on the basis of morality and the "habit and inertia of continued compliance" (Henkin 1979, 49, 58–63). In our view, "right process," "value set," "habit," and "morality" are stand-ins for the concept of *opinio juris* and do not explain why states are pulled toward compliance by customary international law. There are many other theories of international law compliance (see the discussions in Schachter 1968; Koh 1997), but they suffer from similar difficulties.

The Basic Models

Customary international law is best modeled as behavioral regularities that emerge when states pursue their interests on the international stage. In this section, we describe the four models that we believe capture such behavioral regularities. The approach is similar to that of political scientists interested in international relations, such as Martin (1992), but they have not discussed customary international law. The analysis uses as its main example the customary international law rule at issue in the famous *Paquete Habana* (1900) decision, which held that customary international law prohibited a state from capturing a coastal fishing vessel owned by civilians of an enemy state. (We use the coastal fishing vessel rule here for expository purposes; we return to the actual operation of the rule in chapter 2.) For clarity, we initially discuss possible explanations for this rule in interactions between two states. We then discuss the extent to which the conclusions of this discussion can be extended to interactions among more than two states. Finally, we explain how the basic models differ from the traditional conception of customary international law.

Coincidence of Interest

Coincidence of interest is a situation in which a behavioral regularity among states occurs simply because each state obtains private advantages from a particular action (which happens to be the same action taken by the other state) irrespective of the action of the other. Table 1.1 illustrates such a situation.

Table 1.1

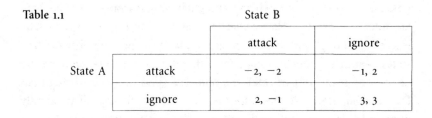

		State B	
		attack	ignore
State A	attack	−2, −2	−1, 2
	ignore	2, −1	3, 3

Table 1.1 might describe the position of two belligerent states whose naval forces patrol a body of water also used by civilian fishing vessels from both states. A state's naval vessels are expensive to operate and have important uses (such as protecting the state from invasion), and the fishing vessels are not worth much. It follows that each state does best if it ignores the fishing vessels of the other (represented by a payoff of 3 for each state). If a state instead attacks the vessels of the other state, we assume that it incurs a loss of 4, so that its payoff is −1 (3 − 4). If the first state's vessels are attacked, it incurs an additional loss of 1, so that its payoff is −2. If a state's vessels are attacked but it does not itself attack the vessels of the other state, it loses 1 but it does not incur the loss of 4, so its payoff is 2 (3 − 1).

To determine the equilibrium of the game, assume first that one player (state B) attacks the vessels of the other player (state A). State A obtains a higher payoff (2) if its navy ignores the fishing vessels of state B than if it attacks and seizes these vessels (-2). Now assume that state B ignores the vessels of state A. State A obtains a higher payoff if it ignores (3) than if it attacks (-1). Accordingly, state A ignores state B's vessels regardless of state B's behavior. Because state B's payoffs are symmetric to state A's, state B ignores state A's vessels as well. Thus, in equilibrium, each state ignores the vessels of the other state. By an "equilibrium" we mean that the two states will continue engaging in this behavior as long as the underlying payoffs do not change. Thus, when an equilibrium occurs, one would observe a behavioral regularity—in this case, a behavioral regularity consisting of each state ignoring the vessels of the other.

Political scientists have noted that what we call coincidence of interest may explain why states often appear to comply with treaty regimes: the treaties do not require the states to do anything different from what they would do on their own (see Oye 1986; Martin 1992; Downs, Rocke, and Barsoom 1996).[1] Coincidence of interest is also a possible explanation for behavioral regularities associated with customary international law. Notice that the states act according to their self-interest. Although an observer might applaud the outcome because the states refrain from belligerence (and therefore seem to be cooperating or obeying some sort of rule), the outcome is no more surprising than the fact that states do not sink their own ships. States independently pursuing their own interests will engage in symmetrical or identical actions that do not harm anyone simply because they gain nothing by deviating from those actions.

Coercion

A second strategic position in which states find themselves can be called *coercion*. One state, or a coalition of states with convergent interests, forces other states to engage in actions that serve the interest of the first state or states. To understand this strategic situation, imagine that a large and powerful state initially can threaten to punish a small and weak state that engages in any action X. The cost of punishing the small state is trivial. The small state then chooses to engage in the action or not, and the large state responds by punishing the small state or not. The game then repeats itself. The large state receives its highest payoff if the small state does not engage in X. The small state receives a higher payoff if it does not engage in X and is not punished than if it does engage in X and is punished. In equilibrium the large state makes the threat, the small state does not engage in X, and the large state does not punish the small state. The small state does not deviate because the large state would punish it if it did. The threat of punishment is most credible when the cost of punishing the small state is low.

As an example, suppose that a powerful state, A, wishes to prevent weak state B from attacking A's civilian fishing boats. State A threatens state B by announcing that if state B does not stop its attacks, state A will destroy B's navy. If state A cares enough about preventing B's attacks, and the cost of punishing state B is low enough, state A's threat will be credible, and state B will cease attacking the fishing vessels. If, because it has better uses for its navy, state A also does not attack state B's fishing boats, then observers will perceive a behavioral regularity consisting of states A and B not attacking each other's civilian fishing boats. They may conclude that a rule of customary international law prohibits the seizure of fishing boats. But this harmonious result actually is produced by force or threatened force.

In a situation of coercion, both the coercing state and the coerced state act rationally to further their interests based on the perceived interests and strengths of the other state. In the example above, state A becomes better off as a result of coercing B, and B is better off than it would have been had it not responded as it did to the coercive acts or threatened acts. Note, however, that although coerced state B acts rationally to avoid an even worse result than would have occurred had A carried through on its threat, B *is* worse off from the baseline of the status quo prior to the threat. Note also how coercion differs from coincidence of interest. Coincidence of interest exists when a state's incremental payoff from an action is independent of the action of the other state. Coercion exists when the strong state's payoff depends on the weak state's action and the strong state would punish the weak state if the weak state chose the action that does not maximize the strong state's payoff. (For a related discussion of coercion, see Martin 1992, chap. 2.)

Cooperation

The third strategic position in which states find themselves is that of the bilateral repeated prisoner's dilemma. Table 1.2 illustrates one stage of such a game.

Table 1.2

		State A	
		attack	ignore
State B	attack	2, 2	4, 1
	ignore	1, 4	3, 3

Recall that the coincidence of interest example (Table 1.1) also assumes that each state receives 3 if both states ignore the fishing vessels of the other. But whereas the earlier example assumed that states lose 4 when they attack, because this strategy is a waste of naval resources, the example here assumes that a state gains 1 when it attacks, holding constant the response of the other state. So a state's payoff increases from 3 to 4 if it attacks the vessels of a state that plays "ignore," and its payoff increases from 1 to 2 if it attacks the vessels of a state that plays "attack" (see Table 1.2). The payoffs in Table 1.1, where there is a coincidence of interest, describe conditions under which naval resources are expensive, fishing vessels have little value to an enemy, and fishing plays a minor role in an economy. The payoffs in Table 1.2, where there is a prisoner's dilemma, describe conditions under which naval resources are cheaper, fishing vessels are valuable as prizes, and fishing plays an important role in the economy.

The analysis of the prisoner's dilemma is familiar. State A obtains a higher payoff from seizing state B's fishing vessels regardless of whether state B also seizes state A's vessels (2 > 1) or not (4 > 3). State B's payoffs are symmetrical. Therefore, if Table 1.2 describes the whole game and there is no possibility of future action or international sanctions, both states will seize the fishing vessels of the other and obtain the jointly minimizing outcome.

When the prisoner's dilemma is repeated over an indefinite period of time, however, the optimal outcome (ignore, ignore) becomes possible in each round (see Baird, Gertner, and Picker 1992, 164–72; Gibbons 1992, 82–99). If the states expect to interact over time, each state could adopt the following strategy. Each state ignores the other state's fishing vessels in period n + 1 as long as there were no attacks (that is, "cooperation") in period n. If one state does attack the other's vessels (that is, "cheat") in period n, the victim will not cooperate in period n + 1 or in any future period. This strategy—and similar strategies that we need not discuss here—can yield cooperation over time, as long as several conditions are satisfied. We focus here on the four most relevant to our analysis.

First, the parties must know what counts as cooperation and what counts as cheating. In our simple setup, we assumed away this problem: cooperation means not attacking fishing vessels, cheating means attacking them. In the real world, there is infinite complexity. The customary international law rule extended only to "small" fishing vessels, but what is small and what is big? It extended only to "coastal" fishing vessels, but at what point in the ocean does "coastal" end and "deep sea" begin? It permitted states to attack a fishing vessel that is a threat, but what counts as a threat? A vessel that contains weapons that are being transported from here to there? A vessel whose sailors might be spies, or who might simply report the whereabouts of the enemy navy to their own forces? (We discuss these controversies in chapter 2.) These problems of ambiguity (that is, multiple equilibria) have always made customary international law very weak and have spurred states to use treaties to clarify customary international law (see chapter 3).

Second, the players must have sufficiently low discount rates; that is, they must care about the future relative to the present. Individuals who are impulsive or impatient or who do not care about the future have high discount rates. Because such individuals value the short-term gains from cheating over the discounted long-term gains from cooperation, they cannot sustain cooperative relationships with others. The international analogy to the impulsive individual is the *rogue state.* Rogue states are states controlled by irrational or impulsive leaders, or states with unstable political systems, or states in which citizens do not enjoy stable expectations. At the other extreme, a state whose institutions successfully aggregate the preferences of citizens and are able to extend them across time (so that, for example, a new government finds it difficult to depart too much from the old government's foreign policy) and whose citizens care about future payoffs can be said to have a low discount rate.

Third, the game must continue indefinitely, in the sense that players either expect it never to end or to end only with a sufficiently low probability. Care should be taken when analyzing the end of a game. Laws of war (such as the prohibition on the use of poison gas) might exist because (1) belligerents foresee interaction ceasing at the end of the war but do not know when the war will end, and so refrain from cheating during the war (for example, by using poison gas) in the expectation that the enemy will do the same; or (2) belligerents foresee interaction continuing after the war ends and fear that cheating during the war may invite retaliation after the war. Analyses of customs between states should not overlook the influence of future interaction between the states outside the narrow context of the game.

Fourth, the payoffs from defection must not be too high relative to the payoffs from cooperation. Because payoffs may change over time, a relationship may succeed for a while and then, after a sudden change in payoffs, collapse.

The bilateral prisoner's dilemma can be overcome and result in a jointly maximizing outcome only if the above conditions are met. By contrast, the coincidence of interest case results in a jointly maximizing outcome regardless of whether these conditions are met. The bilateral repeated prisoner's dilemma differs from the coercion case along two dimensions. First, the cooperative equilibrium in the prisoner's dilemma depends on mutual threats of deviation rather than the powerful state unilaterally threatening to punish the weaker state (as in the coercion game). Second, in the prisoner's dilemma, both states prefer the cooperative equilibrium that is sustained by mutual threats over the equilibrium that results when both states deviate. In contrast, in the coercion game, the powerful state prefers the equilibrium sustained by its threats, and the weaker state prefers the equilibrium in which the threat is not credible and not carried out.

Coordination

The fourth strategic position in which states find themselves is one of *coordination*. In the simplest form of this game, the states' interests converge, as in the case of coincidence of interest; but unlike the latter case, each state's best move depends on the move of the other state. Consider Table 1.3.

Table 1.3

		State A	
		action X	action Y
State B	action X	3, 3	0, 0
	action Y	0, 0	3, 3

Each state prefers to engage in X if the other state engages in X, and each state prefers to engage in Y if the other state engages in Y. There are two desirable equilibria: {X, X} and {Y, Y}. Once the states coordinate on one action, neither state will deviate. The main problem is the first move. If state A does not know whether state B will choose X or Y, then state A does not know whether to choose X or Y. Both states might choose their first and subsequent moves at random, resulting in a mixed-strategy equilibrium in which the parties fail to obtain the full gains from coordination (Baird et al. 1992, 37–39).

We will abandon our fishing vessel example, which does not lend itself to the coordination case, and instead consider the simpler case we discussed in the introduction: the border between two states. Suppose that action X is "patrol up to the river" and action Y is "patrol up to the road." The river and road cross but divide the territory evenly. The states are indifferent whether the river or the road should divide their territories, but they want to avoid conflicts between their patrols. Once it is established that the equilibrium action is X (or Y), neither state will deviate from that action. To see why, suppose that state A knows that state B engages in X. Then state A does better by also engaging in X than by engaging in Y. If, instead, state A knows that state B engages in Y, state A does better by engaging in Y than by engaging in X.

Coordination problems also arise in the course of solving the repeated prisoner's dilemma. As we noted earlier, although repeated play can overcome the incentives to cheat in one round of the prisoner's dilemma, there remains a problem of identifying which moves count as cooperative moves and which moves count as defections. For example, part of state A's and state B's problem in overcoming the incentives to seize each other's fishing vessels involves identifying which seizures are permitted and which are not permitted. Can one seize a fishing vessel if it contains spies? What if the sailors are not spies but have observed secret maneuvers? A repeated prisoner's dilemma, when discount rates are low enough, is not the same thing as a one-shot prisoner's dilemma; it is instead a kind of coordination game.

There are many variations on the pure coordination game. One equilibrium might produce higher payoffs for both parties than the other; then coordination may be easy. Or one party might do better in one equilibrium while the other party does better in a second equilibrium, in which case coordination may be difficult. This is the "battle of the sexes" game. Morrow (1994a) analyzes a treaty on wireless communications as a battle of the sexes game because all states preferred coordinating on some standard rather than on none, but some standards benefited certain states more than others. He points out that although the states can coordinate on one of the equilibria by using a treaty, a state that prefers the other equilibrium has an incentive to undermine the treaty by deviating from it occasionally, in the hope of forcing other states to switch to the preferred equilibrium outcome. (See also Krasner 1991.)

Similar problems afflict efforts to coordinate in the absence of treaty negotiations. The matrix for the battle of the sexes is provided in Table 1.4. The outcomes {X, X} and {Y, Y} are both equilibria: given that state A chooses X, state B can do no better than choose X; given that state A chooses Y, state B can do no better than choose Y. But state A prefers {Y, Y}; state B prefers {X, X}. State B might be expected to choose X because {X, X} provides a higher payoff for it than {Y, Y} does; but state B must also worry that state A will choose Y for analogous reasons, in which case B's payoff is 0 rather than 3 or 2. Thus, there is no obvious solution to the game.

Table 1.4

		State A	
		action X	action Y
State B	action X	3, 2	0, 0
	action Y	0, 0	2, 3

Nonetheless, a solution might arise through custom. Through repeated play, the states might coordinate on one equilibrium or the other, and then it may stick. This process is the same as in the pure coordination case. But the pure coordination game's outcome is more stable. As noted earlier, in the battle of the sexes the state that does less well in equilibrium has an incentive to disturb the equilibrium by deviating. If the status quo is {X, X} but state A has a sufficiently long time horizon, it might deviate and choose Y in the hope that state B will switch as well. State B will switch if it prefers the short-term gains from {Y, Y} to the long-term payoff from {X, X} following a period of coordination failure. Thus, a rule of customary international law that solves a battle of the sexes game will be both less robust—more violation will be observed—and more susceptible to change and even cycling than a rule of customary international law that solves a pure coordination game.

On the Possibility of Multinational Customary International Law

One of the central claims of the standard account of customary international law is that customary international law governs all or almost all states, or at least all "civilized" states. Our theory shows how many apparently cooperative universal behavioral regularities may in fact be illusory. Suppose, for example, that we observe that no state seizes civilian fishing vessels from enemies in times of war. Our theory contemplates many possible explanations for this observation based on some combination of the four models described earlier.

First, states might not seize fishing vessels because their naval forces have better uses, for example, attacking enemy warships or large merchant vessels. This is coincidence of interest. Second, many states receive no benefit from seizing fishing vessels (coincidence of interest), and the few states that would benefit from seizing fishing vessels are deterred from doing so by powerful states that want to prevent seizures of their own vessels (coercion). Third, two states decline to seize each other's fishing vessels in a bilateral repeated prisoner's dilemma, and all the other states decline to do so because of coincidence of interest or coercion. Or it may be that the other states also face each other in bilateral repeated prisoner's dilemmas and therefore refrain from seizing fishing vessels because they fear retaliation from their (single) opponent. Fourth, some or all states face each other in bilateral coordination games that they solve, and other states engage in the same action because of coincidence of interest or coercion.

There are numerous other possible combinations of coincidence of interest, coercion, bilateral prisoner's dilemmas, and bilateral coordination. In all these cases, some states refrain from seizing fishing vessels because they have better uses for their navy, because they fear retaliation from the state whose fishing vessels they covet, or because they fear a failure of coordination. In none of these cases does multilateral cooperation occur.

Multilateral cooperation occurs when many states cooperate to overcome a collective action problem. A multistate repeated prisoner's dilemma is very different from the two-state version of this game. An example of the multistate game would be a fishery surrounded by many states. Table 1.2, which was used to illustrate the two-state prisoner's dilemma, can also be used to illustrate the multistate version, except with the interpretation that the row player represents any given state and the column player represents any other state. With this arrangement, each state does better by overfishing, whether or not other states overfish. Therefore, every state has an incentive to overfish.

In contrast to the two-player game, a multistate prisoner's dilemma is theoretically much more difficult for states to overcome. There are many reasons why this is so. The four conditions needed to overcome a bilateral prisoner's dilemma—that the cooperative moves be clearly defined, that the states have low discount rates, that they expect the game to continue indefinitely, and that their payoffs from defection are not too high relative to the payoffs from cooperation—become more difficult to maintain as the number of participating states increases. In addition, as the number of states increases, the cost of monitoring increases, and therefore the likelihood of erroneous punishment and undetected or unredressed free-riding increases.[2] In our fishing example, as the number of states increases, it becomes increasingly less likely that a state will refrain from overfishing to avoid retaliation by other states. The fishery could be preserved if all states adopt the strategy of, for example, overfishing for all future rounds if any single state overfishes in any previous round (Kandori 1992). But this draconian strategy would result in the depletion of the fishery if any single state cheated, or even if a single state mistakenly believed that another state cheated. And it is unlikely in a multistate situation that every state would adopt this strategy rather than any of the indefinitely large number of alternatives.

For these reasons, we are skeptical that customary international law's supposed multilateral or "universal" behavioral regularities are best explained as examples of overcoming multistate prisoner's dilemmas (Oye 1986, 6–7). Game theory does not rule out the possibility of such multistate cooperation. And, as we explain in our discussion of treaties, states can increase the likelihood of overcoming multistate prisoner's dilemmas and establish at least shallow multistate cooperation through formal negotiation and specification of what counts as cooperation and through formal and elaborate monitoring mechanisms. But in the context of customary international law, which develops in an uncoordinated and uneven fashion and where states lack the information and monitoring structures needed to overcome a multilateral prisoner's dilemma, genuine multistate cooperation is unlikely to emerge. Indeed, as we argue, there is no evidence that customary international law reflects states solving multilateral prisoner's dilemmas: we see neither direct evidence, such as third-party enforcement, where unaffected state X punishes state Y when state Y violates customary international law in a way that harms only state Z, nor indirect evidence, in the form of customary international law governing collective goods like fisheries.

Similar points apply to multistate coordination games. Examples of such coordination problems include the division of the world into time zones and the choice of international communication or transportation standards. In the latter case, every state wants to facilitate transportation between territories, but all states must agree on, for example, a railroad gauge. Once a particular standard is established, no state gains anything from deviating from it. If everyone uses the same gauge, a state will likely lose by switching to another gauge because it will increase the cost of interstate transportation.

To say that states can in theory solve multilateral coordination problems is not, however, to say that these problems can easily be solved in the informal, unstructured, and decentralized manner typically associated with customary international law. Such problem solving is difficult because the costs of coordination rise exponentially with the number of states. Imagine ten contiguous states that must choose between different railroad gauges. If there are only two possible gauges and each state chooses a gauge independently, the odds that they will all choose the same gauge in the first round are 2 in 2^{10}, or 1 in 512. In later rounds, one state might, at great cost, switch to the gauge used by another state, but at the same time one or more other states might switch to the gauge of the first state. And if there are more than two gauges, if there are dozens or hundreds of possibilities from which to choose, the odds against coordination are astronomical. Over a very long period of time, it is conceivable that the states might eventually settle on the same gauge, especially if some gauges are economically superior.[3] But this is unlikely.

One can imagine other exceptions to the general proposition that multinational coordination games are not likely to be solved in an informal and unstructured fashion. Suppose that two states that are technological leaders play a coordination game that establishes a particular gauge. A third state that later develops the technology might independently adopt this standard to minimize the cost of transportation to the first two states. Other states then imitate the first three states. Here, the original bilateral coordination game can establish the focal point for multilateral coordination. Similarly, a high-profile international event might supply a focal point that would be the basis for multilateral coordination. While multilateral coordination problems thus can be solved, they are difficult to solve in the absence of formal negotiation and specification typically associated with treaties, especially when the coordination problem has distributional consequences as it does in the battle of the sexes model. (We return to the topic of how treaties solve multilateral coordination problems in chapter 3.)

Comparison of the Basic Models and the Traditional View

Mainstream international law scholars would not view a behavioral regularity that arises from any of the four strategic situations outlined earlier as an example of customary international law. Begin with coincidence of interest. In this situation, parties acting independently achieve their best outcomes regardless of the behavior of the other party. In this strategic scenario, the behavioral regularity of states not sinking enemy ships is functionally identical to the behavioral regularity of states not sinking their own ships. There are an infinite number of behavioral regularities of this form that no one would claim constitute customary international law. None of these behaviors has anything to do with a state's "sense of legal obligation," which is so central to the traditional account.

Similarly, behavioral regularities explained by coercion would not be viewed as customary international law from the traditional perspective. The behavioral regularity results from the dominion of the powerful over the weak. Weak states do not act in the strong state's interest out of a sense of legal obligation. They do so to avoid some worse fate.

Now consider a behavioral regularity that results from a solution to a bilateral prisoner's dilemma. This behavior seems more meaningful than in the other two situations, because in any particular iteration of the game, each state has a private incentive to cheat. When a state cooperates in a round, it acts in a fashion that is not in its immediate self-interest. In this sense, the resulting behavioral regularity looks like compliance with a norm. For these reasons, the bilateral iterated prisoner's dilemma approaches the traditional conception of customary international law more than the other two models.

But this explanation for an international behavioral regularity differs from the traditional account. A state's compliance with the cooperative strategy in the bilateral prisoner's dilemma has nothing to do with acting from a sense of legal obligation. States do not act in accordance with a rule that they feel obliged to follow; they act because it is in their interest to do so. The rule does not cause the states' behavior; it reflects their behavior. As a result, behavior in bilateral iterated prisoner's dilemmas will change with variations in the underlying payoffs. Cooperation will rise or fall with changes in technology and environment. Although most international law scholars acknowledge that states are more likely to violate customary international law as the costs of compliance increase, they insist that the sense of legal obligation puts some drag on such deviations. Our theory, by contrast, insists that the payoffs from cooperation or deviation are the sole determinants of whether states engage in the cooperative behaviors that are labeled customary international law. This is why we deny the claim that customary international law is an exogenous influence on states' behavior. And because we are skeptical about the possibility of cooperation by custom in multiplayer prisoner's dilemmas, we are skeptical that customary international law fosters true multilateral cooperation.

Similarly, pairwise coordination may emerge spontaneously, or evolve into a behavioral regularity. Multilateral coordination is, for reasons explained earlier, unlikely to evolve by custom, but if it were to evolve, states would not act as they do out of a sense of legal obligation, but to further their interests.

We think that customary international law is best understood as a product of state self-interest that accords with one of the four models described. What scholars view as compliance with customary international law driven by a sense of legal obligation is, we contend, a behavioral regularity that results from states pursuing their interests. Scholars who think that customary international law results from a sense of legal obligation fail to distinguish between a pattern of behavior and the motives that cause states to act in accordance with that pattern. A business analogy may be instructive. Firms may offer identical prices and terms for identical services, but their motive for doing so is not a desire to conform to this pattern. Their motive is self-interest; the resulting pattern is due to the dynamics of the market. Firms that charge too much make no sales; those that charge too little do not cover costs and go out of business. Similarly, in our hypothetical example, apparent compliance with the fishing vessel rule did not result from the motive on the part of states to comply with customary international law. The motive was self-interest; the resulting pattern was due to the dynamics of international relations.

The Origin and Evolution of Customary International Law

The four basic models provide an account of the behaviors associated with customary international law. We now show how each of the models might explain the origin and change of these behaviors. The following examples are illustrative but not exhaustive. Our purpose is to show that, under our theory, the way customary international law originates and changes is no mystery.

First, when customary international law reflects coincidence of interest, a change in customary international law can occur whenever the states' interests change, and the states' interests will change when the environment changes. For example, states A and B seize each other's fishing vessels at time 0, perhaps because they gain more by engaging in mutual predation than by engaging in unilateral or mutual restraint. At time 1, state C enters the scene and threatens the security of both state A and state B. Now, states A and B have a better use for their navies: defense against state C's navy rather than seizure of fishing vessels. If one defines customary international law as any behavioral regularity, then the law changes (from mutual predation at time 0 to mutual restraint at time 1). If one defines a customary international law only as behavioral regularities that are harmonious in some sense, then the law emerges at time 1 from the disorder that existed at time 0.

Second, when customary international law reflects coercion, a change in customary international law may again occur whenever the states' interests or relative power changes. State A loses its war with state C and also its power to coerce state B, so state B starts seizing A's fishing vessels. The old customary international law against the seizure of fishing vessels is either replaced by a new law or by nothing, again depending on how one defines customary international law.

Third, when customary international law refers to the behavioral regularity in a bilateral repeated prisoner's dilemma, a more complicated story is needed. One possibility is that customary international law of this type can arise when neutral behavioral regularities already exist because of coincidence of interest, but payoffs change, creating a conflict of interest. To illustrate, suppose that at time 0 two states refrain from seizing each other's fishing vessels just because their navies have more valuable opportunities. At time 1, these opportunities disappear (a naval war with other states ends), and consequently the one-round payoff from seizing fishing vessels becomes higher than the payoff from not doing so. Each state must now decide whether to begin seizing the other's fishing vessels.

At this point, the status quo—not seizing fishing vessels—is focal, in the sense that each state recognizes it as a possible desirable state of affairs and this recognition is common knowledge (that is, state B knows that state A recognizes the status quo as a desirable state of affairs, and state A knows that state B knows this). One state might rationally hold off seizing the other state's vessels in the hope that the other state recognizes that this is a mutually desirable strategy. Or, one state might not realize that payoffs have changed, and the other state declines to alert the first state to that fact by seizing its fishing vessels, given that the other state prefers to preserve the status quo. In either case, one might say that a "mere" behavioral regularity based on coincidence of interest gives way to a behavioral regularity that reflects cooperation. In contrast, if the status quo is that of mutual seizure of fishing vessels, it will be much more difficult for a pattern of not seizing vessels to arise, given that each state knows that if it stops unilaterally, the other state will be tempted to continue seizing vessels.

It is not the case, however, that a neutral behavioral regularity is a necessary predecessor to bilateral cooperation. Any focal point can stimulate the emergence of a behavioral regularity that produces cooperative gains. Suppose that state A and state B face the payoffs described by Table 1.2, a prisoner's dilemma, because of an exogenous change. Prior to this change, each state seized the fishing vessels of the other. The change could be, for example, wars involving other states, which require the attention of each state's navies. Each state still prefers seizing fishing vessels to ignoring them in a single round, but both would be better off over the long term if both refrained from seizing the vessels. There is no time for a treaty. State A might simply announce, "We will no longer seize the fishing vessels from state B, unless state B seizes our fishing vessels." If state B knows state A's payoffs, it might well believe state A. The joint action of ignoring unless provoked is focal because of the announcement, which (as we explain at greater length in chapter 6) is credible because each state knows that this strategy leads to the optimal outcome. Thus, bilateral cooperation can arise despite the absence of a long historical practice.

Fourth, when customary international law reflects coordination, it can arise and change as a result of trial and error. Recall the example of a coordination game in which armies patrol an area of disputed land that is divided about evenly by a river and a road, and the river and the road cross at various points (see Table 1.4). Suppose the soldiers want to avoid conflict, and they know that conflict will arise if they patrol overlapping areas. Both sides do best if they patrol up to the same boundary (either river or road); they come into conflict if they patrol up to a different boundary. If the river is a superior boundary, say, because it keeps opposing soldiers farther apart, then the payoffs from the river boundary would be higher and patrolling along the river is a natural focal point. But even if both states do not choose this strategy, so long as payoffs for identical actions are equal one would expect eventual coordination on the same action, albeit perhaps after an initial period of conflict (see H. Young 1998, 25–90). Once the pattern is established, no state has an incentive to deviate.

In sum, our theory contemplates that behavioral regularities will arise at an international level as a result of states maximizing their interests. We identify four strategic situations in which behavioral regularities are likely to emerge: coincidence of interest, coercion, bilateral repeated prisoner's dilemma, and bilateral coordination. Behavioral regularities that reflect these patterns might not be considered remarkable or desirable. But we claim that they, rather than the notion of universal state practices followed from a sense of legal obligation, account for the actual state behaviors associated with customary international law. Some critics of our earlier work think that we "deny[] the existence of" customary international law (Guzman 2002a, 1876). Our claim is not that customary international law does not exist, but rather that it is not an exogenous influence on state behavior. Our theory does, however, suggest that the behavioral regularities associated with customary international law lack the universality or robustness posited by the traditional account.[4]

CHAPTER 2

CASE STUDIES

Customary international law fills volumes of treatises, and we cannot try to show that all of it follows the logic of our models. Instead, we examine in detail four areas of customary international law chosen on the basis of their prominence and on the availability of a detailed historical record. The four case studies we examine are the "free ships, free goods" rule of wartime maritime commerce; the breadth of the territorial sea; ambassadorial immunity; and the wartime exemption from prize for coastal fishing vessels. We show that these areas of supposedly robust customary international law never reflected universal behavioral regularities and that the actual state behaviors associated with these laws are most easily and parsimoniously explained using our four models.

Free Ships, Free Goods

The customary international law of neutrality governs relations between neutrals and belligerents during times of war. One important neutrality issue is the status of enemy property on neutral ships. Before 1856, many belligerents, especially Britain, seized enemy property on neutrals' ships. Conventional wisdom among courts and treatise writers holds that the principle of "free ships, free goods"—all property on a neutral's ship, including enemy property but excluding contraband, is immune from seizure—became a well-established rule of customary international law after the Declaration of Paris in 1856 (Colombos and Higgins 1926, 164–67; Jessup 1928, 20–23; Moore 1906, 382; Woolsey 1901, 302–3). The Declaration followed the Crimean War, in which France,

Britain, Turkey, and Piedmont defeated Russia. One of the Declaration's four principles was the free ships, free goods principle. All parties to the Crimean War (including Great Britain) signed the Declaration, and during the next fifty years most of the major states of the world acceded to it. In addition, the states that did not accede to the Declaration consistently announced adherence to the free ships, free goods principle at the outset of wars in which they were belligerents. The broad accession to the Declaration, consistent state pronouncements in support of free ships, free goods, and the relative paucity of overt violations of free ships, free goods are the bases for the claim that the free ships, free goods principle was a rule of customary international law after 1856.

We argue that the historical evidence supports our theory of customary international law better than the traditional understanding. There was no universal behavioral regularity, and the actual behavior of states is best explained by our models. Academic claims to the contrary exemplify several errors common to analyses of customary international law.

U.S. Civil War

For its first seventy years, the United States was the world's most ardent defender of neutral rights. This stance was designed to promote trade and keep the United States out of European entanglements. It included a firm commitment to free ships, free goods, a strict conception of blockade, and a narrowly defined conception of contraband (Savage 1934, 1–82). The United States did not sign the pro-neutral Declaration of Paris because, as a relatively weak naval power, it objected to the Declaration's provision outlawing privateering (Pierce 1856/1897, 412–14). But in light of its historical support for free ships, free goods, it was no surprise that, when its Civil War began five years after the Declaration, the United States announced adherence to the principle that "free ships make free goods . . . with the exception of articles contraband of war" (Seward 1861/1965, 34).

The United States' novel status as a dominant naval belligerent provided the first real test of its commitment to neutrality principles. It failed that test. In the "single incident in which the question of free ships, free goods arose during the Civil War," a U.S. prize court apparently rejected the principle (Bernath 1970, 7). More insidious to the principle than this overt violation was the United States' use of an unprecedentedly broad conception of blockade and contraband to justify widespread disruption of neutral ships carrying enemy goods.

At the outset of the Civil War, Lincoln declared a blockade of the entire coastline of the Confederate states. A blockade justified a belligerent in seizing all ships, including neutral ships, attempting to violate the blockade. The traditional U.S. position was that blockades were legitimate only if they were "effective" in the sense of preventing access to the enemy's coast (Moore 1906, 788–97; Savage 1934, 25, 38–45). Anything short of this strict definition of effective blockade would allow a belligerent to declare a paper blockade and "assert a general right to capture any ship bound to his enemy," thereby undermining free ships, free goods and other neutral rights (Jessup 1928, 24). American insistence on the principle of effective blockade was one reason for the War of 1812 (id., 25).

When Lincoln declared the blockade of the Confederacy, one Union ship covered sixty-six miles of Confederate coast, and nine out of ten vessels successfully breached the blockade; during the war five of six blockade runners made it through (Owlsey 1935, 194–201; Bernath 1970, 11). This porous blockade would have been deemed ineffective under prior U.S. views about customary international law (Owlsey 1935, 197–204). But Lincoln changed the U.S. stance, arguing that a blockade did not have to be totally effective to be legally effective (Coogan 1981, 22; Savage 1934, 87–90; Bernath 1970, 11–14). The Supreme Court, sitting as a prize court, later ratified Lincoln's view as consistent with customary international law (*The Springbok* 1866, 21–28; *The Peterhoff* 1866, 50–52; Moore 1906, 708–15).

U.S. practice with respect to effective blockades undermined the force of the free ships, free goods principle because it justified the United States in preying on neutral vessels anywhere at sea that were bound for a blockaded port. By itself, this practice did not completely undermine free ships, free goods, for a neutral could, in theory, take enemy property to a neutral port for subsequent shipment to the Confederacy. But the United States closed this loophole, too. In the early nineteenth century, it had vigorously protested the British practice of seizing U.S. ships sailing between two neutral ports, which the British justified on the ground that the goods were on a "continuous voyage" to a blockaded port (Bernath 1970, 66–67). In the Civil War, the United States reversed course and began to capture neutral vessels sailing between neutral ports if the ultimate destination of the goods on board the ship was the blockaded Confederacy (J. Baxter 1928, 18–19; J. Baxter 1929, 517). In so doing, the United States engaged in generous presumptions about the goods' ultimate destination that expanded the concept of "continuous voyage" beyond even Britain's broad interpretation. The Supreme Court, sitting as a prize court applying customary international law, upheld this broad conception, too (*The Springbok* 1866, 21; *The Peterhoff* 1866, 54; *The Bermuda* 1865, 551–58; Baty 1900, 13–17).

The United States' liberal policy concerning blockade and continuous voyage undermined the free ships, free goods principle. As Arnold-Forster (1942, 31–32) observed: "By [an] irony of fate, the first country to contribute to [the] stultification of the Free Ships rule was the very state which had been the rule's most consistent champion—the United States." This policy was guided by expediency, not principle. The goal was to be as aggressive as possible in shutting down trade with the Confederacy without provoking the British to enter the war on the side of the South. In pursuing this goal, some U.S. officials (such as Secretary of State William Henry Seward) were indifferent to customary international law or tried to manipulate its requirements for strategic purposes; other officials (such as Secretary of the Navy Gideon Welles) were ignorant or disdainful of customary international law (Bernath 1970, 12–17; O'Rourke 1963). There is no evidence that the free ships, free goods rule, to which the United States announced adherence at the outset of the war, had any influence on the government's decision-making process, and the announcement of fidelity to free ships, free goods was belied by the government's subsequent practice.

Following the U.S. Civil War, other states also expanded collateral maritime doctrines to water down the free ships, free goods principle. For example, in the Franco-Chinese conflict of 1885, the French embraced a broad doctrine of continuous voyage and contraband to seize a ship carrying rice between neutral ports. Japan engaged in similar acts during the Sino-Japanese War of 1894, as did the Italians in their 1896 war with Abyssinia (Verzijl, Heere, and Offerhaus 1992, 367–69).

Spanish-American War

In the next major war, the Spanish-American War (1898), the United States and Spain engaged each other primarily at sea. Although neither state was at the time a signatory to the Declaration of Paris, both states announced adherence to its principles, including free ships, free goods, at the outset of the war. During the war Spain did not disrupt neutral ships that contained U.S. property (McKinley 1898/1917; Spanish Royal Decree 1898/1901). And despite controversial blockades of a few Spanish ports and a mildly expansive contraband list (Benton 1908, 196–204), the United States enforced its belligerent rights in a very narrow fashion (Coogan 1981, 25–26).

One could interpret these events as support for the free ships, free goods principle. But closer inspection reveals that neither state had an interest in disrupting neutral commerce during the short three-month war. Spain's Atlantic navy consisted of a handful of "inadequately equipped, out of repair, and wretchedly manned" ships (Sprout and Sprout 1966, 232) that were blockaded in Santiago Harbor in Cuba before they were destroyed (Trask 1981, 257–69; Westcott et al. 1947, 230–32). Spain's naval force in the Philippines was destroyed less than two weeks after the war began and thus never presented a threat to neutral commerce. Clearly, Spain declined to prey on neutral commerce in the war not because of international law, but because of its lack of naval capacity. The United States had different reasons for not preying on neutral commerce during the three-month war: there were few Spanish goods on neutral ships for it to capture (Bowles 1900, 205), and the United States' overwhelming military and strategic superiority meant that it had no need to prey on neutral ships.

Boer War

The Anglo-Boer War (1899–1902) between Britain and the two Boer republics (Transvaal and the Orange Free State) did not portend a dispute over maritime rights. The landlocked Boer republics had no navy, no merchant ships, and no coast to attack or blockade. And the British were disinclined to attack neutral trade because they believed that the Boers did not depend on it and because the British wanted to avoid reprisals from neutrals. For these reasons, among others, the British announced at the war's outset that they would not search or detain any neutral ship (Coogan 1981, 30–31).

The British attitude toward neutrals changed following early military setbacks and reports that the Boers were receiving supplies through Lourenco Marques, the neutral port for Portuguese Mozambique that was forty miles by rail from the Transvaal frontier. For several months in 1899–1900, the British Navy seized U.S. and German ships sailing from neutral ports to Lourenco Marques. In so doing, the British government acted on the basis of military expediency and ignored legal advice that such seizures would violate customary international law (Coogan 1981, 31–42). The British government justified the seizures on the grounds that the ships carried contraband goods and that there was "ample ground" to believe that the ultimate destination of the goods was the Boer republics (Campbell 1908, 230–64). The British conception of contraband goods was extremely broad, including, for example, foodstuffs. Britain also employed a broad conception of continuous voyage (id., 232–37, 248–49).

The British expansion of the contraband and continuous voyage doctrines vitiated the free ships, free goods principle, just as U.S. actions had done during the Civil War. In contrast to the British response to the U.S. practice during the Civil War, however, the British practice during the Boer War caused the United States and Germany—states that were targets of British action—to threaten retaliation (Coogan 1981, 36–41). In response, Britain defended the legality of its actions, but it eventually stopped preying on neutral commerce and compensated some of the affected German commercial interests (Campbell 1908, 38–42; Coogan 1981, 38–42).

The resolution of the maritime rights disputes in the Boer War thus ultimately resulted in a behavioral regularity consistent with the free ships, free goods principle. But Britain did not obey the principle out of a "sense of legal obligation." Britain began the war with no interest in preying on neutral shipping. When its strategic needs changed, it reversed this policy even though doing so violated the ostensible requirements of customary international law. It then retreated in the face of threats, which, if carried out, would have offset any gains from interrupting neutral trade.

Russo-Japanese War

During the Russo-Japanese War (1904–1905), Russia took an even more aggressive stance toward enemy property on neutral ships than had the United States during its Civil War and Britain during the Boer War. Both Russia and Japan proclaimed adherence to the free ships, free goods principle at the outset of the war. But Russia also claimed the right to seize and sink neutral ships carrying contraband, and its contraband list "included food, fuels, and other items of general use" (Coogan 1981, 44). Pursuant to these rules, the Russian Navy harassed, seized, and sometimes sank U.S., German, and British ships, many of which contained only foodstuffs and were not bound for a Japanese port (Birkenhead and Sibley 1905, 7; Takahashi 1908, 310–30). Enemy property on neutral ships received no protection (Birkenhead and Sibley 1905, 227).

Russian policy and actions provoked threats of retaliation from Britain and (especially) the United States (Coogan 1981, 44–50). The Russian foreign ministry came to believe that "Russia stood to lose far more by provoking Britain and the United States than it could possibly gain by seizing a few cargoes of food" (id., 50). Accordingly, as Britain had done during the Boer War, Russia maintained the legality of its policies but backed away from its aggressive antineutral actions. Once again, the Russian action is best understood as bowing to threats of retaliation in the pursuit of short-term interests, rather than compliance out of a sense of legal obligation with a rule of customary international law.

World War I

The absence of a customary practice concerning the rights of maritime neutrals, which was so evident in the U.S. Civil War, the Boer War, and the Russo-Japanese War, was confirmed at the Second Hague Peace Conference of 1907 and the London Naval Conference of 1908–1909. The Hague Conference was unable to reach agreement about the content of maritime doctrines—contraband, blockade, continuous voyage, and the like—that belligerents had invoked to skirt the free ships, free goods rule (Colombos 1962, 440–41, 766). The Conference also split on the U.S. proposal to immunize all private property from capture during war. When delegates from the maritime powers met at the London Conference, they were able to reach agreement on a substantive law of maritime rights, including concrete definitions concerning contraband, continuous voyage, and blockade. But many states (most notably Britain) rejected the agreement, and no state ever ratified it.

World War I began a few years later. It is well known that the war destroyed any pretense of a law of maritime rights. Contraband lists expanded to include any item unless there was proof that it was not destined for an enemy (Jessup 1928, 37; Turlington 1936, 8–33). Blockades were clearly ineffective and were extended to neutral ports (Jessup

1928, 38–42; Turlington 1936, 34–66). Blacklists, embargoes, and mine laying further disrupted neutral commerce (Jessup 1928, 42–50; Turlington 1936, 36–48, 67–73, 80–86). In short, all property on neutral ships, especially enemy property, was subject to seizure.[1] Scholars like to say that the belligerents violated customary international law; it is more accurate to say that any behavioral regularities that emerged during prior wars did not recur during World War I, no doubt because of changes in technology, stakes, and interests.

Assessment

The free ships, free goods principle illustrates how our theory explains the behaviors associated with customary international law better than the traditional conception. The theory better explains both the behavioral patterns that are consistent with the ostensible customary international law rule and the deviations from the rule.

In some of the wars during the period, belligerents and neutrals acted consistently with the free ships, free goods rule. The best explanation for this result is not, however, adherence to a customary international law rule out of a sense of legal obligation. In each of the wars discussed, a belligerent's decision whether, and to what extent, to forgo capturing enemy property on neutral ships was the product of an assessment of its (usually short-term) interests. Belligerents sometimes gained little from interrupting neutral trade and thus did not try to do so. Coincidence of interest best describes the position of Britain at the outset of the Boer War and the United States throughout the Spanish-American War. At other times, belligerents gained much from capturing enemy goods on neutral ships but lost more from neutral retaliation. This coercion situation was the position of Britain later in the Boer War and Russia late in its war with Japan. In those cases in which the belligerent's desire to disrupt enemy property on neutral ships was not checked by a credible threat of retaliation, the ostensible free ships, free goods rule did nothing to prevent it from doing so. This result, which can be seen as coercion as well as a coincidence of interest, was the situation in the U.S. Civil War.

The free ships, free goods example illustrates many changes in the practices of states that are consistent with our view that international behavior is a function of states' changing interests and relative power. In contrast, the changes make no sense under the view that states abide by customary international law from a sense of legal obligation. State practice and the rationalization of practice with regard to the status of enemy property on neutral ships changed in important ways from war to war. The United States asserted neutral rights liberally throughout the nineteenth century except for the one time that it was a belligerent (its Civil War), when it asserted unprecedentedly broad belligerent rights. Similarly, Britain asserted broad belligerent rights in the Boer War but protested when Russia asserted similar rights in the Russo-Japanese War just a few years later. Germany vehemently protested the British antineutral practices during the Boer War but engaged in aggressive antineutral acts little more than ten years later.

In addition, the free ships, free goods example illustrates several common errors committed by international law scholars. The first is to infer customary international law from verbal commitments to adhere to customary international law. We have seen that there was no behavioral regularity of not seizing enemy property on neutral ships during the period in question; belligerents invoked a variety of related maritime rights to continue preying on enemy property on neutral ships in much the same fashion as in the pre-1856 period. As one commentator observed:

> While granting that the letter of the law [of free ships, free goods] has been observed strictly, the conclusion that is forced upon the student of recent practice is that, through unwarranted extension of belligerent rights based upon related portions of the law of maritime warfare, the rule that private enemy property is free when transported in neutral ships very nearly approaches nullity, and is only preserved in some semblance of vigor by the influence of neutral opposition to the devices of belligerents for rendering it a "dead letter." (Quigley 1917, 26; see also Arnold-Forster 1942, 3; Baty 1900, 12; Benton 1908, 146; Colombos and Higgins 1926, xiii; Randall 1908, 464)

By focusing on pronouncements and the relative paucity of "direct" violations of the free ships, free goods principle, commentators have overlooked the many ways in which the practice of seizing enemy goods on neutral ships continued unabated.

A second error is to view coincidence of interest situations as examples of states being motivated by a desire to comply with law. For example, in the Spanish-American War the United States did not want, and Spain did not have the ability, to seize enemy property on neutral ships. The states were not motivated by customary international law.

A third error is the belief that the behavioral regularities associated with an ostensible customary international law rule possess a unitary underlying logic. The free ships, free goods example shows that such behavioral regularities have multiple, and quite different, explanations. States sometimes refrained from seizing enemy property on neutral ships because they lacked any affirmative interest in doing so, and sometimes because they feared neutral retaliation.

A fourth error is the belief that behavioral regularities in one maritime context generalize to all maritime contexts. As the Boer and Russo-Japanese Wars demonstrate, if a powerful neutral makes a credible threat of retaliation, the belligerent might refrain from seizing neutral ships. But such belligerent acts are a function of war-specific allocations of power and other contingent factors that inform belligerent and neutral payoff structures. There is no reason to believe that payoff structures that result in this behavioral regularity in some wars will be present in all, or even most, wars.

There is a final aspect of the free ships, free goods story worth noting. Although state practice during the period cannot support the claim that free ships, free goods rule reflected a general and consistent practice of states followed from a sense of legal obligation, it is nonetheless striking that every belligerent during the post-1856 period announced adherence to free ships, free goods as a principle of international law, and every state attempted to justify departures from this principle as consistent with international law. This is admittedly a puzzle for our theory, a puzzle that we address in chapter 6.

Ambassadorial Immunity

Commentators have long agreed that customary international law usually requires states to protect foreign ambassadors and related personnel (Fenwick 1948, 467–70; Ogdon 1936, 105–14; Oppenheim 1912, 457–60; Satow 1957, 174–212; Westlake 1910, 273–81; Woolsey 1901, 133–38). This requirement has two main components. First, the host state may not harm foreign diplomatic personnel, either through civil or criminal process or through extralegal means. Second, the host state must protect foreign diplomatic personnel from threats posed by citizens of the host state. Although these requirements have limitations and have fluctuated to some extent over the years, the customary international law of ambassadorial immunity, now codified in the Vienna Convention on Diplomatic Relations, Article 31, has always been considered one of the most robust rules of customary international law.

Empirical evidence supports this conclusion. States almost always grant immunity to diplomats who commit crimes. For example, between August 1982 and February 1988, there were 147 alleged criminal cases involving foreign diplomats in the United States, none of whom was prosecuted (U.S. Department of State 1988). Similarly, from October 1, 1954, to September 30, 1955, there were 93 criminal cases against diplomatic personnel in England and Wales that were not pursued because of diplomatic immunity (Wilson 1967, 79).

The immunity rule is remarkable, because the payoff from not protecting diplomats can be high. Iranians mobbed the U.S. embassy in 1979 in part because they believed that the United States was responsible for the shah's regime. If the Iranian government had restrained the mob, it would have suffered a decline in its popularity among citizens. The local population can be similarly aroused when diplomatic personnel violate local criminal laws. Members of the British public were upset when a U.S. ambassador was not prosecuted after shooting to death an intruder (Wilson 1967, 88). The U.S. Congress has considered several bills designed to restrict immunity for certain crimes, such as drunk driving (id., 37). More recently, the American public was aroused when a Georgian diplomat ran over and killed an American teenager in Washington, D.C., while driving under the influence of alcohol. There are many similar examples. In all of these cases, governments responsive to popular agitation would receive a relatively high short-term payoff by either seizing or allowing others to seize diplomatic personnel.

In these circumstances, diplomatic immunity can prevail only if the conditions of two-state cooperation are met. They usually are. Relations between two states are almost always indefinitely long games. The benefits from diplomatic communication are high, but these benefits are always spread out over the long term. Short-term deviations may be tempting because of local or temporary political circumstances, but are unlikely to exceed the long-term benefit of communication. When a diplomat from state B commits a crime, state A has an interest in enforcing its criminal laws against the diplomat to preserve the integrity of the criminal law and prevent local unrest. But if A prosecutes the diplomat, it suffers more than just a breakdown in communication with B, for B has a hostage in the person of A's ambassador and may retaliate by harming A's ambassador.

These adverse consequences from enforcing local criminal law against B's diplomat mean that A will receive a larger payoff from non-enforcement if B refrains in similar circumstances. Although a diplomat may impose costs on a host state by committing crimes, the host state refrains from punishing him or her because it wants to maintain its own diplomat in the foreign state. This cooperative strategy (immunity) has a clear all-or-nothing quality that is relatively easy to monitor; indeed, the all-or-nothing quality of states' responses is probably intended to avoid ambiguity. Each state's response to a violation of the immunity rule (retaliate) is clear.[2] And states that successfully maintain long-term diplomatic relations are usually relatively stable states, rather than rogue or revolutionary states, consistent with the assumption that cooperation can be achieved primarily when parties have low discount rates.

At first glance, the ambassadorial immunity rule appears to be a counterexample to our claim that cooperative multilateral behavioral regularities are not likely to exist. In fact, it shows the opposite: it illustrates our claim that a broad behavioral regularity may develop as an amalgam of independent, bilateral repeated prisoner's dilemmas. The logic of ambassadorial immunity—the sending and receiving of diplomats, the monitoring of diplomatic activities, the breakdown in communication and retaliation that follow harm to a diplomat, and so forth—takes place within bilateral relations. The fact that states A and B have diplomatic relations with numerous other states is irrelevant; relations with third countries do no work in explaining the operation of the diplomatic immunity rule. Far from being multilateral cooperation, ambassadorial immunity reflects equilibria that arise from strategic behavior in pairwise interactions among all states.

Abundant evidence supports this claim. When diplomatic immunity is denied or postponed, the diplomat's country often retaliates, but third countries do not. For example, in 1961 the Soviet Union expelled the Dutch ambassador in protest of the Dutch police's alleged mistreatment of the Soviet ambassador, but no other states retaliated (Wilson 1967, 68 n. 145). Only in egregious cases do otherwise uninvolved states retaliate against another state for violating diplomatic immunity, and even in these cases, retaliation is neither universal nor significant. Consider the Iranian invasion of the U.S. embassy. No state pulled its embassy from Iran, and the United Nations failed to impose sanctions (Frey and Frey 1999, 480, 519). Only the United States' closest allies, the European Community states and Japan, imposed economic sanctions. They did so late, grudgingly, and in response to enormous pressure from the United States (Frey and Frey 1999, 519; *Economist* 1980a, 77). The sanctions they finally did impose were generally acknowledged to be ineffectual, empty gestures (Frey and Frey 1999, 480, 518–19; *Economist* 1980b).

In addition, while our theory accounts for a general behavioral regularity of states protecting diplomats, it does not predict equilibrium behavior to be identical among all states. It is one thing to say, at a high level of generality, that states respect diplomatic immunity and that immunity equilibria resemble each other. This is not surprising because the same basic strategic game is being played by states in the same basic position. States exchange ambassadors for communicative benefits, they are sometimes tempted to prosecute foreign ambassadors or to fail to protect them from harm, they risk a breakdown in communications and retaliation against their ambassador if they fail to protect foreign ambassadors, and they can hold foreign ambassadors as hostages if foreign states harm their own ambassadors. But our theory predicts that details of behavior will vary in important respects when the relationships between states vary. The evidence is too sketchy to confirm or falsify these hypotheses with rigor, but it is highly suggestive.

The first claim is that rogue states violate the rules of diplomatic immunity more often than "civilized" states do. When states have unstable political institutions, their leaders weigh short-term payoffs more heavily than leaders in other states do. As a result, they are more willing to risk retaliation to obtain any payoffs from violating diplomatic immunity in the present. Available empirical evidence shows that developing states, states in the throes of revolution, and states controlled by unstable dictators violate diplomatic immunity more frequently than "civilized" states do (Frey and Frey 1999, 503–7; McClanahan 1989, 142–46). The Iran hostage crisis is a prominent example, but so too are the 1967 attack on the British embassy by supporters of the Cultural Revolution in China and the 1958 Iraqi military coup that resulted in the burning of the British embassy (McClanahan 1989, 145, 181; Wilson 1967, 68–70). There are many similar examples (Wilson 1967, 51–52, 62–63, 82, 86). A survey of U.S. Foreign Service officers indicated that "the extent of protection in so-called 'civilized countries' was greater than in the newly emerging nations" and that in these emerging nations, "the degree of protection apparently sometimes coincided with the level of political stability and the role of the political leader" (Wilson 1967, 50).

The second claim is that states are more likely to violate diplomatic immunity when stakes change, so that the benefits of violating immunity (for example, quelling a popular outcry) are very high or the benefits of respecting immunity (for example, maintaining communication with a state) are low. Several observations are consistent with this claim. Perhaps the most frequent denial of diplomatic immunity occurs when the diplomat does something in the host state that threatens its national security (see generally, Wilson 1967, 82–86). To take two examples: the British seized Swedish Ambassador Count Gyllenborg in 1917 in connection with a plot to overthrow George I (*Law Journal* 1929) and in 1914 the United States arrested and seized the papers of an attaché of the German embassy who was conspiring against the neutrality of the United States (Wilson 1967, 83). When a state's security is threatened, it receives a higher payoff from compromising diplomatic immunity. Another example is the well-documented mistreatment of diplomats behind the Iron Curtain at the onset of the cold war (McClanahan 1989, 143–44; Wilson 1967, 55). The communist states were closed societies that often arrested, detained, and harassed diplomats to deter their travel, inquiries, and photography within the host state (Wilson 1967, 62–70). Wilson (id., 71) refers to this trend as a "retrogression" from traditional practice. The retrogression makes sense: the communist states suffered more than noncommunist states from enforcement of the traditional customary international law of diplomatic immunity, because in a closed society ordinary observation is more damaging than in an open society.

The third claim is that respect for diplomatic immunities, far from being universal, is sensitive to variations in bilateral relations between states over time. The Soviet Union mistreated foreign diplomats with greater regularity than did Russia before and after the Soviet Union; the United States and the Soviet Union subjected each other's diplomats to more harassment during the cold war than at other times; and states in the Eastern bloc treated diplomats from the West with less respect than they treated diplomats from fellow Eastern bloc states (Wilson 1967, 55–56, 62–70, 71–72). The explanation for these variations is that the diplomats of one's enemies pose a greater threat to security than the diplomats of one's friends; so, when dealing with one's enemies, the payoff from violating diplomatic immunity will often be higher than the cost. By contrast, the traditional view cannot explain the many deviations from the immunity rule.

Territorial Sea

Prior to the eighteenth century, many powerful maritime states proclaimed control over large areas of the ocean. These states were unable to sustain their claims, however, and by the eighteenth century the seas became viewed as free areas that no state could appropriate (Heinzen 1959, 598–601). One limitation on this so-called freedom of the seas was the power that a state retained over the territorial sea adjacent to its coast. According to the doctrine of territorial jurisdiction, a state had plenary jurisdiction within its territorial sea and no jurisdiction beyond it. Other states could freely exploit and navigate the sea up to the boundary of a state's territorial sea, but they could no more operate within a state's territorial sea without the state's permission than they could operate in a state's territory without permission.

Jurists originally conceived the territorial sea as the water a state defended to protect its territorial sovereignty (Jessup 1927, 5). Bynkershoek (1923, 44) famously captured the idea with the statement "The power of the land properly ends where the force of arms ends." In the seventeenth and eighteenth centuries, the territorial sea did not have a settled breadth (Brownlie 1960, 187–88). During this time, Bynkershoek's dictum evolved into the idea that a state's sovereignty over the sea extended as far as it could fire a cannonball from its shores. By the end of the eighteenth century, many who embraced the cannon-shot rule began to identify it with a three-mile breadth, the approximate distance that cannonballs could be projected at the time (Churchill and Lowe 1983, 59).

Conventional wisdom holds that a three-mile territorial sea was customary international law during most of the nineteenth and the first half of the twentieth century (Calvo 1896, 479; Heinzen 1959, 629, 634; Hyde 1922, 251–53; Jessup 1927, 62–66; Oppenheim 1912, 257; Phillimore 1879, 274–75; Westlake 1910, 167). The basis for this conventional wisdom is as follows. In the nineteenth and twentieth centuries, the three-mile rule was officially championed by several states, most notably Britain and the United States, as a rule of customary international law (Colombos 1962, 85–88; Heinzen 1959, 617–19; Jessup 1927, 62–63). Many states that attempted to assert a broader jurisdiction than three miles retracted these claims in the face of threats or protests, usually from the United States or Britain (see Heinzen 1959, 630–32). Sometimes states paid damages after asserting jurisdiction beyond the three-mile range (id., 636). The three-mile rule also appeared in numerous international agreements (for example, *The North Sea Fisheries Convention*, 1882). And it was broadly, though not unanimously, supported by jurists (Riesenfeld 1942, 29–98).

The immediate problem with the traditional account is that as many states rejected the three-mile rule as adhered to it (Riesenfeld 1942, 129–250). The Scandinavian countries always asserted at least a four-mile territorial sea (Heinzen 1959, 605–12; Riesenfeld 1942, 188–94). Spain and Portugal consistently asserted that the territorial jurisdiction band was six miles wide (Jessup 1927, 26–31; Riesenfeld 1942, 175–80); Russia (and later the USSR) frequently asserted claims beyond the three-mile band (Jessup 1927, 26–31; Riesenfeld 1942, 194–203); and various other countries claimed jurisdiction beyond the three-mile band (Riesenfeld 1942, 208). It is true that some of these states sometimes asserted jurisdiction only up to three miles in the face of threats of retaliation, usually from Britain or the United States. To take one of many examples, in 1821 Russia claimed jurisdiction up to "100 Italian miles" off the coasts of eastern Siberia and Alaska, but ultimately agreed to a three-mile rule by treaty with Britain and the United States following protests from both states (Riesenfeld 1942, 144–46; Heinzen 1959, 630). In these latter cases, the resulting behavioral regularity is best explained by coercion. It is no coincidence that the most successful enforcers of the three-mile rule were Britain, the preeminent naval power, and the United States, a burgeoning naval power, both states with a strong interest in limiting encroachment on the freedom of the seas and the power to enforce these interests. However, even these powerful states were often unable to make credible threats to enforce the rule; threats and complaints were often not heeded, and practices inconsistent with the three-mile rule frequently went unabated. Thus, for example, Spain ignored some British complaints in the nineteenth century about Spanish jurisdictional claims and seizures beyond the three-mile limit (Riesenfeld 1942, 147).

The absence of a customary state practice is confirmed by the debates and resolutions in various official conferences throughout the period, which reveal stark disagreement about the breadth of the territorial sea (Riesenfeld 1942, 99–111). In addition, the treatise writers were split (id., 279–80). Those who claimed that customary international law required a three-mile band were predominantly English-speaking jurists who reflected their states' views of customary international law (Fulton 1911, 681).

Turning to the details of state practice, throughout the period many states enforced antismuggling and related security laws outside the three-mile band (Fulton 1911, 594; Jessup 1927, 19, 25, 76–96). The standard view explains away these examples as "exceptions" to the three-mile rule or as actions that other states did not challenge for reasons of "comity" (Jessup 1927, 76–97). A better explanation is that the coastal state has a strong interest in asserting jurisdiction beyond three miles in this context, and other states usually have little reason to support smuggling into the coastal state. This is not to suggest that all antismuggling regimes arose from such a coincidence of interest. Sometimes the assertion of antismuggling jurisdiction beyond the three-mile limit resulted in protests, although these protests did not always, or even usually, result in a retreat to the three-mile line. For example, Britain complained about the 1853 Spanish seizure of the British ship *Fortuna*, but Spain ignored the complaint and Britain dropped the matter after failing to rally support from other states for its position (Riesenfeld 1942, 146–47). Even a relatively weak state is in a good position to patrol coastal waters; so a large state that seeks to preserve the three-mile line may be unable to enforce its will when many weak states violate the rule by claiming a broader territorial sea.

A related problem was the scope of the band of territorial sea in which a neutral state's ships could remain immune from belligerent capture. During the period in question, some states asserted a three-mile zone of neutrality, but many other states asserted zones of neutrality beyond three miles (Jessup 1927, 25, 47–48, 103–5). These regulations were rarely tested because there were relatively few maritime wars in the seventy years prior to World War I (Fulton 1911, 604, 651). But the few international clashes in this context are revealing. During World War I, Britain successfully checked Norway's assertion of a four-mile neutrality zone by capturing Norwegian ships three miles outside of Norway; at the same time, Britain (and the United States) acquiesced in Italy's assertion of a six-mile neutrality zone "out of courtesy" (Jessup 1927, 25 n. 86, 34; Riesenfeld 1942, 163). Scholars have reconciled these actions by arguing that the Norwegian situation exemplifies the true customary international law rule and that the Italian deviation was permitted out of comity. A better explanation is that Britain had the power to coerce compliance with the three-mile rule and a significant interest in intercepting Norwegian shipping destined for Germany. But it did not enforce the three-mile rule against its ally Italy. The relationship between Britain and Norway was one of coercion; the relationship between Britain and Italy was one of coincidence of interest.

The deviations from the ostensible three-mile rule are said to reflect the larger principle that a state can assert jurisdiction beyond the three-mile limit in self-defense or for self-preservation (Jessup 1927, 96–101). This exception to the three-mile rule, analogous to the national security exception to ambassadorial immunity, suggests that the three-mile rule did not limit state action in cases where states had interests in exceeding the limit. A similar story explains the practice of asserting jurisdiction beyond three miles over the rare, valuable, and exhaustible sedentary fisheries such as coral and oysters (id., 13–16).

The same idea is reflected in the single exception to exclusive jurisdiction *within* the three-mile zone: the customary international law right of innocent passage (id., 120). The right of innocent passage permits a foreign ship to pass through the territorial sea unless the ship does something to prejudice the security, public policy, or fiscal interests of the state (id., 120–23). There is indeed a long-term behavioral regularity of states not seizing foreign ships passing close to shore that are deemed innocent. But states have varying and self-serving definitions of innocence; the rule does nothing to prevent a state from seizing a ship that the state perceives to be a threat to its interest. What international scholars consider to be customary international law is nothing more than a description of states acting in their interest: states seize ships passing through their territorial sea exactly when they have reason to do so. As Hall (1924, 216) has noted: "The state is . . . indifferent to . . . what happens among a knot of foreigners so passing through her [territorial sea] as not to come in contact with the population. To attempt to exercise jurisdiction in respect of acts producing no effect beyond the vessel, and not tending to do so, is of advantage to no one." All of these deviations are inconsistent with the traditional account of the three-mile rule; all have straightforward explanations within our framework.

Another embarrassment to the traditional account that makes sense in our theory concerns the double standards of the three-mile rule's proponents. During the same period when Great Britain championed and enforced the three-mile rule, it acted to preserve its ability to assert jurisdiction beyond three miles when doing so suited its needs (Riesenfeld 1942, 131, 148–54). For example, during the eighteenth and nineteenth centuries, the English Hovering Acts asserted customs jurisdiction beyond the three-mile range. And in legislation and treaty making during the late nineteenth century, Britain was careful not to commit itself to the three-mile rule generally and to preserve its rights to assert jurisdiction beyond the three-mile limit with respect to certain fishing rights, bays, folded coasts, pearls, and coral banks (id., 148–71). Similarly, the United States protested Russian restrictions on sealing beyond three miles in the Bering Sea when Russia owned the sea. But after the cession of Alaska to the United States in 1867, the United States, pursuant to an act of Congress asserting U.S. dominion over the entire Bering Sea, seized seal hunters in the Sea beyond the three-mile limit (Jessup 1927, 54–57). This is one of many examples of the United States "var[ying] her principles and claims as to the extent of territorial waters, according to her policy at the time" (Fulton 1911, 650). These examples show that, as in the other case studies, states will assert changing and inconsistent readings of customary international law consistent with their interests.

Throughout the period, the greatest clashes over territorial jurisdiction concerned the area of water to which a state's citizens would have exclusive fishing rights. Coastal states with weak navies sought to maximize the breadth of exclusive fishing rights; states with powerful navies sought to minimize the scope of exclusivity. There was little stability in practice.

As one would expect from their proximity and shared body of narrow water, Britain and France (and to a lesser degree Britain and Belgium, and Britain and Holland) frequently clashed over the three-mile rule for fishing (Fulton 1911, 605–50). To the extent that the three-mile rule was effectively embraced, it was by virtue of carefully negotiated bilateral and multilateral treaties rather than customary practice; yet even these treaties were frequently violated. Both sides captured ships of the other that were fishing beyond the three-mile limit, and both sides had ships that fished within the other's three-mile limit. To be sure, the history was not one of unremitting chaos. There were short periods in which two states engaged in what might be called cooperative behavior, usually pursuant to a treaty. One explanation for such cooperation is that two states with access to a fishery find themselves in a bilateral repeated prisoner's dilemma, and when conditions are favorable, cooperation will occur. Consistent with this theory, the most successful instances of cooperation, such as the harvesting of oysters, occurred when both sides would clearly be harmed by overexploitation and violations were relatively easy to identify.

Similarly, Spain and Russia tried to assert fishing rights beyond the three-mile zone. Sometimes, they succeeded. More often, they were met with threats of force from Britain and the United States and backed away to defend only a three-mile band. This is thought by some to evidence a rule of customary international law. A better explanation is that Britain and the United States had much stronger navies and powerful interests in maximizing areas in which their nationals could fish. It is not surprising that states with powerful navies would tend to desire the narrowest possible territorial sea and would usually get their way.

The only puzzle is why the United States and Britain recognized even a three-mile territorial sea. The likely answer is that neither the United States nor Britain was powerful enough both to provide safe passage to their civilian fishing vessels along the coast of a hostile power and to defend their fishing vessels close to home. Most states have a stronger interest in protecting their own coastal seas than in maintaining rights for their ships in distant seas for the simple reason that their fishing industry can more cheaply harvest the coastal seas, which are close to shore, than distant seas. In addition, it is considerably easier to defend coastal seas, both by ship and from the shore, than to maintain power over distant waters.

Thus, every state of roughly similar power has an interest in not interfering with the coastal fisheries of other states in return for noninterference with their own coastal fisheries. The only problem, which is characteristic of such games, is coordinating on a particular area. What is needed is a focal point. Any band defined by a constant distance from the coastline is more simple, more "focal," than the alternatives, such as particular longitudes and latitudes. So it is no surprise that the fights about defining the territorial sea for fishing purposes were couched in terms of band widths. That the three-mile rule was frequently invoked during the period in question can be explained by the fact that three miles comported with the eighteenth-century cannon-shot mark: the rough distance from which a state could protect its seas from shore (Fulton 1911, 694). But, of course, states would have different interests over the size of the band, as the optimal size for each state would vary according to local technologies, economic needs, and types of fish available. These considerations suggest that the battle of the sexes game is a better model than the pure coordination game; here, we would expect the powerful states to prevail over the weak states.

Finally, the fishing example illustrates how various exogenous shocks led to changes in behavior. A prominent example is trawling, a late nineteenth-century development (on this point, see Fulton 1911, 698–703; Riesenfeld 1942, 152–55). Trawling was a profitable but destructive form of fishing; trawling just outside the three-mile band disrupted fishing within the band much more than prior fishing methods. The rise of the steamship (also in the late nineteenth century) made trawling possible at much farther distances. These developments heightened conflicts over fishing zones and precipitated the expansion of asserted and defended zones early in the twentieth century (Brown 1994, 8). They also explain why Britain began to hedge on its formal assertion of the three-mile rule in the late nineteenth century. Britain wanted to assert trawling broadly abroad but protect fisheries at home. This led it to refrain from asserting a well-defined rule, relying instead on standards that it, the preeminent naval power, could interpret flexibly to suit its needs.

Another example of how exogenous shocks can change behavior: as more states gained independence, the behavioral regularities became less common (Brown 1994, 8). Cooperation and coordination become exponentially more difficult as the number of participants increases. Although a rule may evolve that governs fishing among a few large states, it is less likely that a rule could evolve to foster cooperation or coordination among dozens of states.

The customary international law of the territorial sea was never uniform and never static. States followed different behavioral patterns in different maritime contexts, in accordance with their interests and power. Behaviors changed during relatively short periods of time. The ostensible three-mile rule did little, if any, work in affecting the actual behavior of states. Sometimes one state had an interest in asserting jurisdiction beyond the three-mile limit and no other state had an interest in preventing this act; this was coincidence of interest. At other times, a state tried to assert jurisdiction but was met by a threat of retaliation from a more powerful state; this was coercion. In yet other contexts, states engaged in mutually beneficial cooperative behavior by refraining from exercising jurisdiction beyond a three-mile limit; this can be seen as a prisoner's dilemma or a coordination game. The many puzzles, inconsistencies, and violations that appear under the traditional view make sense when viewed through the lens of the various and changing interests at stake.

Rather than following an exogenous rule, then, states acted in their self-interest, and their behavior changed as their interests changed. In arguing for an exogenous rule of customary international law, jurists commit the errors of (1) inferring a rule of customary international law from a few cases that amount to a behavioral regularity in a specific context during a short period of time; (2) labeling behavioral patterns inconsistent with the ostensible rule as "exceptions" or "comity"; (3) viewing a coincidence of interest or coercion situation as evidence of cooperation; and (4) analyzing behavioral patterns without considering the different underlying logics that these patterns exemplify.

The Paquete Habana

Perhaps the most famous case identifying and applying customary international law is *The Paquete Habana* (1900). As noted in chapter 1, this case involved a seizure by the U.S. Navy of a Cuban fishing smack during the Spanish-American War. At the time of the decision, the customary international law of prize permitted a belligerent to capture ships and goods at sea during times of war. *The Paquete Habana* held that customary international law excluded enemy coastal fishing vessels from this right of capture. Most contemporary commentators agreed with the U.S. Supreme Court's analysis. Although prize law today has little importance, *The Paquete Habana* remains an important international law decision for its illustration of the process by which the fishing vessel exemption ripened from a customary practice into an "established rule of international law." The decision is reproduced in almost all international law casebooks (Damrosch et al. 2001, 62; Janis and Noyes 1997, 66; Carter, Trimble, and Bradley 2003, 226). It is generally viewed as a model of how customary international law becomes established (Rogers 1999, 5–19).

Our main goal here is to show that the famous customary international law analysis in *The Paquete Habana* is riddled with errors characteristic of the mainstream approach to customary international law, and that the behaviors associated with the coastal fishing vessel rule make more sense under our theory than under the traditional account. We do this through a close examination of the evidence that was invoked in support of the rule. Like the *Paquete Habana* Court, we begin with an examination of customary practice prior to the nineteenth century. We next examine the nineteenth-century evidence that convinced the Court that a customary international law norm had ripened. We then consider the influence of *The Paquete Habana* on subsequent practice. We conclude with some reflections on what the decision teaches about the nature of customary international law.

Practice through the Early Nineteenth Century

In *The Paquete Habana*, the Court acknowledged that the fishing vessel exemption was not customary international law at the beginning of the nineteenth century. The Court nonetheless examined the prehistory of the customary international law rule, as if to claim that the rule was latent prior to the nineteenth century, ready to spring forth when conditions ripened.

Beginning in the fifteenth century, pairs of states would occasionally agree not to attack each other's civilian fishing vessels. The Court cited a treaty signed by France and Britain in 1403; treaties, joint edicts, and mutual understandings between France and the Holy Roman Empire in 1521; and treaties and understandings between France and Holland in 1536 and again in 1675. With one exception, the Court neither discussed whether these treaties were tested by war nor provided any evidence of state practice pursuant to the treaties. The exception was the 1675 "mutual agreement" between France and Holland. The Court noted that as early as 1681, France stopped complying with this agreement because of what a French writer called the "faithless conduct of the enemies of France" (*The Paquete Habana* 1900, 689).

The Court then skipped one hundred years to the late eighteenth century. It cited a 1779 French declaration not to seize vessels carrying fresh fish, as well as the release pursuant to this declaration of a British fishing vessel seized in 1780. In that same year, however, the British High Court of the Admiralty issued a standing order concerning procedures for prize captures of fishing vessels. Nonetheless, the Court noted that Britain and France "abstained from interfering with coastal fisheries" during the American Revolutionary War (*The Paquete Habana* 1900, 690). The Court did not say why they did so—whether, for example, they did so because custom required or just because they had better things to do with their navies.

After citing three U.S.-Prussian treaties that embraced the fishing vessel exemption rule in case of war, the Court moved to the wars of the French Revolution. Following France's Declaration of War in February 1793, Britain authorized the capture of French vessels, and late that year the French National Convention asked the executive to conduct reprisals. In 1798, Britain again authorized the seizure of French (and Dutch) fishing vessels, and several fishing vessels were captured as prizes of war. One British prize court described the state of the law in 1798 as follows: "In former wars it has not been usual to make captures of these small fishing vessels; but this rule was a rule of comity only, and not of legal decision; it has prevailed from views of mutual accommodation between neighboring countries, and from tenderness to a poor and industrious people. In the present war there has, I presume, been sufficient reason for changing this mode of treatment" (*The Paquete Habana* 1900, 693, quoting *The Young Jacob and Johana* 1798).

When Britain and France officially stopped seizing each other's fishing vessels at the beginning of the nineteenth century, Britain announced that this action was "nowise founded upon an agreement but upon a simple concession," and "this concession would always be subordinate to the convenience of the moment" (*The Paquete Habana* 1900, 693). Although in 1801 the French Council of Prizes released a captured Portuguese fishing vessel and stated that the capture contradicted "the principles of humanity and the maxims of international law" (id., 693, quoting *La Nostra Senora de la Piedad* 1801), the British view of early nineteenth-century customary international law was, as the Supreme Court appeared to acknowledge, a truer description of affairs.·

Four observations are in order about this pre-1815 evidence. First, the paucity of evidence is noteworthy. The Court's analysis focuses on relations between Britain on the one hand and France (predominantly), Holland, and the Holy Roman Empire on the other. It tells us little about the practice of any other maritime state during the many wars from the fifteenth century to the nineteenth, including the Hundred Years' War, the Thirty Years' War, the Seven Years' War, the Great Northern War, the various wars between the Ottoman Turks and European powers, and scores of other, smaller wars involving naval conflict. In a case famous for its extensive examination of custom, this highly selective survey makes clear how difficult it would be to do the work needed to discover a universal customary practice. It also shows how cautious one must be about generalizing from a limited sample of cases scattered over several centuries. For example, if state A and state B conclude an agreement in 1450, and A and C have a similar agreement in 1550, it does not follow that all are part of any "implicit" agreement thereafter, especially because the circumstances of A and B's relations inevitably differ from the circumstances of A and C's.

Second, the evidence adduced by the Court has dubious value. The Court relies primarily on states' agreements and announcements rather than the conduct of their navies. Such evidence might count in favor of *opinio juris*, but it does not, at least on the traditional positivist view, count as custom. The Court offers scattered examples of states not seizing fishing vessels during wars. But it fails to consider the many reasons a state might abstain from seizing a belligerent's coastal fishing vessels. Seizing such a vessel is a costly activity in terms of lost opportunities and military expenditures, and it provides the state with little gain. A state's navy often has more valuable opportunities to pursue, such as defending the coastline or attacking the enemy's navy. The Court assumes that states that did not seize the enemy's coastal fishing vessels acted pursuant to customary international law. But it might well be that states did not seize the vessels for the same reason that they did not sink their own ships: they simply had no interest in doing so because the activity was costly and produced few benefits.

This latter conclusion finds support in a third feature of the pre-nineteenth-century evidence: each state's position on the content of customary international law, most notably France's and Britain's, reflected its interests and capacities. France, which had a broad fishing coast and a relatively weak navy (Lloyd 1975, 76–80; Phillips et al. 1936, 24–26), consistently used treaties, pronouncements, and nonreprisals to obtain consent to a rule that protected its coastal fishery. Britain, which had the world's most powerful navy, saw no reason to yield its advantage. The Court, however, viewed France's support for the fishing vessel exemption in sentimental rather than strategic terms. It quoted Napoleon Bonaparte—not someone known for his humanitarian impulses in war or for his compliance with international law—who piously declared in 1801 that Britain's attack on French fishermen is contrary "to all the usages of civilized nations . . . even in time of war." Napoleon added that the French would respond magnanimously to the British atrocities, for having always made it "a maxim to alleviate as much as possible the evils of war, [France] could not think, on its part, of rendering wretched fishermen victims of a prolongation of hostilities, and would abstain from all reprisals" (*The Paquete Habana* 1900, 693). This was pure propaganda (Hall 1924, 535).

Finally, the bilateral nature of the relations the Court examined is noteworthy. All of the conflicts involve two states with neighboring or proximate coasts. This is significant for two reasons. First, as explained in chapter 1, we might expect the opportunity for international cooperation to be at its height when only two states are involved. And yet the Court's opinion makes clear that cooperation in protecting coastal fisheries was rare and fragile before 1815. Second, the Court provides no evidence that the incipient custom extended beyond the bilateral context. It cites no evidence of treaties or customary practices involving more than two states. Nor does it cite evidence that third countries protested against, much less retaliated as a result of, a violation of the fishing vessel exemption rule. There may have been isolated bilateral customs; there were no multilateral ones.

Nineteenth-Century Evidence

We now turn to the evidence that persuaded the Court that by the late nineteenth century customary international law had developed to protect coastal fishing vessels. Britain declared in orders in 1806 and 1810 that it would not seize the fishing vessels of Prussia and France, respectively. The United States did not seize coastal fishing vessels during the Mexican War on the east coast, though it did authorize its navy to capture "all vessels" under Mexican flag on the west coast, with no mention of an exemption for fishing vessels. The 1848 Treaty of Peace between the United States and Mexico prohibited the seizure of fishing vessels in future wars. France ordered its navy not to seize coastal fishing vessels in the Crimean War in 1854, in its war with Italy in 1859, and during the Franco-Prussian War in 1870, though with a significant exception: "unless naval or military operations should make it necessary" (*The Paquete Habana* 1900, 699–700). Moreover, France's ally during the Crimean war, Britain, destroyed Russian fishing vessels. The Court also noted that during the period since the British orders of 1806 and 1810, "no instance has been found in which the exemption . . . has been denied by Britain, or any other nation" (id., 700). Finally, the Court surveyed a large number of commentators, most of whom thought customary international law included the fishing vessel exemption.

This is the sum total of the evidence that the Court recounted in support of its conclusion that, by the end of the nineteenth century, the fishing vessel exemption rule had grown "by the general assent of nations, into a settled rule of international law" (*The Paquete Habana*, 694). Yet the evidence for this conclusion is weak. A few states announced an intention not to seize the fishing vessels of a few states during times of war, and other states remained silent on the issue, without denying the exemption, to be sure, but without affirming it either. These scattered, untested executory commitments hardly constitute a universal practice followed out of a sense of legal obligation.

The evidence looks even weaker when one considers that the period from 1815 to 1900 was one of relative peace in Europe and that there were very few naval wars to test the fishing vessel exemption rule. The European wars during this period did not last long, they took place mostly on land, and they did not generally involve the disruption of sea trade in a way that affected maritime rights (Hattendorf 1994, 110; Coogan 1981, 21, 25; Howard 1976, 95–99). To take a typical example, the Franco-Prussian War lasted only ten months, and France was essentially defeated much sooner. The French Navy, which was more powerful than the Prussian Navy, proved "totally ineffective" (Kennedy 1989, 186). The quick defeats on land meant that many French naval forces never made it to the Prussian coasts, and the ones that did were quickly recalled to France to assist in the futile defense of Paris (Howard 1962, 75–76). In short, the French Navy never had the opportunity to raid Prussian coastal fishing vessels. We have not been able to discover why the French government ordered its navy not to seize coastal fishing vessels at the outset of the Franco-Prussian War. But because the commitment was never tested, the French order should not count as evidence that it was following customary international law.

Indeed, what is striking about the Court's nineteenth-century evidence is that during the one war in which the fishing vessel exemption rule was clearly tested, the Crimean War, the rule was violated. As the Court acknowledged, during this war Britain destroyed coastal fishing vessels in the Sea of Azof (Verzijl et al. 1992, 296). In this light, the Court's claim that Britain did not deny the validity of the fishing vessel exemption rule after the Napoleonic Wars means very little, for Britain did not participate in the continental wars during this period. It never had the opportunity as a belligerent to confront or defend the fishing vessel exemption rule—except, of course, during the Crimean War, when it violated the rule. It is difficult to understand how the Court can conclude that the fishing vessel exemption rule had grown "by the general consent of civilized nations" into "a settled rule of international law" when Great Britain, the leading maritime power and the leading defender of the right to attack coastal fisheries, did not accede to the rule (*The Paquete Habana* 1900, 708).

It is against this background that the Court's lengthy discussion of treatise writers must be considered. The bulk of these writers supported the Court's conclusion about the fishing vessel exemption rule, although many of them, most notably British writers, denied the existence of the rule. The important point is that, as best we can tell, the writers added no independent evidence beyond the cases and documents cited by the Court. It is true, of course, that the "works of jurists and commentators" were a traditional source of customary international law. But as the Court made clear, they were a source only because "by years of labor, research and experience" they had "made themselves peculiarly well acquainted with the subjects of which they treat." Accordingly, "such works are resorted to by judicial tribunals, not for the speculations of their authors concerning what the law ought to be, but for trustworthy evidence of what the law really is" (*The Paquete Habana* 1900, 700). Because the scholarly treatises added nothing to the evidence already considered by the Court, the Court should have excluded them from consideration, based on its own theory of their relevance.

Finally, the limited scope of the fishing vessel exemption rule is important. The Court acknowledged that the fishing vessel exemption had exceptions for deep water or commercial vessels and for vessels seized under conditions of military necessity. This means that the bulk of the cases in which states would have an interest in seizing fishing vessels would be the very cases not covered by the customary international law fishing vessel exemption. One would expect states to refrain from seizing vessels that have little economic value (in the first case) or little military value (in the second case), regardless of what customary international law says. It is thus no surprise that, as far as we can tell, the exceptions were invoked in all of the cases involving the seizure of fishing vessels after the Napoleonic Wars. Of course, it is possible that there were no other reported prize cases because states followed customary international law and never seized "true" coastal fishing vessels. This account is consistent with the absence of seizures. There is, however, no affirmative evidence for either account. We discuss the significance of this fact below.

Early Twentieth-Century Practice

One might argue that the preceding discussion is beside the point because, as a matter of positive law, *The Paquete Habana* brought the customary international law into existence. This argument would imply that the new customary international law subsequently influenced the behavior of states. Although there were many pronouncements supportive of the *Paquete Habana* rule, there is little evidence that the rule itself had any influence on the behavior of any state, including the United States, other than the United States' payment of damages to the claimants in that case.

The Paquete Habana has been cited many times by U.S. courts, but almost always for its famous proposition that "international law is part of our law" (for example, in *First National City Bank* 1983 and *Princz* 1994), and never, as far as we can tell, as the basis of a decision in a prize case involving coastal fishing vessels. Although this is no doubt due in part to changes in naval strategy and the decline of prize, it does mean that there is no evidence that it influenced U.S. courts. During World Wars I and II, the United States instructed its navy to exempt coastal fishing vessels from capture (Stucky 1985, 45). We have not been able to determine whether the United States issued this exemption for strategic reasons (to keep the navy from engaging in unimportant tasks) or to comply with customary international law; but there is no reason to think that the United States had any reason to seize coastal fishing vessels during these wars. In the Korean War, however, "the United States openly flouted the *Paquete Habana* principle by seizing and summarily destroying all coastal fishing vessels that its forces could capture" (id., 46). During the Vietnam War, U.S. naval forces avoided mining wooden coastal fishing vessels, although we have not been able to determine why (Clark 1973, 175).

The Paquete Habana also had little influence on the behavior of other states. To be sure, the coastal fishing vessel exemption was embraced by the Hague Convention of 1907, where Britain for the first time agreed to the exemption as a legal principle (Oppenheim 1912, 477–78). And many delegates said the purpose of the exemption was to protect coastal fishing on the humanitarian grounds that it was a small industry and fishermen were poor. But a careful reading of the text and the delegates' debates gives grounds for skepticism about the delegates' own optimism. During the debates, delegates pointed out that fishing vessels may be used for military purposes: the fishermen might convey information about naval movements to the enemy; the enemy might plant spies or transport contraband on fishing vessels; and the fishing vessels might be used as weapons (Scott 1921, 617). These fears explain the final rule's limitation to vessels "exclusively" used for fishing. It also accounts for the failure to specify what constituted a fishing vessel or what it meant to fish along the coast, leaving these important issues to be determined by the states involved (Colombos 1940, 147). In short, the rule adopted at the Hague Convention was too narrow and ambiguous to prevent a state from seizing a fishing vessel when it would have any interest in doing so.

Turning to state practice, treatise writers say that states did not seize fishing vessels between 1898 and World War I, as though this showed that states respected the fishing vessel rule. But it does not, because the major European powers and the United States were not at war with each other during that time. The two major wars during the period, the Boer War and the Russo-Japanese War, do not support the existence of such a rule. The Boers were landlocked, and they had no means to threaten British fishing. The Japanese seized numerous Russian fishing vessels during their war, and the Japanese prize courts rejected claims by owners of the vessels, generally on the grounds that these vessels were engaged in deep-sea fishing and were operated by companies (Bray and Hurst 1913, 80–82, 92–93). These courts acknowledged the existence of the Hague Convention, but they distinguished it on the grounds that it applied only to small, coastal fishing vessels owned by individuals; they did not speculate as to whether the Hague Convention might be binding in other circumstances. There is thus no evidence that either the Hague Convention or *The Paquete Habana* influenced behavior during the Russo-Japanese War.

The same is true of British prize courts during World War I. In *The Berlin*, the court condemned a fishing vessel, holding that the exemption did not apply because of the vessel's size (110 metric tons) and the locations where it had been engaged in fishing (J. Gardner 1927, 241–43). Although the court cited *The Paquete Habana*, among other cases, as evidence of the fishing vessel exemption's status as customary international law, the court held that the seizure was permitted; the court's reference to *The Paquete Habana* is thus dicta that cannot count as evidence of its influence on state behavior. In *The Marbrouck*, a French Prize Court held that the exemption did not apply to the vessels in question because they supplied blockaded ports (Colombos 1940, 147). We have found no other relevant cases arising from World War I, although there is evidence that Germany sank many fishing vessels during World War I, and as many as two hundred fishing vessels during World War II (J. Gardner 1920, 362, n. 2). We have not examined non-U.S. practice after World War II.

Significance

When one looks closely at the evidence offered in *The Paquete Habana* in support of the fishing vessel exemption rule, two points become clear. First, we see many violations of the rule and no affirmative evidence of states refraining from preying on fishing vessels out of compliance with the rule. Second, in the wars in which there are no reported cases of fishing vessel seizures, the best explanation is probably coincidence of interest. For example, the Court makes much of the fact that "no instance has been found in which the exemption . . . has been denied by Britain or any other nation" (*The Paquete Habana* 1900, 700) after 1810. This lack of conflict is less significant than the Court thinks, for there were few maritime wars during the nineteenth century in which the rule could have mattered. Britain, the most ardent critic of the rule, did not fight major naval wars during that period except for the Crimean War, and during that war it violated the rule. Because it had no desire or opportunity to seize coastal fishing vessels in the other cases, Britain's failure during this period to seize fishing vessels or criticize the exemption cannot count as evidence of adhering to a rule of customary international law.

Sometimes, of course, fishing vessels will be an attractive target because they obstruct a coastline, contain spies or weapons, or are a vital part of the enemy's economy. Our theory would expect a higher likelihood of attack on fishing vessels in such circumstances because the benefits are higher. It is thus no surprise according to our theory that there was an exception to the fishing vessel exemption rule for fishing vessels that serve a military or important economic function. This is just the sort of exemption that our theory would expect, as the exception tracks those instances in which states would have powerful incentives to seize fishing vessels.

To bring these points together, consider a passage from Hall (1924, 536), a respected British treatise writer, on the pattern of adherence to the fishing vessel exemption rule: "England does not seem to have been unwilling to spare fishing-vessels so long as they are harmless, and it does not appear that any state has accorded them immunity under circumstances of inconvenience to itself. It is likely that all nations would now refrain from molesting them as a general rule, and would capture them so soon as any danger arose that they or their crew might be of military use to the enemy; and it is also likely that it is impossible to grant them a more distinctive exemption."

Perhaps inadvertently, this passage gets the logic of the fishing vessel exemption rule exactly right. Britain did not attack "harmless" fishing vessels; it had no interest in doing so. Nor did it accord fishing vessels immunity when it was "inconvenient" to do so, such as when the fishing vessels had a military use. The *Paquete Habana* Court and international law scholars view this pattern as adherence to a fishing vessel exemption rule with an exception for fishing vessels with military uses. Our theory views it as states following their self-interest in all circumstances, refraining from seizing ships when there is no advantage in seizure and seizing when there is a balance of advantage.

We believe that coincidence of interest accounts for most, but probably not all, of the behavioral patterns associated with the *Paquete Habana* rule. It is easy to see how the coastal fishing vessel rule might also reflect cooperation. In some of their many wartime encounters, Britain and France might both have had an interest in seizing each others' fishing vessels (to disrupt local economies, for example), but both states would be better off if both refrained from doing so (because, perhaps, both are better off if they preserve their own fishing vessels and forgo the expenditure of naval resources in an attack on the other's). The danger for each state was that it might refrain from seizing the other's vessels while the other state seizes its own, leaving the state that refrained worse off than if it had acted aggressively. This is a bilateral prisoner's dilemma in which meaningful cooperation is possible. We think the best evidence in *The Paquete Habana* for this logic comes from the bilateral treaties and understandings between various pairs of European countries in the fifteenth and sixteenth centuries.

While some of the examples cited in *The Paquete Habana* thus might be evidence of bilateral cooperation, the historical record recounted in the case supports our theory's skepticism about multilateral customary international law. All of the ostensible examples of cooperation—whether by treaty, understanding, or practice—occurred in *bilateral* contexts. The Court cited no evidence whatsoever that third-party states protested or retaliated against actions inconsistent with the fishing vessel exemption rule.

We close with a consideration that might be viewed as cutting against our theory. The *Paquete Habana* decision itself applied customary international law to override the United States' apparently self-interested action in seizing the Spanish fishing vessels, even though the navy and the executive branch strenuously argued to the Supreme Court that the fishing vessels served a military purpose. Nothing in rational choice mandates the particular domestic arrangement by which a state pursues its self-interest in connection with customary international law, and it is consistent with the theory that a state would commit itself to certain courses of action via judicial enforcement. (We explore this possibility, and its effects, in our discussion of treaties in part 2.) Thus, the Court might simply have been holding the president to his prewar proclamation that the United States would conduct the war consistently with the "law of nations" and the "present view of states." But we think it likely that most states would decide that political rather than judicial figures should determine the state interest with respect to customary international law. And in fact, U.S. courts almost always defer to the executive's view about customary international law, and the political branches have the final say about whether and how it applies in the United States and whether or not the United States will comply with it. Indeed, although *The Paquete Habana* did not defer to the executive's views in Court, it did famously state that courts must apply customary international law "where there is no . . . controlling executive . . . act" (*The Paquete Habana* 1900, 700), suggesting that the Court did not believe it was acting contrary to the United States' interest as officially declared by the president. Nonetheless, *The Paquete Habana* remains an exception to the rule of judicial deference to the executive's views, an exception rarely repeated, especially in cases with more significance than a determination of the validity of the seizure of a fishing smack—a determination that occurred after the conclusion of a one-sided war that resulted in a decisive victory.

PART 2

TREATIES

Part 2 examines the second form of international law: treaties. Care must be used with the term "treaties," for it can be used in two different senses. Under international law, a treaty is an agreement between states "governed by international law" (Vienna Convention on Treaties, Article 1[a]). Under U.S. domestic constitutional law, a treaty is an agreement between states governed by international law but made in a certain way: by the president with the consent of two-thirds of the U.S. Senate (U.S. Constitution, Art. 2, sec. 2, cl. 2). This domestic law treaty process is not the only way under U.S. law to make a treaty in the international law sense (i.e., an international agreement governed by international law). Congressional-executive agreements (which are made by the president and approved by majorities in both Houses) and "sole" executive agreements (which are made on the president's authority alone) are two other mechanisms under U.S. domestic law for making treaties in the international law sense. In general, unless otherwise made clear by context, we use the term "treaty" in its international law sense.

Treaties raise many interesting issues. The most fundamental issue is: Why ever have a treaty? Why doesn't customary international law suffice? Other important issues include: When and why do states comply with treaties? When and why do states enter into multilateral rather than bilateral treaties? How do multilateral treaties (and the international organizations they often create) work? What role do domestic courts and bureaucracies play in treaty enforcement?

Another important set of issues concerns the distinction between treaties (legalized agreements) and agreements that are not binding under international law. Nonlegal agreements come under different labels: memoranda of understanding, nonbinding resolutions, exchanges of notes, joint communiqués, joint declarations, *modi vivendi*, political agreements, administrative agreements, voluntary guidelines, handshakes, verbal promises, arrangements, letters of intent, statements or declarations of principles, "best practices," exchanges of letters, gentlemen's agreements, and side letters. Examples of nonlegal agreements include the SALT I extension, the OPEC quota agreements, and the understandings that resolved the Cuban Missile Crisis. The literature usually labels nonlegal international agreements "soft law." We avoid this label because nonlegal agreements are not binding under international (or any other) law, so it is confusing to call them law, soft or otherwise (Raustiala 2003).

The dominant positivistic approach to international law views nonlegal agreements as aberrational or of secondary importance (Weil 1983). And yet nonlegal agreements are prevalent and clearly play an important role in international politics. Why do states use nonlegal agreements? How do nonlegal agreements facilitate cooperation among states? If states can cooperate using nonlegal instruments, why do they ever enter into treaties governed by international law? What does legalization add? This part presents a theory of treaties and nonlegal agreements that seeks to answer these and related questions.

CHAPTER 3

A THEORY OF INTERNATIONAL
AGREEMENTS

Conventional Wisdom

The conventional international lawyers' wisdom about treaties is un-
complicated. When a state enters an agreement that evinces an
intent to be governed by international law, it puts itself under an international law obligation to comply with the agreement. The legalization of the agreement, on this view, creates a special obligation beyond that which is created by a mere nonlegal agreement. This special
obligation is usually captured by the *pacta sunt servanda* doctrine:
"Every treaty in force is binding upon the parties to it and must be
performed by them in good faith" (Vienna Convention on the Law of
Treaties, Art. 26).

Under mainstream international law theory, legalization enhances
compliance by increasing the normative strength of the agreement and
thus a state party's sense of obligation. The mainstream view acknowl-
edges that states sometimes violate treaties when their interests are
strong enough to outweigh their sense of obligation. Desiring to
strengthen the international legal system, the more theoretically inclined
international lawyers see their task as that of strengthening the normative obligation created by treaties. As with customary international
law, these scholars explore the conditions for normativity and urge that
these conditions—for example, "right process," the participation of liberal democracies, domestic law penetration, management and deliberation—be strengthened whenever possible (Franck 1990; Tesón 1998;
Koh 1997; Chayes and Chayes 1995). They also argue that treaty compliance would be more widespread if treaties were more precise and

formal and if more power were given to third-party institutions charged with the task of monitoring compliance and resolving disputes.

Conventional wisdom about nonlegal agreements is more varied. At one time, scholars viewed nonlegal agreements as less interesting and less important than treaties, and indeed many viewed them as outside the study of international law (R. Baxter 1980 is an exception). To some, nonlegal agreements and related quasi-legal instruments were "pathological" (Weil 1983) because their existence supposedly damaged the normative integrity of treaties. Nonlegal agreements have been studied, and defended, more seriously in recent years (Lipson 1991; Abbott and Snidal 2000; Abbott et al. 2000; Raustiala 2003).

This chapter sets forth our theory of treaties and nonlegal agreements. We begin with issues common to both: the ways that both foster cooperation and coordination better than customary international law, how multistate international agreements work, and the relevance of coincidence of interest and coercion. We then explain why states sometimes choose treaties over nonlegal agreements. The basic answer is that the processes and conventions associated with treaties provide information to treaty parties that can enhance cooperation. Next, we consider theories of treaty compliance. And we close by considering the role that domestic bureaucracies play in treaty enforcement.

The Logic of International Agreements

The Basic Logic

The basic logic of international agreements—both treaties and nonlegal agreements—follows directly from the models of cooperation and coordination set forth in part 1. As we explained in part 1, to achieve joint gains under these models, states must know which actions count as cooperation or coordination. This knowledge need not be embodied in a written or oral agreement; indeed, there need not be any formal communication between the parties. Cooperation or coordination can emerge spontaneously as long as each state has enough information about the payoffs of the other states. As we saw in part 1, two states with clearly defined interests and capabilities might, without any communication or agreement, implicitly accept a particular river as the border between territories, or an exemption for coastal fishing vessels in the prize system. This is the domain of customary international law.

Part 1 expressed skepticism about how often such cooperation or coordination by custom really occurs, especially as the number of states increases. It is often not obvious where a natural border is located; even a river moves, raising questions about the border after a flood or years of erosion. And it is often not obvious what kind of ship counts as a coastal fishing vessel. For these reasons, among others, customary international law has always been weak; the areas of genuine customary cooperation and coordination are limited.

If customary international law is weak because of its ambiguity, then states will have strong incentives to clarify customary international law by communicating with each other. Communication may clarify the expectations of each state, or, in the jargon, describe the actions that will count as cooperative moves, or the focal points at which coordination will occur. (We examine how this communicative process works in more detail in chapter 6.) Games of cooperation and coordination usually have multiple equilibria, that is, multiple outcomes that are consistent with the logic of the game, and no single focal point that will provide a basis for decentralized action. When communication facilitates cooperation or coordination, states can make oral or written agreements to identify opportunities for joint gains and to bring into alignment expectations about the actions to be taken by each state to achieve the gains. In repeated prisoner's dilemmas, when the agreement sets out clearly what counts as a cooperative action, unintended defections are reduced, and it becomes more difficult for a state to engage in opportunism and then deny that the action violated the requirements of a cooperative game. In coordination games, when the agreement sets out what the coordinating action is, it becomes less likely that a failure of coordination will occur because of error.

Multilateral Treaties and International Organizations

As we explained in part 1, game theorists have shown that the logic of bilateral cooperation and coordination can be extended to any number of agents. Suppose that numerous states must cooperate to preserve a commons like an ocean fishery. As we noted, if each state adopts the right strategy—for example, not overfishing in the first period, but overfishing in subsequent periods if another state overfished in an earlier period—then in theory, the commons can be preserved. But for reasons we gave in part 1, we doubt that happens much in the world of customary international law. To solve collective action problems, players must be able to monitor each other and commit to punishing any player who free-rides, and that includes any player who fails to punish another player who free-rides. The amount of information that a state would need to do this is far beyond what is usually available through the informal mechanisms by which customary international law is created.

But multilateral international agreements, especially ones that create international organizations, seem to present a different picture. The past sixty years have witnessed an explosion of such agreements, especially treaties, many of which have near universal assent. Some multilateral treaties established freestanding international organizations, such as the United Nations, the World Trade Organization, the International Atomic Energy Agency, and the North Atlantic Treaty Organization. These multilateral treaties, and their attendant international organizations, require a more complex explanation than do bilateral agreements. (The analysis below focuses on treaties rather than nonlegal agreements, but the logic of nonlegal multilateral agreements would be similar.)

The international relations institutionalist literature has a standard account for how multilateral treaties, especially ones that create freestanding multilateral organizations, can overcome the hurdles to multilateral cooperation. A multilateral treaty, like a bilateral treaty, can identify focal points that align expectations about which behaviors count as cooperation. By setting up a permanent international institution, a multilateral treaty can increase the transparency of international relations, making it easier to identify and punish cheaters, thereby reducing the incentives to cheat. Multilateral negotiations and institutions can also lower the communication and related transaction costs of continued cooperation (Keohane 1984; Krasner 1983).

We have sympathy for this analysis, which rests on standard rational choice models, but we think that the proponents of this view have made claims on its behalf that are not always supported by the evidence. The best case that can be made for it is in the fields of communications and transportation. Most states want to enable their citizens to communicate with citizens of other states, and communication requires agreement on a common standard. Once a few big states agree on common communication standards, these states have no reason to switch to a new standard—they just lose the ability to communicate with other states—and the smaller states have no choice but to accept the common standard if they want to communicate with the big states (and each other). The treaty regime may create some institutions that help resolve technical problems, and the states will pay for these institutions. This story seems straightforward and plausible to us (though we have ignored some complications). It is also true that a small number of states can cooperate, at least partially, for the sake of achieving relatively narrow goals such as defense against a common enemy by a military alliance (NATO), or the control of world prices of a single commodity that dominates the economies of the state parties (OPEC) (Sandler and Hartley 2001).

But the case is weaker for true international public goods such as the protection of fisheries, the reduction of atmospheric pollution, and peace. These are multilateral prisoner's dilemmas, not coordination games. Merely embodying the rules in a treaty instrument does not solve the problem; in addition, every state would need to commit to punish every state that violates the treaty, and to punish every state that fails to punish every state that violates the treaty, and so forth. While international organizations established by treaty can enhance monitoring and related information-providing mechanisms, punishment still depends on state action and is subject to free-riding and related collective action difficulties. For these reasons, we are skeptical that genuine multinational collective action problems can be solved by treaty, especially when a large number of states are involved. (For similar skepticism, see Downs and Rocke 1995.)

What, then, is the point of multilateral treaty regimes? We argue that these regimes have an implicit two-step logic: in step 1, states come together and negotiate common terms; in step 2, states cooperate (or not) *in pairs*, with each state in a pair complying with the common terms as long as the other state in the pair does. When the common terms—the treaty terms—do not maximize value as between the states in a pair, they may agree to alternative terms that do; but often, renegotiation is too costly and the common terms are used instead.

Three general observations about this process are appropriate at this point. First, step 1 involves the solution of a coordination problem: where and when the states' delegates will meet and which common terms are value-maximizing. Typically, a few big states or blocs of states will agree on these issues. Agreeing to the terms is not as hard as it seems, because (1) states can opt out of terms they do not like by using reservations, and (2) states know that inappropriate terms will be ignored or renegotiated pair by pair.

Second, step 2 involves the solution of a repeated bilateral prisoner's dilemma. Although the terms are common, the victim of a violation almost always has to enforce the terms itself through the threat of retaliation. This is a strong pattern in international law, one that is often condemned but rarely explained by international lawyers. If states X and Y trade with each other, and state X violates a WTO rule in a way that harms Y, state Y might retaliate *but no other state will.* The lack of third-party enforcement, except in unusual instances, is strong evidence against the view that multilateral collective goods are created, as the game theoretic models all require that third-party enforcement occur.

Third, because enforcement of multilateral treaty regimes is usually bilateral, the behavior of states will often drift apart, even though they are formally governed by the same treaty. Powerful states will behave differently toward powerful states than they behave toward weak states, though in all cases some cooperation may occur.

We do not want to insist too rigidly on this two-step theory, but we think that the ideas have general applicability. The Vienna Convention on the Law of Treaties, discussed later in this chapter, fits this theory. We examine human rights law and trade law in the next two chapters and show how they too reflect this theory. Other areas of the law may as well, but they must be left for future research.

Coincidence of Interest and Coercion

Thus far we have discussed only two of our models—cooperation and coordination—in connection with international agreements. International agreements can also reflect elements of the coincidence of interest and coercion models. But these latter two models cannot fully capture what international agreements accomplish.

Consider coincidence of interest. If each state would engage in the same action for self-interested reasons regardless of what the other state does, then there would be no reason to invest resources to enter an agreement codifying the behavior. The same is true of coercion. If one state coerces another state into action that it would otherwise not take, an agreement seems redundant. Unlike many examples of customary international law, states enter into agreements self-consciously and for a reason, and on our theory, the basic reason is that they gain more than they lose, on balance, from the agreement. What, then, do states gain from agreements when the logic of their situation appears to be coincidence of interest or coercion?

The answer is that even agreements that seem dominated by coincidence of interest or coercion have a cooperative element, however thin. Consider the Treaty of Moscow signed in May 2002, in which Russia and the United States agreed to reduce their nuclear warheads to no more than 1,700 to 2,200 by 2012. Most observers believed that each state independently had powerful interests in reaching this result. President Bush had announced his intention to unilaterally reduce nuclear arms regardless of what the Russians did. And the Russians were under independent pressure to reach the same result because they had diminished need for the weapons and could not afford to maintain them anyway. So why make a treaty if both sides would do the same thing in any event? We are not sure, but our theory suggests that this was probably not a pure coincidence of interest. Each state might have been tempted to reduce its nuclear stockpile less rapidly if it knew that the other state would be reducing its own stockpile unilaterally, so that it could maintain some nuclear advantage in case of an escalation of tensions, however remote this possibility might have seemed. If this is so, the agreement would increase each state's sense of security about the other state's nuclear policy: an apparent coincidence of interest is in fact an example of real but thin cooperation.

Coincidence of interest plays a more substantial explanatory role in multilateral treaties. The final version of these treaties often requires many of the parties to do nothing different from what they have done in the past. Human rights treaties often have this character, as we discuss in chapter 4. So do many multilateral arms control treaties. When Burkina Faso, Costa Rica, Gabon, the Holy See, and Malta ratified the Comprehensive Test Ban Treaty, they did not have to alter their pre-ratification behaviors. Compliance in these cases is best explained by coincidence of interest (see Downs et al. 1996).

Thin cooperation can also explain compliance with treaties that result mainly from coercion. When a victorious party imposes a treaty of peace on a defeated enemy, it sets terms that the defeated party would not accept in the absence of the coercion. But there is still a cooperative element here: the defeated party promises to comply with the treaty in return for good treatment, preservation, or some other benefit. And the rights and expectations of all parties are made clearer than they would be in the absence of the treaty. In these senses, even the famously onerous Versailles Treaty contained cooperative elements. It created a new German border, established the criteria for military disarmament, set up a prisoner of war exchange process, and clarified allied air travel and waterway rights in Germany. These provisions established what counted as cooperation and thus made the treaty parties better off than if there had been no treaty.

Summary

Thus far we have analyzed both treaties and nonlegal agreements under the same basic models of cooperation and coordination. In other words, we have explained the logic of treaties without reference to notions of "legality" or *pacta sunt servanda* or related concepts. As was the case with customary international law, the cooperation and coordination models explain the behaviors associated with treaties without reliance on these factors, or on what international lawyers sometimes call "normative pull." States refrain from violating treaties (when they do) for the same basic reason they refrain from violating nonlegal agreements: because they fear retaliation from the other state or some kind of reputational loss, or because they fear a failure of coordination.

The cooperation and coordination models can be contrasted with the view that international agreements are like domestic contracts or statutes (see Janis 2003, 9–10). In our view this analogy has limited value. Unlike statute and contract violations, violations of international agreements, though sometimes subject to self-help remedies, are not subject to reliable sanctions by independent third parties. A better domestic analogy is the nonbinding letter of intent, in which individuals exchange promises without consenting to legal enforcement. Letters of intent, which are common, depend for their efficacy on retaliation and reputation. International agreements are a formal kind of communication like the letter of intent. Both create a record, rely on more careful language than in everyday speech, clarify the terms of cooperation or coordination, and provide a springboard for mutually beneficial interaction. Neither depends on external enforcement.

If this view is correct, then we must interpret treaties and the international behavior that flows from them with care. When a firm complies with the terms of a letter of intent, the reason is that it sees an advantage in doing so. The letter of intent announces a firm's intention to merge with another; subsequently, the firms merge. We do not say that the firms merged because of the letter of intent, nor that the letter of intent caused or forced the firms to merge. We say that the letter of intent laid the groundwork and clarified expectations for the subsequent merger. Similarly, when the United States complies with NAFTA, the most plausible explanation is that it sees an advantage to continuing reciprocal reduction in trade and investment barriers.

The Choice between Nonlegal Agreements and Treaties

We have discussed how both treaties and nonlegal agreements—bilateral or multilateral—can foster cooperation and coordination. But nothing in the logic of the cooperation or coordination models explains why states sometimes prefer treaties to nonlegal agreements. To answer this question, we must examine what legalization adds to an international agreement. We discuss three basic answers: (1) treaties usually require legislative consent, a process that conveys important information about state preferences for the treaty; (2) treaties implicate certain interpretive default rules; or (3) treaties convey a more serious commitment than nonlegal agreements do.

Legislative Participation

In most states, the legislature must consent to most agreements before they can be binding under international law. When negotiating with another state, the executive thus has a choice, bounded by constitutional and related political constraints, between making a nonlegal agreement that does not require legislative consent, or a legalized agreement that requires legislative consent. (There is a third and narrow class of agreements that we ignore for present purposes: legalized international agreements that the executive can make on his own authority. See the second endnote in this chapter.) In situations where he or she has a choice, why might the executive choose to involve the legislature and legalize an international agreement?

The Treaty of Moscow illustrates these issues. When President Bush announced his intention to achieve significant arms control reduction with the Russians, he initially proposed that the deal be sealed with a handshake between him and Vladimir Putin. Putin and several U.S. senators balked at this form of agreement. They insisted that the agreement be written down, consented to by the U.S. Senate and the Russian Duma, and formally ratified. And this is what happened. Bush and Putin signed the Treaty of Moscow in May 2002 and their two countries ratified the treaty in 2003. Why insist on a fully legalized treaty, consented to by the U.S. Senate, instead of a handshake?

From the Senate's perspective, insistence on participation in the treaty process is easy to understand: participation enhances its influence over foreign policy. It is not the only such device: the Senate (and the House) can also influence foreign policy through ordinary domestic legislation (for example, funding the military or imposing sanctions on a foreign state); by retaliating against a president whose foreign policy it dislikes (for example, not implementing his domestic agenda); by restricting the powers of the president when permitted by the Constitution; by exercising advice and consent power with regard to foreign policy appointments; and, in a parliamentary system, by withdrawing support from the executive. It is not surprising that in democratic states, legislatures would insist on formal influence over foreign policy and that in many written and unwritten constitutions, legislatures have a great deal of influence.

This explains why the Senate would want to participate. But why would Putin want the Senate to participate? And what might Bush gain from its participation? The answer is that legislative participation can convey information in a manner advantageous to all involved. First, legislative consent requires hearings, expert testimony, floor debates, public discussions, questions from Congress to the executive, amendments (proposed and actual), and the like. This process reveals information about the policy preferences of the legislature, and thus (in a reasonably democratic state) of the public and/or the elite (Schultz 1998). The revealed information is a clearer indication to a potential treaty partner about the U.S. attitude toward the agreement, and thus its likelihood of compliance, than the word of the president alone. Putin might have demanded a treaty because he wanted to know whether the U.S. legislature and public shared Bush's apparently strong interest in arms reduction. If they did not, Putin would have faced a heightened risk that Congress and subsequent presidents would not comply with the treaty.

Second, legislative consent can serve as a commitment that is separate from the commitment that the executive alone makes (Martin 2000). Bush might keep his promises with the Russians (among other reasons) in order to retain his power to make future promises. For that reason, Putin might have believed that Bush would try to reduce U.S. arms while he was in office. But Putin might have worried that Bush's successor would not. Or he might have worried that even if Bush's successors remained committed to arms control, Congress would not cooperate. If the Senate or individual senators also try to maintain a reputation for keeping promises (as they presumably do), a separate promise from the Senate (in the form of its consent) would reduce concerns that a future Congress would act contrary to the agreement.

Third, the legislative consent process can send a credible signal about the *president's* degree of commitment to the treaty. A president who sends an agreement to the Senate (or to Congress) for its consent incurs several costs. Executive branch officials must forgo other initiatives to explain and defend the agreement orally and in writing. In addition, the Senate Foreign Relations Committee can consider only a limited number of treaties each session, and prior to each session the president must inform the Committee of his treaty priorities. Every treaty considered by the Senate thus comes at the cost of neglect of other treaties or laws that could further the president's agenda. In these and other ways, legislative participation can send a credible signal about the seriousness with which the president views the treaty.

Bringing these considerations together, Bush might have understood that Putin would not make a commitment unless he received more information than Bush by himself could credibly provide: information about the attitudes and preferences (and intensity of preferences) of senators (and their constituents) and of Bush himself. In addition, in light of a threatening letter that Bush received from Senators Biden and Helms (Letter 2002), he might have understood that the costs of a possible Senate retaliation would be greater than the costs (minus the informational benefits) of a Senate confirmation process. Some combination of these reasons probably explains why Bush agreed to use the Senate consent process.

Finally, legislative participation may be desirable because it can enhance the role that domestic courts play in enforcing treaties. Some treaties are self-executing and thus apply as domestic law and are enforceable by courts. If a treaty is not self-executing, the legislature can render it judicially enforceable by enacting implementing legislation for the treaty. Both self-executing treaties and treaties with implementing legislation can create domestic institutional obstacles to reneging on treaties, and thus strengthen the credibility of the treaty commitment. The effect provided by judicial enforcement, which is available for treaties but not generally available for nonlegal agreements, is real but should not be overstated. In the United States, most treaties are nonself-executing and lack implementing legislation. In addition, courts usually defer to the views of the executive branch in interpreting treaties. This means that later executive branches can influence the content of a self-executing treaty, thereby lessening the impact of independent courts. And a commitment to judicial enforcement is always reversible (at some cost) by the legislature.

For all of the reasons outlined above, an executive wishing to foster successful international cooperation will, all things being equal, choose to involve the legislature. But, of course, all things are not equal. Legislative participation can be a lengthy, expensive, and risky process. The executive has to commit important resources to securing consent that could be used for other purposes. If the executive does not accurately determine the policy preferences of the legislature, he or she might fail to obtain the desired consent, such as when the Senate refused consent to the Test Ban Treaty and the Versailles Treaty. Or perhaps the executive will obtain consent, but only after a lengthy and costly delay, as occurred with the Panama Canal Treaty in 1977. Moreover, the executive might have to make political payoffs to legislators with opposing foreign policy objectives.

The executive can avoid these costs by entering into a nonlegal agreement that does not require legislative consent. Nonlegal agreements are on the whole less costly, for they can be negotiated and concluded more quickly, and they are (usually) less public than legal agreements. These advantages, of course, all come at the price of a reduction in the information and commitment benefits that flow from legislative participation, described earlier (Lipson 1991).

We can summarize as follows: when domestic law permits, executives will tend to opt for legalized agreements with legislative participation when (1) the other state demands a strong or lasting commitment; (2) the executive's and legislature's foreign policy goals converge sufficiently that consent can be obtained; and (3) immediate action is not required. By contrast, executives will tend to choose nonlegal agreements, and to avoid the legislative process, when one or more of these three conditions is not satisfied and when a nonlegal agreement will otherwise bring benefits.[1] In choosing the route of nonlegal agreements, the executive must consider, among other things, whether any divergence in objectives with the legislature will invite costly legislative countermeasures.

It is important to note that these trade-offs can be described without reference to the concept of normativity. Legalized agreements (i.e., treaties) are the name we give to instruments that emerge from processes that are motivated by factors mostly related to information conveyance. The strength of a state's commitment to an agreement is not a function of its legality, but of the strength and uniformity of public and elite preferences.

Default Rules

A second reason to choose treaties over nonlegal agreements is to take advantage of the interpretive rules that apply to treaties. An important difference between treaties and nonlegal agreements is the existence of a law of treaties, as codified in the Vienna Convention on the Law of Treaties (1969). By entering a treaty, a state invokes a set of expectations about how it will be interpreted and understood. A nonlegal agreement does not create the same expectations, because the Vienna Convention does not govern such agreements (Art. 2[1][a]). To understand how a treaty creates these expectations, we must look first at the Vienna Convention.

The Vienna Convention clarified, modified, and codified disparate state practices concerning various aspects of treaty interpretation, including which agreements count as treaties, the various mechanisms by which states consented to treaties and took reservations to certain treaty provisions, the rules of treaty interpretation, the effect of treaties on third states, the process of treaty modification and termination, and so forth. For example, the Vienna Convention tells us what counts as a treaty and what doesn't (Arts. 1–3). This is important, because the rules that it lays out apply only to treaties and not to nonbinding agreements. The Vienna Convention also specifies the various ways that a state can consent to a treaty (Arts. 11–17). Sometimes the representative's signature suffices; sometimes an exchange of instruments is necessary; sometimes the method is ratification. Each of these methods entails a different significance for the treaty signature and for the subsequent duties and expectations of each state. It is important that each state have the same expectations about the significance of these acts. The Vienna Convention clarifies these different expectations.

The same is true for the Vienna Convention's rules of interpretation (Arts. 31–33). Many sources potentially inform the meaning of a treaty, including text, the treaty's purpose, negotiation records, and legislative hearings. When a dispute arises, it is important that the treaty parties agree on how to interpret the treaty. The Vienna Convention's rules of interpretation facilitate this process. They say that the treaty shall be interpreted in "context and in the light of its object and purpose," and they exclude consideration of "supplementary means of interpretation, including the preparatory work of the treaty and the circumstances of its conclusion," unless the presumptive source "leaves the meaning [of the treaty] ambiguous or obscure," or "leads to a result which is manifestly absurd or unreasonable" (Arts. 31–32).

As a final example, consider the rules on reservations. A reservation is essentially nonconsent to a particularly treaty term. Reservation rules are simple for a bilateral treaty, where a reservation is like a counteroffer: both parties to the treaty must agree to every reservation before the treaty becomes valid. For multilateral treaties, matters are more complex. The traditional rule was that a reserving state was not a party to a treaty unless every other party to the treaty accepted the reservation. With the expansion of multilateral treaty making after World War II, the unanimity rule came to be viewed as insufficiently flexible. In its 1951 advisory opinion in *Reservations to the Convention on the Prevention and Punishment of the Crime of Genocide,* the International Court of Justice held that a reserving state could be a party to the Genocide Convention even if some parties to the Convention objected to the reservation. The ICJ stated, however, that if a state makes a reservation incompatible with the object and purpose of the Genocide Convention, the state "cannot be regarded as being a party to the Convention" (id., 29).

This holding, and the problem of multilateral treaty reservations more generally, raised several difficulties that the Vienna Convention aimed to solve. Article 19 of the Convention allows a party to formulate a reservation to a treaty unless "the reservation is incompatible with the object and purpose of the treaty." Articles 20 and 21 then establish rules for acceptance or rejection of reservations and the consequences that follow from acceptance or rejection. When a contracting state accepts another state's reservation, the reserving state becomes a party to the treaty in relation to the accepting state. A reservation is deemed accepted by any state that does not raise an objection to the reservation within twelve months of notification or by the date on which it expressed its consent to be bound by the treaty, whichever is later. An objection to a reservation does not preclude entry into force of the treaty between the reserving and objecting states unless the objecting state says so definitively; rather, the provision to which the reservation relates is simply inapplicable between the two states to the extent of the reservation. In sum, the Vienna Convention's reservation rules specify the meaning of silence and objection in the face of a reservation and outline the consequences. Once again, the aim is to facilitate cooperation.

Much of the Vienna Convention clarifies general expectations about what actions count as cooperative moves in treaty relationships. These rules are, in the parlance of contract theory, default rules or interpretive presumptions (Ayres and Gertner 1989), the rules to which states appeal when they advance interpretations of contested language in a treaty. The default rules created by the law of treaties are sometimes vague, as the "object and purpose" test for reservations shows. But they are more precise than, and distinct from, the more general intuitions that inform moral evaluation of a violation of an agreement. One important reason why states enter into legal agreements, then, is to inform each other that the default rules set forth by the law of treaties will apply if a dispute arises, and not the more general intuitions that apply to disputes about nonlegal agreements.

Our view of the Vienna Convention's role contrasts with Setear's (1996) "iterative perspective." Setear argues that the Vienna Convention facilitates iteration between treaty parties, which in turn can promote cooperation in relationships modeled as prisoner's dilemmas. It does so, according to Setear, by setting forth at least two iterations, signature and ratification; by requiring notice of treaty termination and dispute resolution procedures; by permitting parties to withdraw only in narrow circumstances; by preserving the right to retaliate to deter cheating; and in other ways. We fail to understand how the Vienna Convention promotes iteration beyond that contemplated in the underlying treaty itself. A state that violates a treaty without providing notice to the other party does not incur any extra sanction or reputational loss over and above the underlying violation because it also violated the Vienna Convention's notice provision. It is thus hard to see how the Vienna Convention itself affects a state's cost-benefit analysis in assessing whether to comply with the underlying treaty, and thus difficult to see how the Vienna Convention increases the number of iterations beyond what would occur in its absence. States might indeed design a treaty to promote iteration by, for example, breaking up obligations into discrete steps spread over time, with each state taking the next step only if the other state took the prior step. The Vienna Convention does not add to this iteration beyond its general clarification of expectations described earlier.

Seriousness

A final reason to choose a treaty over a nonlegal agreement is to convey the seriousness of a state's commitment to the agreement. In domestic affairs, a legalized contract is a more serious commitment than a letter of intent, which in turn is a more serious commitment than a handshake. In part, the contract is more serious because it is enforceable in court; but in part, it is just a conventional way of conveying the seriousness of the commitment. And the greater seriousness of a letter of intent over a handshake is purely a convention. Similarly, legalized agreements reflect a greater commitment as a matter of convention than a nonlegalized agreement.

On this view, the legalization of agreements may serve a channeling function similar to that served by the consideration doctrine and other conventional legal formalities in domestic contract law (Fuller 1944). In domestic law, as in international law, individuals have a choice between making legal and nonlegal commitments. Under the consideration doctrine, a promise made in exchange for another promise or performance is presumptively a legal obligation, but the promisor can avoid legalizing the agreement by explicitly disclaiming any intention to make it legally binding. Under older law, a gratuitous promise was presumptively not legally binding, but the promisor could convert the promissory obligation into a legal obligation by putting it under seal. Outside contract law, a statement of intent to bequeath an estate to an individual is not legally effective, but a person can convert the statement into a legally effective will by signing a document in front of witnesses and satisfying other formalities. In all of these cases, legal form provides a device by which an individual communicates to courts his or her desire to create or avoid a legal commitment, as the case may be. In addition, as Fuller emphasized, the channeling function of formalities communicates intention not only to courts, but also to other parties who carry on business extrajudicially.

The channeling function of formalities in international law is similar, though more complex. There are certain formalities associated with legal and nonlegal agreements, respectively. Generalizing, legal agreements tend to use the term "agree," to speak in terms of obligation, to be organized in terms of a preamble and articles, and to talk about entering into force. Nonlegal agreements, by contrast, tend to use the term "decide" or "determine" or "understand," to speak in terms of responsibility rather than obligation, to be organized in terms of an introduction and sections, and to enter into effect rather than force.

When one state contemplates an agreement with another, the use of legalistic conventions (or not) helps to determine whether the agreement will count as a (legalized) treaty or a nonlegal agreement. One reason for using legalistic conventions is to convey the parties' intent about the strength of the commitment to comply. In the jargon of rational choice, the convention is a focal point that helps to solve the coordination problem that can arise when states want to convey the level of seriousness of an endeavor to cooperate. Over time, the use of legalistic language, perhaps because of the analogy to domestic arrangements, has come to convey that the commitment is especially serious, and the state is less likely to violate it than a nonlegal agreement, all things being equal. (We have more to say about why states use legalistic language in chapter 6.)

Summary

When the executive seeks to make an international agreement, he or she can, within domestic constitutional and political constraints, choose to legalize it or not to legalize it. Legalization usually (but not always) requires legislative participation and thus is politically costly, but for that reason can be used to signal the depth of political support for the commitment.[2] Legalization of an agreement is also a useful way to invoke a host of international conventions, gap fillers that facilitate cooperation and that minimize the time and cost needed to negotiate the obligations on each side. Finally, legalization is by diplomatic convention a way to demonstrate the seriousness of the commitment.

Compliance

There are many theories about compliance with treaties. These theories can be divided into two schools. The first school holds that states comply with treaties for noninstrumental reasons. A state complies with a treaty because complying is the right thing to do, or because the people who run the state believe that complying is the right thing to do. As we discussed in the introduction, this is a view emphasized by many international law scholars and by some in the "legalization" camp in political science. Chapters 1 and 2 argued that this view does not provide a good explanation for customary international law. Chapters 4 and 5 will argue that this view does not provide a good explanation for two areas of treaty law: trade law and human rights law.

A second school views compliance in instrumental terms: states comply with treaties when it is in their rational self-interest to do so, and not otherwise. Within the rational choice school, two types of explanation are given for compliance: retaliation and reputation. (We should note that many scholars committed to noninstrumental explanations of international law [such as Henkin 1979] also invoke reputation arguments, to which our analysis of such arguments below applies.)

The simplest explanation for why a state might comply with a treaty, and the explanation we generally emphasize, is that it fears retaliation or some other failure of cooperation or coordination if it does not. Suppose that two states share a fishery and have ratified a treaty that limits each state to a sustainable yield. Each state complies with the treaty because it fears that if it violates the treaty by overfishing, the other state will retaliate by overfishing, and the cooperative surplus will be dissipated. In this example, the treaty has no force beyond the underlying strategic situation: the parties could, in principle, cooperate without a treaty, but the treaty is useful because it clarifies the actions that count as cooperation and defection, and it works because of the logic of retaliation in the face of defection.

Or suppose that two states ratify a treaty that establishes standards for wireless communication. Once each state has adjusted its technology so that it conforms to the treaty, neither state has any incentive to cheat by violating the standard, even if the other state did not retaliate in some way. In this coordination situation, the treaty once again works not through its exogenous force, but rather by aligning expectations. Although the coordination case does not, strictly speaking, involve retaliation, we include it within a retaliation approach, because in a coordination situation the party that deviates from the coordinated solution will do worse.

The second instrumental approach to treaty compliance concerns reputation. Reputation refers to other states' beliefs about the likelihood that the state in question will comply with a treaty. These beliefs should be distinguished from the actual determinants of future compliance. The determinants are those elements of a state's domestic political institutions, traditions, and interests that influence foreign policy decisions. When a state repeatedly violates treaties, other states will (all things being equal) infer that its domestic political institutions, traditions, and interests do not generate foreign policy decisions that remain consistent over time. One can thus, by treating each state as having private information about the quality of its foreign policy determinants and as having limited information about the quality of other states' foreign policy determinants, rely on economic models of reputation that are based on asymmetric information (for example, Kreps and Wilson 1982; on the political science literature, see Mercer 1996). States with poor institutions violate treaties, thereby revealing that they have poor institutions, with the result that other states will be reluctant to cooperate with them in the future. States with good institutions comply with treaties even when it is against their immediate interest, because by complying with treaties against this interest they avoid the inference that they are unreliable and instead reveal the quality of their institutions and attract future cooperative partners.

To understand the difference between the reputation story and the retaliation story, consider the case of sovereign debt. Suppose state B borrows money from state A and then defaults on the loan. The retaliation story implies that state B will be punished, if at all, by state A. State A might retaliate by cutting off trade, or taking military action, or simply refusing to lend to state B in the future, even though the loan in the future might seem profitable. No other state will punish state B. The reputation story implies that state A, and all other states, will update their beliefs about the likelihood that B would repay any future loans, and in the future they will refuse to lend to B (or lend at a higher interest rate) because B is now a higher risk. Lending is no longer attractive because it is too risky and thus less profitable. Indeed, states might conclude that B is untrustworthy in a range of possible cooperative relationships, including military alliances and trade.

A rational choice theory need not choose between the retaliation and reputation stories. Both are consistent with rational choice premises, both may be at play when states cooperate, and we have relied on both explanations in this chapter and throughout the book. Nonetheless, the reputation argument must be made with care. We have two concerns in particular. First, scholars sometimes exaggerate the reputational costs of treaty noncompliance, thereby overstating the possibilities for interstate cooperation, especially multilateral cooperation. Second, scholars sometimes lean too heavily on a state's reputational concern for complying with *international law*. The reputational costs of noncompliance, and the extent of a state's concern with international law compliance, are empirical questions. We will discuss some of the evidence in chapters 4 and 5. Here we provide theoretical reasons why we are skeptical about the strong claims made for the reputation theory, though we do not dismiss them out of hand.

First, it is not clear how much the violation of one treaty says about a state's propensity to violate other treaties. A state might have a good record complying with trade treaties and a bad record complying with environmental treaties. This might result from the differential performance of the state's political institutions; perhaps political coalitions for trade policy are more stable than coalitions for environmental policy. But then reputation must be disaggregated, and it makes little sense to talk about a state's general propensity to comply with treaties (Downs and Jones 2002). In addition, treaty violations may be driven by events having nothing to do with the state's internal institutions, and thus might have little or no effect on reputation for future compliance (Mercer 1996).

Second, a state has multiple reputational concerns, many of which have nothing to do with, or even are in conflict with, a reputation for international law compliance. As Keohane (1997) has observed, a reputation for compliance with international law is not necessarily the best means, and certainly not the only means, for accomplishing foreign policy objectives. States can benefit from reputations for toughness or even for irrationality or unpredictability. Powerful states may do better by violating international law when doing so shows that they will retaliate against threats to national security. Weak states with idiosyncratic domestic arrangements may benefit by being unpredictable. One might conclude that, all things being equal, states will strive to have a reputation for compliance with international law, but a reputation for compliance will not always be of paramount concern because all things are not equal.

Third, many treaties are mistakes or are quickly rendered irrelevant by rapidly changing international relations. They assume near-term distributions of power that turn out to be false or that quickly change. The treaties of Versailles and Sèvres at the end of World War I are only the most obvious examples. The terms of the first could not be enforced by a weak Britain and France and indifferent United States against a resurgent Germany. The terms of the second could not be enforced against a revitalized Turkey. The latter was soon renegotiated on terms that better reflected the distribution of power in the region. It is hard to believe that Germany's and Turkey's reputations for complying with treaties were weakened. Perhaps their reputations for complying with poorly negotiated treaties were weakened, but that would add another element of noise to an already ambiguous variable. One could say the same thing about all the states that were parties to the Kellogg-Briand Pact of 1928, a treaty that outlawed aggressive war and is still in effect.

Fourth, as we explained in the introduction, there are methodological reasons for resisting the assumption that states incur a reputational cost whenever they violate a treaty (or, for that matter, customary international law). Once one makes that assumption, it becomes more difficult to explain why some treaties generate more compliance than others. Although a sufficiently precise theory of reputation might enable one to make progress with this question and others, we have not found such a theory in the literature.

Having said all this, we want to emphasize that we do not deny that states and their leaders care about their reputations. They clearly do care, and we have relied on reputational considerations earlier in this chapter. Our point is simply that reputational arguments must, for the reasons outlined above, be made with care, especially when the posited reputational concern involves a reputation for complying with international law. A state and its leaders might care about their reputation for keeping promises, or defending allies, or toughness, or giving aid to poor countries, or repaying loans. But these are competing reputational concerns, and they are all different from a reputation for compliance with international law per se.

Compliance, Bureaucracy, and Agency Costs

States often create bureaucracies, sometimes large bureaucracies, to ensure that they act consistently with international treaty obligations. In the United States, the Defense Department incorporates the laws of war in military manuals and rules of engagement; the U.S. trade representative monitors compliance with trade treaties; and many other agencies take steps to comply with international agreements that affect their field of regulation. All of this is consistent with our theory. States enter into treaties, in our view, because the benefits of the treaty outweigh its costs. Because states want to obtain the benefits of cooperation and coordination that the treaty represents, it is natural for them to delegate this task to the institutions through which the states act.

Some scholars argue that such delegation, and the attendant "repeated participation in the legal process" by government actors, leads government officials to internalize and get into the habit of complying with international law, even when doing so would not serve their government's interests (Koh 1997). There is little empirical evidence for this view (see Posner 2004, for further discussion). It is true that a bureaucracy charged with ensuring compliance will often insist on compliance in instances that do not serve the state's immediate interest, either because the bureaucracy is trading off relatively unimportant short-term interests for more important medium-term interests (as is the case with treaties that solve prisoner's dilemmas), or because, as is sometimes the case, bureaucratic self-aggrandizement leads to continued bureaucratic support for a treaty regime, or for bureaucratically self-serving interpretations of the treaty, even in instances that do not serve the state interest. The former case is an example of the state following its interest; the latter is an example of agency costs that encumber all political systems. Neither is an example of international law becoming part of a state's "internal value set" (Koh 1997), and neither prevents a state's leadership from changing course in a sufficiently important case.

As an analogy, consider a CEO who delegates routine contract disputes to corporate counsel, with instructions that the corporation's lawyers should ensure that the corporation obeys contract law. It might happen that the corporation will, as a result, comply with many contracts when breaching particular contracts and paying damages would be profit-maximizing. But the reason is not that the CEO, or his lawyers, have an intrinsic preference for having the corporation comply with the law. The CEO has decided that, in the aggregate, obeying contracts will maximize profits compared to examining each one and determining whether the benefits of breach exceed the cost. Such an examination would not be a good use of the CEO's time, and it would often be impractical for a subordinate lawyer, who might not have enough expertise about the corporation's business interests. In a sufficiently important case, however, the CEO would withdraw authority from the general counsel and decide for himself or herself whether the corporation should perform or breach. Delegation of authority, with directions that the agent should obey the law, will lead to a great deal of routine compliance with the law even when it is not in the corporation's self-interest in each individual case. This is surely the case for international law as well. But such routine bureaucratic compliance is based on an aggregate cost-benefit analysis, and is not the same thing as a general willingness or habit of complying with international law against the state's interest.

Two other points cut against the bureaucratic internalization thesis. First, there is no reason to think that international law compliance will always be the top priority for an agency. Even when the state has delegated compliance monitoring to the agency, the agency has other delegated authorities and responsibilities and numerous constituents. So, for example, the Department of Agriculture may generally favor strict enforcement of treaties within its purview for reasons stated above, but in particular cases it might pressure the government to violate or alter trade treaties that harm U.S. farmers. Similarly, the Department of Homeland Security may favor compliance with international laws that advance its mission but may pressure the government to violate or alter a treaty that, say, interferes with the development of a new antiterrorism technology. Second, and relatedly, different bureaucracies with different institutional interests might have very different attitudes toward compliance with the same treaty. In the examples above, the U.S. trade representative might resist the Department of Agriculture, and the State

Department might resist the Department of Homeland Security. The point is simple but important: even bureaucracies with delegated authority to comply with international law have competing preferences that sometimes win out, and when bureaucracies differ on compliance issues, the compliance view does not always prevail.

CHAPTER 4

HUMAN RIGHTS

International human rights law regulates the way states treat individuals under their control. The modern multilateral human rights regime consists primarily of treaties regulating genocide (1951), racial discrimination (1969), civil and political rights (1976), economic, social, and cultural rights (1976), discrimination against women (1981), torture (1987), and the rights of children (1990). (There are also various regional human rights treaties.) Each party to these treaties promises other signatories to protect the human rights of individuals under its control. The treaties also create various monitoring mechanisms that aim to promote compliance. As Table 4.1 shows, the vast majority of states have ratified most of these important human rights treaties.

Many believe these treaties are novel post–World War II developments. This view is misleading. International law regulation of "internal" state action is obviously not new. Bilateral investment treaties have long prevented states from expropriating private property within their territory. Similarly, individual rights protection is an old concern for international law. Treaties dating back to the Peace of Westphalia (1648) protected religious freedoms. The nineteenth century saw the rise of an international law prohibition on the slave trade. And international law has long protected individual aliens from denials of justice. Finally, concerns about human rights affected states' decisions to recognize foreign states and governments in the nineteenth century (Grewe 2000).

What was new in the postwar period was the effort to institutionalize an international human rights regime in a series of multilateral treaties. The novelty lay in the scale of the undertaking and the creation of international institutions to monitor compliance. But if this is new,

Table 4.1 Participation of States in Human Rights Treaties

Treaty	Entry into Force	Percent of UN That Ratified
Convention on the Prevention and Punishment of the Crime of Genocide	1951	70
International Covenant on the Elimination of All Forms of Racial Discrimination	1969	88
International Covenant on Civil and Political Rights	1976	78
International Covenant on Economic, Social, and Cultural Rights	1976	77
Convention on the Elimination of All Forms of Discrimination against Women	1981	91
Convention against Torture and Other Forms of Cruel, Inhuman, and Degrading Treatment	1987	70
Convention on the Rights of the Child	1990	99

Source: United Nations, Office of the High Commissioner for Human Rights, data available at www.unhchr.ch/pdf/report.pdf (as of July 7, 2003).

it is of a piece with other modern developments in international law. The use of multilateral treaties and the creation of multilateral international institutions are found in many other areas of international law as well. Modern human rights law, like modern security and trade law, addresses concerns that date back centuries, but in a new way.

This chapter shows how our theory of international law accounts for human rights law. We begin with a general account of state interests related to human rights. We then show how the basic ideas that form the core of our theory—coincidence of interest, cooperation, coordination, and coercion—explain the human rights practices of states. Against this background, we argue that modern multilateral human rights treaties have little exogenous influence on state behavior, and examine why states nonetheless devote resources to such relatively inefficacious treaties. We close by considering how the customary international law of human rights operates.

State Interests

I n every state, the government balances a concern for the well-being of persons under its control with concern for security (internal and external) and the government's own perpetuation. Different governments accommodate these concerns in different ways. At one end of the spectrum, liberal democracies embrace democratic governmental change and judicially enforceable individual rights protections (usually on the basis of constitutional or other "higher law" principles not subject to democratic derogation). At the other end, authoritarian regimes do not permit democratic change and deny legally enforceable fundamental freedoms to the people under their control. But although authoritarian governments usually deny citizens *legal* recourse against the state for violating their freedoms, they often permit many citizens various freedoms for the sake of internal peace and stability.

The degree of reconciliation of governmental authority with individual rights depends on a number of factors, including economic development; social, religious, and political culture; and the presence or absence of internal or external armed conflict (Poe 2004). For our purposes, we need only assume that liberal democratic states have a greater interest in respecting the human rights of those under their control than authoritarian states do. This simply means that, as a matter of fact, liberal democratic governments value liberties—either intrinsically, instrumentally, or both—more than authoritarian governments do. (As we noted in the introduction, our identification of the state interest does not refer to the policy that would best enhance the welfare of persons under the control of the state.)

In addition to having an interest in the well-being of persons under their control, governments also have a weaker interest in the well-being of persons in other states. Hathaway (2003b, 1823) claims that rational states should not care much about how other states treat their citizens. This is misleading. People in states care about people in other states, and sometimes, especially in democracies where voter preferences matter, these cares influence government action. Three aspects of this state interest may be distinguished.

First, people who live in one state care about the well-being of coreligionists, coethnics, and conationals living in other states, and this concern can translate into governmental interest and action. The United States has been involved in foreign conflicts over two hundred times in its history; most of these interventions were designed to protect the interests of U.S. persons in foreign lands. Similarly, in the nineteenth century, Great Britain, France, and Russia intervened in Ottoman lands as a result of outrage at massacres of Christians (S. Murphy 1996, 52–55). Interwar German pressure on states with German-speaking populations had warm popular support in Germany.

Second, people are sometimes concerned about the well-being of persons in other states with whom they lack ties of religion, ethnicity, or citizenship. Important segments of the British public opposed the slave trade and Belgian atrocities in the Congo in the nineteenth century. Suffering in Somalia and Kosovo influenced U.S. policy in the 1990s. States frequently give small amounts of aid, some of it untied, to poor and developing countries (Lumsdaine 1993), although the aid rarely reflects altruism for the poorest in any straightforward way (Akram 2003) and often goes to states with which the donor has security or trade relationships or colonial ties (Goldsmith 2003).

Third, an important school of thought holds that liberal democracies do not go to war with one another, and are better trading partners and more stable than nondemocracies are (Lipson 2003). Some states therefore have an interest in improving the way other states treat their citizens in order to expand trade, minimize war, and promote international stability. This was a primary impetus for the human rights movement following World War II.

While it is clear that states (and citizens in states) often take an interest in the well-being of persons in other states, especially conationals or coethnics, this interest has historically been weaker than the state's interest in local economic or security matters. We discuss some reasons for this in chapter 8. For now, it suffices to note that most states' foreign aid reflects mixed humanitarian/economic/strategic concerns, and a concern for people in other states tends to translate into humanitarian intervention only when it dovetails with a state's economic or security interests.

The Logic of Human Rights Compliance

Given this understanding of state interests related to human rights, why might states act consistently with international human rights law?

Coincidence of Interest

States rarely commit genocide or crimes against humanity (see Chalk and Jonassohn 1990). An international lawyer might view this fact as evidence that states comply with the Genocide Convention and the customary international law prohibition on crimes against humanity. A better explanation is that the relative absence of genocide and crimes against humanity reflects a coincidence of interest. Both before and after the twentieth-century development of international law prohibitions on these crimes, states have had many good reasons, independent of human rights law, for refraining from committing these crimes against local populations. There are almost always insufficient animosities among citizens to provoke such crimes, it is morally abhorrent to kill large groups of people, and such acts radically disrupt society and the economy (and thus threaten even autocratic leaders). It is misleading to call the resulting behavioral regularity among states compliance with international human rights law, for the law does not supply the motivation.

Genocide and crimes against humanity are not the only human rights crimes that most states most of the time have no interest in committing. As just noted, if for no other reason than internal stability, all but the most authoritarian of states usually have no interest in mistreating large groups under their control. Domestic political exigencies generated increasingly liberal toleration in states long before the modern international human rights movement sprang into existence. The Ottoman Empire tolerated religious diversity. Most Western European governments stopped using torture as a routine investigative tool in the nineteenth century; political freedom advanced throughout that century as well. The rise of women's and children's rights in the nineteenth and twentieth centuries was a phenomenon unrelated to international law; so was the decline of racial and religious discrimination. By the second half of the twentieth century, most liberal democracies could comply with most aspects of the modern human rights treaties without changing their behavior. And the few aspects of these treaties that would have required liberal democracies to change behavior were easily circumvented by reservations, understandings, and declarations (RUDs).

Consider the most comprehensive modern human rights treaty, the International Covenant on Civil and Political Rights (ICCPR). Over one third of the parties to the ICCPR have qualified their consent through

RUDs that deflect the impact of scores of ICCPR provisions. The United States declined consent to the ICCPR's capital punishment limitations, hate speech prohibitions, postconviction sentence reduction rules, and its ban on treating juveniles as adults, and interpreted several other ICCPR provisions to be no more restrictive than domestic law. The United Kingdom opted out of certain ICCPR immigration restrictions contrary to U.K. domestic law and reserved the right not to comply with some of the ICCPR rules concerning hate speech and war propaganda, mandatory free legal assistance, equality of marriage rights, voting, and segregation of juvenile and adult prisoners. France declined consent to the ICCPR's limitations on emergency powers and entered RUDs to ensure that its ICCPR obligations concerning military discipline, immigration, appellate criminal review, and certain minority rights were no more stringent than French law. Sweden declined to consent to the ICCPR's prohibition on double jeopardy or its requirement that juvenile and adult defendants be segregated. Belgium conditioned consent to the ICCPR to protect its practices concerning discrimination in the exercise of royal powers, juvenile criminal offenders, criminal procedure, and marriage. And so on. RUDs permit liberal democracies to conform ICCPR obligations to the contours of extant domestic law, permitting compliance without any change of behavior.

In sum, most states do not curtail their interests by complying with treaties that prevent gross atrocities such as genocide and crimes against humanity, and many states (because of prior behavior under domestic law, RUDs, or both) do not curtail their interests by ratifying and acting in accord with treaties like the ICCPR. To the extent that human rights treaties reflect a coincidence of interest, they raise a puzzle, analyzed below, about why states expend resources to create the treaties in the first place. The point for now is simply that the consistency of much state action with human rights law largely reflects coincidence of interest.

Cooperation

While genocide and crimes against humanity are relatively rare, many governments do commit less extreme human rights abuses, especially during times of civil unrest or war. Many governments find it expedient to discriminate against women, to jail political opponents, and to deny civil rights such as freedom of speech.

At first glance, human rights cooperation seems impossible. If states A and B both abuse their citizens, they appear to gain nothing, based on their self-assessment of interests, from a mutual agreement to withhold abuse. If state A abuses its citizens and state B does not, then state A gains nothing but loses something if both states agree to stop abusing citizens, while state B loses nothing but also gains nothing from such an agreement. If states A and B both protect human rights, an agreement to protect human rights seems to add nothing. Cooperation is obviously no more likely among multiple states. Under these assumptions, cooperation-based human rights law will not exist.

This analysis is flawed, however, because it overlooks a point made earlier: some states (and persons in these states) care about human rights abuses committed in other states. Once this possibility is acknowledged, human rights cooperation becomes possible in two circumstances. The first can be called *symmetric* cooperative human rights law. In this case, each state contains a different ethnic or religious majority that cares about the well-being of coethnics or coreligionists who form a minority in the other state. The states enter a treaty that requires each state to grant rights to the minority living within its territory. The resulting cooperation is roughly the pattern in Europe after the two Treaties of Westphalia (1648) that ended the Thirty Years' War. These bilateral treaties, one between the Holy Roman Emperor and the King of France (who represented his allies) and one between the Holy Roman Emperor and the King of Sweden (who represented his allies), are famous for establishing the principle that the prince determines the religion of his territory. But they also contained significant restrictions on the prince's ability to regulate religious practices in his state, akin to modern human rights treaties. For example, they gave minority religious practitioners the right to practice religion and educate their children at home, prohibited religious discrimination in employment and burial, and guaranteed proportional religious representation in certain cities and certain Holy Roman Empire assemblies (Krasner 1999, 80–81).

These provisions were largely effective. Against the background of the brutally destructive Thirty Years' War, Protestant and Catholic countries both agreed to forgo persecuting religious minorities for the sake of coreligionist minorities in other countries. The Treaties of Westphalia clarified the precise terms of such cooperation, enhancing monitoring capabilities and minimizing mistakes that might jeopardize cooperation. Enforcement was provided by a clear and easy-to-implement threat of retaliation: Protestant states would conduct reprisals against their own minority Catholic populations, and vice versa (Krasner 1999, 81–84). Henkin (1995, 206) has claimed, "The threat that 'if you violate the human rights of your inhabitants, we will violate the human rights of our inhabitants' hardly serves as a deterrent." But this claim is too broad, as the Treaties of Westphalia show. In these cases of symmetric cooperative human rights law—human rights law in which states benefit each other by taking the same actions against locals—the normal cooperation story holds (compare Krasner 1999, 82).

Asymmetric cooperative human rights law is also possible. In this situation, state A abuses its citizens, and state B does not abuse its citizens but cares about the well-being of state A's citizens. The possible reasons for B's concern were mentioned earlier: (1) sympathy for coethnics and coreligionists; (2) weak altruism provoked by atrocities; and (3) an instrumental interest in human rights based on the belief that human rights violations will destabilize A when B has an interest in maintaining A as a viable state. In the case of asymmetric human rights law, cooperation is achieved by a payment—in the form of recognition, cash, aid, credit, military assistance, and so forth—from B to A in return for A's commitment to refrain from abusing people under its control.

Cooperation of this sort was an important part of Great Britain's nineteenth-century strategy to end the slave trade worldwide. Britain had an interest in ending the slave trade after it unilaterally ceased the practice in 1807, and was willing to pay a lot to achieve this end. (Whether this interest was attributable primarily to the influence of religious dissenters motivated by moral concerns [Kaufmann and Pape 1999] or to material economic concerns [Grewe 2000, 554–58] is still debated, but of no relevance to our argument.) In early nineteenth-century treaties, Spain and Portugal agreed to prohibit the slave trade (in certain areas) and to confer peacetime visitation rights on the British in exchange for loans, debt forgiveness, and outright payments (H. Thomas 1997). In addition, Brazil in 1826 agreed to abolish the slave trade and authorized British visitation rights in exchange for recognition by the British government, a benefit that consisted of trading and treaty rights, immunity, and other cash substitutes (id.). In both cases, the economic benefits offered by Britain were presumably more valuable to the slave-trading states than continuing the slave trade.

This kind of cooperation is easy to understand. Britain's treaty partners agreed to a continuing obligation to refrain from the slave trade, and if Britain had refused to keep its promises, they could have brought the slave trade back into existence. Britain's obligations were in form not long term and continuous; payment, forgiveness, and recognition are discrete acts, or a series of acts with an identifiable end. But Britain's real promise was not to use force against the treaty partners, and this promise was open-ended. Indeed, Britain did use force against them when it felt that they were not living up to their side of the bargain, as we discuss later. Repeated interaction with the threat of retaliation sufficed to maintain cooperation for a lengthy period of time; then, as planters deprived of their labor source switched to substitutes, the demand for slaves declined, and any incentive for the slave-trading states to cheat and resurrect the slave trade fell significantly (id.).

Our examples thus far have concerned legal agreements. But human rights cooperation can take nonlegal forms as well. When it works, U.S. foreign aid conditioned on improved human rights practices in recipient states can plausibly be viewed as an example of nonlegalized asymmetric cooperation (Steiner and Alston 2000, 1089–1108). The Helsinki Accords, an explicitly nonlegal document, can also be viewed this way. In the Helsinki Accords, Western states agreed to recognize the Soviet sphere of influence in Eastern Europe (and, implicitly, to expand economic contacts with the East), and the Soviet Union agreed to respect human rights and fundamental freedoms. This exchange was an example of genuine cooperation, though of the shallowest kind, because the West was not positioned to challenge Soviet domination in Eastern Europe and the Soviet Union knew that its commitment to human rights was externally unenforceable. Such thin cooperation is the type one expects between enemies whose primary common interest was avoiding mutual extinction in a nuclear war. But the agreement did reduce tensions between the Western and Soviet blocs during the cold war. And it may have given a significant boost to dissident groups in some states under Soviet influence (D. Thomas 1999).

Coercion

The analysis thus far suggests that, absent special circumstances giving rise to bilateral human rights cooperation, states not inclined to protect human rights for domestic political reasons will not act in accordance with human rights treaties. There is another possibility, however, that has played a prominent role in the history of human rights: coercion. For example, weak state X would, in the absence of external pressure, use torture to quell political dissent. Powerful state Y threatens to cut off military and economic aid if X goes down this path, an outcome that X prefers less to torture. If Y is not otherwise inclined to use torture itself, the result is a behavioral regularity across two states: an absence of torture. But the regularity is the result of Y's independent interest in X not torturing its citizens followed by its coercion of X, not the result of both countries trying to adhere to international law.

There are many examples of coercion in the human rights context. We discuss one example, humanitarian intervention, briefly in chapter 8. Another example is the International Criminal Tribunal for the Former Yugoslavia (ICTY) in The Hague. The tribunal has had modest success in trying war criminals, including Slobodan Milosevic. But it was not the gravitational pull of the ICTY charter that lured these defendants to The Hague. Rather, it was NATO's (and primarily American) military, diplomatic, and financial might. U.S. military and diplomatic power ousted Milosevic's and other unattractive regimes in the Balkans, making a trial of Balkan leaders a possibility. And the United States has consistently threatened to withhold hundreds of millions of dollars in U.S. and International Monetary Fund monies unless the successor regimes in Yugoslavia continue to send war criminals to the ICTY.

Coercion was also a part of Britain's strategy to eliminate the slave trade in the nineteenth century (Krasner 1999, 107–9). Britain had the military force, especially the naval power, to see its abolitionist wishes carried out. In addition to the cooperative agreements outlined earlier, Britain used (or threatened) military force to end the slave trade. The 1815 treaty with Portugal did not apply to slave trading south of the equator. When Britain was unable, by 1839, to reach agreement with Portugal on its south-of-the-equator activities, it ordered its navy to board and seize Portuguese ships in this area, in technical violation of international law. These acts successfully coerced Portugal into ending its slave trade later in the century. Similarly, when Brazil failed to live up to its agreement to abolish the slave trade following British recognition, British warships entered Brazilian ports and burned ships thought to be involved in slave trading. These actions yielded results. As the Brazilian foreign minister said in the Brazilian Chamber of Deputies when he proposed to end the slave trade in 1850: "With the whole of the civilized world now opposed to the slave trade, and with a powerful state like Britain intent on ending it once and for all, can we resist the torrent? I think not" (quoted in id., 106). These and similar events resulted in the legal prohibition, and effective elimination, of the slave trade by the end of the nineteenth century. British coercion, often in violation of international law, made possible compliance with this new rule of international law.

Coercive human rights enforcement need not, and usually does not, take place on the scale suggested by the previous examples. Along many points of diplomatic and economic interaction, more subtle, low-level coercive sanctions can be brought to bear on states that abuse their citizens. While coercion of various sorts no doubt explains some state activities consistent with human rights law, costly coercive enforcement of human rights treaties rarely occurs, and when it does, it usually dovetails with a powerful security or economic interest of the coercing state. States certainly do not exercise coercion out of obedience to international law. If they did, force would be applied systematically and uniformly in the face of human rights violations. But this does not happen. Rather, consistent with states' generally weak interests in persons in other states, coercion is applied episodically and inconsistently, depending on the economic and political interests of the enforcing state and the costs of enforcement.

Consider the patterns of U.S. human rights enforcement. The United States committed significant military and economic resources to redress human rights violations in Yugoslavia (where it had a strategic interest in preventing central European conflict and resolving NATO's crisis of credibility and purpose); Haiti (where turmoil was threatening a domestic crisis in Florida); and Iraq (where it had obvious strategic interests). But the United States has done relatively little in the face of human rights abuses in Africa, where it lacks a strong strategic interest, or in Saudi Arabia, China, and Russia, where its strategic interests conflict with enforcement of a human rights agenda, and where in any event the costs of enforcement are significantly higher.

Cooperation versus Coercion

The above analysis highlights an ambiguity in our use of the terms cooperation and coercion. We described Britain paying a state to end the slave trade as cooperation and its use of force to end the slave trade as coercion. But cash payment is merely a substitute for the threatened use of force. Indeed, Great Britain's decision in each case to pay cash or threaten force probably turned in part on a comparative cost analysis. Similarly, we described the U.S. threat to withhold aid to the former Yugoslavia as coercion, but if the United States had simply paid the former Yugoslavia to turn over its abusers, the example would have better fit our description of cooperation. And yet the threat to withhold payment unless Milosevic is sent to The Hague is identical to the payment of the aid when Milosevic is sent to The Hague. Economic sanctions designed to induce human rights compliance (think of South Africa) share this ambiguity.

For these reasons, cooperation and coercion are in many respects functionally identical. They both consist of (1) acts, threatened acts, or offers of action on the part of state A, that (2) induce state B to change its behavior based on B's conclusion that doing so would make it better off in the face of A's acts, threatened acts, or offered acts. In both cases, state A changes the status quo baseline through acts or threatened acts, and B seeks to maximize its interests in the face of this changed status quo (compare Gruber 2000). The key analytic difference between coercion and cooperation is that when the weaker party cooperates, it is better off from the baseline of the status quo ante, but when it is coerced, it is worse off from this baseline. If Britain is willing to pay £1 million to end Spain's slave trade, and if Spain values this money more than continuing the slave trade, both parties are made better off by such a cooperative deal. If Spain valued the slave trade more than the money, considered alone, but took the money anyway because it was the least bad option in light of the British Navy's additional credible threat to coerce it into submission, this would be an example of coercion.

Although this analytical difference is clear, it is often difficult to determine from the evidence whether cooperation or coercion best describes events. Consider again the U.K.-Spanish bilateral treaty. Although we described the treaty as an example of cooperation, Spain's agreement to accept this treaty was no doubt influenced by its assessment of the costs posed by Britain's sporadic interference with the Spanish slave trade prior to the treaty. If these threatened costs, plus the lost value of the slave trade, were not made up for by Britain's cash payment, the Spanish example is best viewed as coercion. The problem is that it is very hard to tell from the evidence which story is correct.

An analogy from contract law may be helpful here. In ordinary speech we distinguish voluntary and coerced agreements according to whether both parties are better off (voluntary), or one party is better off and the other is worse off (coerced). This distinction assumes a baseline set of entitlements. The person who gives his wallet to a robber to avoid being shot is coerced because the robber has no entitlement to shoot the victim. The person who pays cash for a good, by contrast, has an entitlement not to pay, and thus is not coerced when he does. In the international law context, the baseline set of entitlements is not always clear; for example, a threat to withdraw aid would seem to be a violation of an entitlement if that aid was tied to some prior deal, such as base rights, but not if the aid was purely humanitarian. Despite these difficulties, we follow ordinary usage whenever possible. We call cooperation changed behaviors that result primarily from an exchange of cash and in kind payments, and we call coercion changed behavior that results primarily from threats or use of military force or threatened withdrawal of economic support.

Modern Multilateral Human Rights Treaties

The analysis thus far has touched only briefly on the post–World War II multilateral human rights treaties at the heart of the modern international human rights movement. We now consider these treaties more fully.

The modern human rights treaties do not reflect asymmetric human rights law akin to the British slave treaties, for they do not involve human rights–abiding states offering anything of substance in return for better human rights practices in other states. Rather, the treaties require all states, regardless of their domestic orientation, to do the same thing: treat people under their control well. The treaties also do not reflect symmetric human rights cooperation. Unlike in the Treaties of Westphalia, the parties' symmetrical actions do not involve meaningful reciprocity. For these reasons, we are skeptical about whether modern human rights treaties reflect robust cooperation. Although we later discuss ways that modern human rights law might facilitate cooperation in a thin sense, the point for now is that however these treaties might work, they do not work in the same way as the Treaties of Westphalia or the British bilateral slave trade treaties.

Nor do the modern human rights treaties have an effective or reliable coercive enforcement mechanism. The treaties' reporting obligations are their least onerous provisions, and yet states do not appear to take seriously their obligation to submit reports. More than 70 percent of parties have overdue reports; at least 110 states have five or more overdue reports; about 25 percent have initial overdue reports; the mean length of time for an overdue report is five years; and most of these reports are pro forma descriptions of domestic law, and thus not genuine examples of compliance (which would involve the description of human rights violations) (Bayefsky 2001, 7–8). The treaties do set up committees that can entertain and respond to petitions by individuals. But the recommendations of these committees have no legal force. Perhaps the best indication of the failure of this system is that although 1.4 billion people have the formal right under these treaties to file complaints against their governments, there are only about sixty complaints per year (Bayefsky 2001). Beyond these enforcement mechanisms internal to the treaty, states do not coerce other states into complying with the modern multilateral human rights treaties. States do occasionally coerce other states to improve their human rights practices, but this enforcement is episodic and correlates with the coercing state's strategic interest. Violation of a human rights treaty is neither a necessary nor a sufficient condition for being the target of sanctions motivated by concern about human rights violations.

Two conclusions follow. First, a state incurs little if any cost from violating the treaties. Human rights–abusing states can ratify the treaties with little fear of adverse consequences. Second, for other states the human rights treaties do not require changes in behavior: states comply with the treaties for reasons having to do with domestic law and culture independent of the terms of the treaty.

The scant available empirical evidence is consistent with these conclusions. In addition to the treaty-reporting statistics described above, human rights reports issued by the U.S. State Department, Amnesty International, and Human Rights Watch make clear that human rights abuses in violation of the ICCPR are widespread. These reports suggest that the human rights treaties have not had a large impact, but they say nothing about human rights treaties' possible marginal influence on human rights practices. Two quantitative studies address this latter issue. Linda Camp Keith (1999) examined the relationship between accession to the ICCPR and the degree of respect for human rights.

Oona Hathaway (2002) examined the relationship between accession to the entire array of modern human rights treaties and the degree of respect for human rights covered by these treaties. Both studies find no statistically significant relationship, and Hathaway argues that the relationship in some cases is actually negative. To be sure, one reason for these results might be the difficulty of measuring human rights violations, which are hard to detect and to code (Hathaway 2003a; Goodman and Jinks 2003). Another reason is that liberal states that object to human rights abuses and are willing to devote resources to ending them do not distinguish between human rights abusers that have ratified human rights treaties and those that have not, a point that we develop below. The bottom line remains, however, that there is no evidence that ratification of human rights treaties affects human rights practices. By contrast, empirical studies do find statistical relationships between democracy, peace, and economic development, on the one hand, and protection of human rights, on the other (Poe and Tate 1994; Poe 2004).

The conclusion that the modern human rights treaties have had no significant impact on human rights protection is entirely consistent with human rights being more salient today than sixty years ago, with states respecting human rights in ways they might not have earlier, and with a general improvement of human rights since World War II. Increases in international trade and democratization clearly have had an impact on human rights protection during this period. The end of the cold war was probably the event that had the greatest impact on human rights in the past quarter century. The collapse of the Soviet Union enabled long-oppressed domestic polities throughout Eastern Europe and elsewhere to acquire individual freedoms. In addition, changes in technology have affected human rights enforcement. States have always been willing to pay, but not willing to pay much, to relieve visible suffering in other countries, regardless of what human rights law required. Developments since World War II have increased the benefits and lowered the costs of such enforcement. The rise of television and the Internet has made suffering in other countries more visible; ordinary altruists thus gain more by relieving such suffering than in the past, when relief as well as suffering could (at best) be described only in print. Advances in military technology have reduced the cost of intervening when human rights abuses occur in poor states. So, too, have international institutions that were created to facilitate coordination of security issues, which are also available to coordinate responses to human rights abuse. For example, NATO, a security organization constituted by treaty, lowered the coordination and response costs of intervening to stop human rights abuses in the former Yugoslavia in the summer of 1999.

Additional support for these arguments comes from case studies that provide detailed information about the relationship between international human rights law and the human rights practices of specific states. One prominent study (Lutz and Sikkink 2000) examines three cases from Latin America from the 1970s through the early 1990s. The first two cases involved torture in Uruguay and Paraguay and disappearances in Honduras and Argentina. For each pair, the first state had signed a relevant human rights treaty (the ICCPR and the American Convention on Human Rights, respectively) prior to the human rights violations in question, and the second state had not. For each pair, background conditions were relatively similar, and each state was a dictatorship when the human rights violations occurred. One might have expected Lutz and Sikkink to find that the signatory state engaged in fewer human rights violations than the nonsignatory state did. In fact, human rights violations declined in both states in each pair at roughly the same time, for roughly the same reason: increased international attention to the human rights practices of the two states, followed by a new U.S. policy under the Carter administration, supported by Congress, to withdraw aid from governments that violated human rights. Neither the activists and journalists who highlighted the human rights abuses nor the Carter administration distinguished between signatories and nonsignatories. And the Carter administration's pressure against all four countries was sufficient to reduce human rights violations where they occurred. Public concern followed by coercion, not the human rights treaties, is the explanatory factor here.

The third case study concerns democratization and compares international responses to a coup in Uruguay in 1973 and a coup in Guatemala in 1993. The international community did not respond vigorously to the Uruguay coup; it did to the Guatemala coup. However, this difference cannot be attributed to international law, for the international legal obligations of each country with respect to democracy were the same at the time of its coup. The closest thing to new law was an amendment to the OAS charter that permitted the General Assembly to revoke the membership of a government that came to power through a coup, but this amendment had not been ratified by Guatemala in 1993 and indeed, by its own terms, would not be effective until 1997. For Lutz and Sikkink (2000), all of this is evidence that the law can strengthen an international "norm cascade" in favor of human rights and democracy. But the cases just show that international factors other than international law account for the decline of human rights abuses and the strengthening of democracy in Latin America.

The same conclusion, about the lack of a role for international law in human rights progress, applies to Schmitz's (1999) discussion of human rights abuses in Kenya and Uganda during the past three decades. In Uganda, Idi Amin came to power in a coup and then consolidated his power through a campaign of terror. NGOs protested, and eventually the United States and Britain joined in the chorus, but Amin's real problem was his own people, who did not like his rule, and Tanzania, which he foolishly attacked and which eventually ousted him. After a civil war and much turmoil, during which respect for human rights did not improve, victory was achieved by rebels who obtained popular support by treating civilians relatively well. When their leader, Museveni, obtained power, he declared that his government would respect the human rights of citizens, and created some laws and institutions for this purpose. Human rights abuses declined below the level of the Amin era, though they continued.

In Kenya, Daniel arap Moi came to power under constitutional procedures in 1978, but over the next several years he consolidated and then expanded his power by targeting political opponents and violating human rights. NGOs complained, and the United States exerted diplomatic pressure on Kenya as the human rights abuses there received public attention. This continued for many years. Foreign countries criticized human rights violations in Kenya, and the U.S. Congress threatened to cut off aid. Further pressure through the 1990s led to multiparty (though not entirely fair) elections and some liberalization, as well as accession to the Convention against Torture and Other Cruel, Inhuman or Degrading Treatment or Punishment in 1997. Human rights abuses, however, continued.

Human rights law did not play a discernible role in the reduction of human rights abuses in either country. In Uganda, the atrocities ended before the state signed a human rights treaty. In Kenya, to the extent that human rights practices improved, this occurred before the state signed the treaty; after it signed the treaty, human rights abuses continued. Improvements in both states were mainly due to internal resistance to authoritarian rule. Foreign pressure had diverse motivations, mainly tied to concerns about security and economic disruption. In response to these kinds of realist arguments, Schmitz (1999, 73) says that the pressures of the United States and other countries were marginal and in any event caused by the NGOs' consciousness raising. However, there is no real evidence for the NGO hypothesis either. Probably, the pressures of foreign countries were marginal, and the main pressure for change came from the citizens whose rights were being abused. But, in any event, even in Schmitz's interpretation, the law, as opposed to NGOs' moral commitments, played no role: NGOs were not objecting to violation of a treaty; they were objecting to violation of human rights. It was a moral/political, not legal, claim that had influence, if anything did.

These case studies reveal a pattern. Powerful liberal democracies, usually the United States, take some interest in human rights practices in weak states, but usually not much. Atrocities give rise to protests and expressions of concern without close attention being paid to the state's legal obligations. Liberal democratic governments complain about civil and political rights practices in places like Cuba, Indonesia, Myanmar, Pakistan, Saudi Arabia, and Singapore, even though these states have not ratified the ICCPR. The protests rarely lead to concrete action, and when they do, the patterns of action do not correlate with the requirements of international law. Lower-level human rights abuses also give rise to protests and expressions of concern, but usually to nothing more unless the abuses are tied to governmental instability, regional security concerns, or the disruption of trade. When the abuses are tied to these concerns, powerful liberal democracies either promise goods to states that improve human rights practices or threaten states that do not. The case studies always focus on human rights change in small or weak states that are most susceptible to coercion or economic bribes; they do not focus on larger states like China, Saudi Arabia, or Russia, where human rights progress has been slow and where coercion and bribes are less efficacious.

The rise of transnational NGOs concerned with human rights, a phenomenon greatly assisted by the communications revolutions discussed earlier, does not affect this analysis. Risse and Sikkink (1999) argue (based on some of the case studies described earlier) that NGOs such as Amnesty International can aid in the development and spread of human rights norms throughout the world. This is true but unremarkable. At least since the Reformation, NGO activists have transmitted ideas across borders and engaged in transnationally coordinated political activism, with important implications for domestic governance. Formal NGOs devoted to eliminating the slave trade, to the peace and labor movements, and to free trade flourished and had both domestic and international impacts in the nineteenth and early twentieth centuries (Charnovitz 1997). Relatedly, journalists and activists throughout history have reported on human rights atrocities, provoking domestic audiences to pressure their governments into acting to stop the abuses. In a famous example, Edmund Morel reported on atrocities in the Belgian Congo in the late nineteenth century and engaged in transnational activism, sparking successful worldwide pressure on Belgium to curtail its brutal activities (Hochschild 1999).

Neither these earlier NGO activities nor the ones analyzed by Risse and Sikkink (1999) depended in any special way on international law; nor did they have any clear influence on states' decisions to comply with international law. In modern times as in former times, NGOs, like states, protest atrocities and other objectionable behavior regardless of whether the behavior violates international law. The complaints are sometimes dressed up in the language of illegality (a topic to which we return in chapter 6). But this rhetoric never depends on careful attention to what international law actually requires, or which human rights treaties actually bind on which states. NGOs and other human right monitors (such as the U.S. State Department) simply do not distinguish human rights abuses that do and don't violate a ratified human rights treaty. It is the moral quality of the abusive acts, not their legal quality, that leads to human rights criticism.

Sometimes (but not usually), the rhetoric is followed by changes in the behavior of states. The intervening causal factor does not appear to be international law, but rather domestic political pressure (the people who are being tortured support rebels or foreign armies) or pressure imposed by powerful foreign states. As NGOs complain regardless of whether the state has formally acceded to a human rights treaty, and as the state's response to NGOs' complaints is highly variable in any event, there is no evidence that human rights law plays any special role. The most important NGO contribution is to publicize human rights abuses, which in turn (sometimes) provokes domestic audiences who pressure governmental officials to take action. As the case studies show, the NGO criticisms tend to lead to human rights improvement only when tied to coercive measures that themselves do not depend on the human rights treaties.

Before closing our analysis of multilateral human rights treaties, we must mention an important counterexample to our theory: the European Convention for the Protection of Human Rights and Fundamental Freedoms. The states of Europe agreed by treaty to adhere to certain now standard human rights norms and established a court, the European Court of Human Rights, to interpret the treaty, the decisions of which have been followed by domestic courts and political bodies in hundreds of cases. The most thorough explanation of why this treaty regime works is by Moravcsik (2000), who argues that the states of Europe delegated human rights control to an international organization for the self-interested reasons of "locking in" and consolidating domestic democratic institutions (see also Helfer and Slaughter 1997).

Although this explanation starts from similar premises as our theory, it fails to explain how an international organization can lock in subsequent governments that do not share the same starting assumptions about human rights. To the extent that the European human rights regime is a genuine example of multilateral human rights cooperation, however, it is one that would not have been predicted by our theory. We view the remarkable European human rights phenomenon as part of political and economic cooperation among states that are unifying into a larger state, akin to pre-twentieth-century unification efforts in the United States, Germany, and Italy. On this view, the European system is no more a model for international human rights law than was the United States during the Articles of Confederation period, when it was viewed by many as a "mere" federation governed by international law (Marshall 1819/1969; Yoo 1996). When disparate states integrate into a single state or quasi-state, the influence of international law on their relationship declines, and some kind of federal or regional law (such as European law) takes its place. This new law will reflect the values and interests that are already shared by the states and that are the source of the drive to integrate. This is why international human rights laws have not produced the same level of compliance in South America and Africa, where the human rights regimes are not part of a larger project of economic and political integration, as European human rights law has been in Europe (compare Moravcsik 1995). To be sure, the peripheral members of the European human rights system are not integrating with the EU states, but by the same token these states also do not fully comply with the core states' human rights norms.

Why Ratify Human Rights Treaties?

Our analysis raises a major puzzle. If modern multilateral human rights treaties do not significantly influence human rights behavior, why do states spend the time, effort, and resources to negotiate and create multilateral human rights treaties and related institutions? Why do liberal democracies like the United States and France ratify human rights treaties that don't require any change in behavior? Why don't powerful liberal democracies simply announce a policy of using carrots and sticks to improve human rights in other countries and apply these incentives to weak states whose human rights abuses are especially offensive to world audiences? Why do some authoritarian states ratify the ICCPR when they have no intention of complying, and yet others do not?

There are no precise answers to these questions, and what general answers there are differ based on the type of state and type of treaty at issue. We focus our analysis once again on the ICCPR, the most prominent and important modern human rights treaty. Because we believe that states ratify treaties when the benefits of doing so outweigh the costs, we begin by assessing the costs and benefits of ICCPR ratification.

For most states, the costs of ratifying the ICCPR are low because, as explained earlier, the treaty has no self-enforcement or external enforcement mechanism. This means that authoritarian states like Afghanistan, Iraq, and Rwanda that do not generally act in accordance with the treaty can nonetheless ratify the treaty at little cost, as they have done. Some maintain that ratification of the ICCPR entails a nontrivial cost of monitoring of domestic practices by the Human Rights Committee and its special rapporteurs. But governments, NGOs, and the media closely monitor and criticize human rights practices in every state, regardless of whether it has ratified certain human rights treaties. Against this background, the notoriously weak and all but ignored ICCPR monitoring mechanisms add trivial costs at best.

The lack of ICCPR enforcement means that liberal democracies can ratify the treaty with little cost. A more important explanation for ratifications by liberal democracies is that their practices already conform to the treaty. And when, at the margins, they do not, the incongruence can easily be resolved by RUDs. It is no accident that liberal democracies tend to attach many RUDs to the ICCPR, while most authoritarian states attach few if any RUDs, and most take out none whatsoever (see Table 4.2). This pattern is consistent with our hypothesized reasons that states join the ICCPR: authoritarian states do so because they suffer little cost from their noncompliance, and liberal democracies do so because, after RUDs, they can comply simply by following their prior domestic practices (compare Hathaway 2003b, who reaches a similar conclusion without analyzing RUDs).

We have focused on the low costs of ratifying the ICCPR. What about the benefit side? Why do the ICCPR and treaties like it exist in the first place, and why do states ratify them? Under our theory, there must be at least some small benefit to drafting and ratification to justify the expense of the enterprise. As for drafting: the states and groups that created the ICCPR thought that its report and comment procedures might enhance human rights protections in states that did not otherwise respect human rights. The fact that the treaty has not worked as planned does not undercut this motivation. Nor does it show that the treaty plays no beneficial role. In addition, the ICCPR and related treaties could inform the world of a "code of conduct" that powerful liberal democracies deem important to establish. Smaller states that comply with this code know that they are more likely to receive aid, and less likely to be subject to threats and other forms of pressure, than states that do not comply with the code. Thus, the treatment of human rights may improve as a result of cooperation or coercion in a bilateral relationship; the multilateral treaty provides a rough guide to the kinds of behavior that are deemed acceptable and not.

In this sense, modern human rights treaties operate in much the same way that the "standard of civilization" did in the nineteenth century. As European and American influence expanded around the globe in the nineteenth century, especially into Asia and Africa, the Western powers confronted states that were politically, economically, legally, and culturally much different. In many cases, the Western powers used a "standard of civilization" to determine whether and to what extent to have relations with non-Western states. The standard consisted of basic rights for foreign nationals, a well-organized government with the capacity for international relations, a Western-style legal system, and conformity to international law (that is, the Euro-American version) and to Euro-American customs and norms (Fidler 2001). The standard was designed to determine whether a state was "sufficiently stable to

Table 4.2 Reservations, Understandings, and Declarations (RUDs) to the International Covenant on Civil and Political Rights[1]

States	RUDs
United Kingdom	16
United States	12
Austria	9
France, Netherlands, Trinidad and Tobago	8
Monaco, Switzerland	7
Belgium, Italy, Malta	6
Denmark, Liechtenstein, Luxembourg	5
Bangladesh, Germany, Iceland, Ireland, Mexico, New Zealand, Norway, Thailand, Turkey	4
Algeria, Australia, Belize, Finland, India, Kuwait, Sweden	3
Botswana, Guyana, Romania, South Korea, Syrian Arab Republic	2
Afghanistan, Argentina, Barbados, Bulgaria, Congo, Gambia, Guinea, Hungary, Iraq, Israel, Japan, Libyan Arab Jamahiriya, Mongolia, Russian Federation, Ukraine, Venezuela, Vietnam, Yemen	1
Albania, Angola, Armenia, Azerbaijan, Belarus, Benin, Bolivia, Bosnia and Herzegovina, Brazil, Burkina Faso, Burundi, Cambodia, Cameroon, Canada, Cape Verde, Central African Republic, Chad, Chile, Colombia, Costa Rica, Côte d'Ivoire, Croatia, Cyprus, Czech Republic, Democratic Republic of the Congo, Djibouti, Dominica, Dominican Republic, Ecuador, Egypt, El Salvador, Equatorial Guinea, Eritrea, Estonia, Ethiopia, Gabon, Georgia, Ghana, Greece, Grenada, Guatemala, Haiti, Honduras, Iran (Islamic Republic of), Jamaica, Jordan, Kenya, Kyrgyzstan, Latvia, Lebanon, Lesotho, Lithuania, Macedonia, Madagascar, Malawi, Maui, Mauritius, Moldova, Morocco, Mozambique, Namibia, Nepal, Nicaragua, Niger, Nigeria, North Korea, Panama, Paraguay, Peru, Philippines, Poland, Portugal, Rwanda, Saint Vincent and the Grenadines, San Marino, Senegal, Serbia and Montenegro, Seychelles, Sierra Leone, Slovakia, Slovenia, Somalia, South Africa, Spain, Sri Lanka, Sudan, Suriname, Swaziland, Tajikistan, Tanzania, Timor-Leste, Togo, Tunisia, Turkmenistan, Uganda, Uruguay, Uzbekistan, Zambia, Zimbabwe	0

undertake binding commitments under international law and whether it was able to protect adequately the life, liberty, and property of foreigners" (Schwarzenberger 1955, 220). In short, it was a standard that communicated to non-Western states what criteria they had to satisfy to reap the benefits of relations with Western states.

Because the standard of civilization emerged in a decentralized fashion, and its interpretation could thus vary from state to state, small and weak states that sought to obtain the benefits of international cooperation might have had trouble figuring out just what the rest of the world expected them to do. This is a standard coordination problem. Given that liberal states are willing to provide some benefits to, or refrain from some coercive actions against, other states that meet a certain standard of conduct, it is to the benefit of all liberal states to agree with some specificity on the actions that are permitted under that standard (certain forms of speech regulation) and actions that are not permitted (such as torture). Modern human rights treaties can be viewed as solving a similar coordination problem. Although the liberal states' use of RUDs muddies the standard a bit, there is a clear core of agreement that less liberal states can use as a guide. States know that when they comply with this guide or code, they are more likely to receive benefits (however small) and to avoid diplomatic, military, and economic pressure (even if minor).

These coordination benefits of human rights treaties recall our two-step theory of multilateral treaty making: step 1 consists of negotiations over common terms; step 2 involves enforcement. When the United States rewards or punishes states for their human rights practices, it can refer to the standards codified in the treaties, and it does this regardless of whether the state in question ever signed or ratified the treaties. The treaties, then, clarified the human rights standards of the liberal states. This may explain why ratification is not correlated with compliance. To test whether human rights treaties matter, one would need to compare the human rights practices of states before and after the treaties came into force, not the human rights practices of ratifiers versus nonratifiers. Unfortunately, too many confounding factors would defeat a simple event study, especially given the weak incentives that states have to enforce the treaties.

Then why do the liberal states sign human rights treaties? Why don't they just issue a joint communiqué that embodies their expectations for good human rights practices? All states receive at least this small benefit from ratification: they can no longer be criticized as non-rights-respecting because they failed to ratify the treaty. If there is uncertainty about a state's commitment to treating its own citizens well, failure to ratify a major human rights treaty sends an unambiguous and believable signal that it is not committed to human rights, and thus (perhaps) is not deserving of collateral benefits that might flow to a human rights–respecting state, such as recognition and trade. Ratification is thus especially important for a state making the transition from authoritarianism to liberal democracy, for although human rights treaty ratifications by themselves might not send much information about human rights practices, the failure to ratify the treaties in this context is viewed as evidence of unreliability on the issue (compare Hathaway 2002; Moravcsik 2000). Even liberal democracies benefit from ratification. No liberal democracy is beyond human rights reproach, and thus all can benefit from eliminating the uncertainty about the significance of nonratification. As for authoritarian states, they too are subject to an adverse inference from nonratification, and because ratification is practically costless, there is little reason not to do so. Eventually, however, a cascade of ratification would empty the act of meaning; if all states ratify because it is costless to do so, then ratification does not distinguish states that respect human rights and those that do not. The phenomenon is similar to the process by which clothing or some other expensive item reveals the wealth of its owner until changes in the technology of production reduces its cost and brings its price within the range of the poor. (We return to many of these themes when we discuss international law rhetoric in chapter 6.)

Although these conclusions provide general guidance in explaining the pattern of human rights treaty ratifications, they cannot explain the details of ratification patterns. Why is the United States one of two states (the other is Somalia) that did not ratify the Rights of the Child Convention, a treaty that has no enforcement mechanism and that is ignored by the states that did ratify it? Why have more states ratified the Rights of the Child Convention than the Genocide Convention? Why have authoritarian regimes in Egypt, Russia (in 1976, as the Soviet Union), Iraq, and Iran ratified the ICCPR, while authoritarian regimes in Myanmar, Pakistan, and Cuba have not? Why do Bahrain and Kazakhstan ratify one human rights treaty that they have no intention of complying with (the Convention on the Elimination of Discrimination Against Women), yet decline to ratify another (such as the ICCPR) that they have no intention of complying with? We (like everyone else) have a hard time explaining the details of human rights treaty ratification patterns. We suspect that the reason for the absence of any discernible pattern of ratification is that both the costs and the benefits of ratification of these treaties are very small. Because ratification matters relatively little on the international plane, one way or the other, ratification patterns are unlikely to correlate to systemic international factors, but rather to the vagaries of domestic politics and institutions, which are lost in noise.

Customary International Law of Human Rights

In addition to human rights treaties, there is said to be a large body of human rights customary international law. We say "said to be" because the customary international law of human rights does not reflect a general and consistent state practice followed from a sense of legal obligation. Rather, the customary international law of human rights is based less on actual state practice and more on a human rights consensus found in General Assembly resolutions, multilateral treaties, the writings of scholars, and related sources (Bradley and Goldsmith 1997a).

Consider the famous *Filartiga* decision (1980), which initiated the human rights litigation revolution in U.S. courts. *Filartiga* held, among other things, that customary international law prohibited state-sponsored torture. The court acknowledged that this holding was not based on state practice, because many states of the world torture their citizens. It instead based its holding on the UN Charter, the UN General Assembly's Universal and Torture Declarations, several human rights treaties, and the writings of jurists. *Filartiga* was thought to alter the traditional positivist approach by eschewing close reliance on state practice and by looking to technically nonlegal sources of law (such as unratified treaties and UN General Assembly resolutions) in identifying customary international law. Also, the court relied heavily on moral disapproval of torture. Other domestic and international courts in recent years have embraced a similar approach to the customary international law of human rights (*Military and Paramilitary Activities in and against Nicaragua* 1986; *Regina v. Bartle* 1999).

In our view, the customary international law of human rights, like modern human rights treaties, has little exogenous influence on state behaviors. To the extent that we see behaviors consistent with the customary international law of human rights, they reflect coincidence of interest or episodic coercion. In this respect, the customary international law of human rights is, despite conventional wisdom, very much like many of the traditional customary international law rules analyzed in part 1. It does not generally solve coordination or cooperation problems, but instead tends to be a rhetorical validation of practices that have little if any cooperative element.

Indeed, the customary international law analysis in *Filartiga* has many similarities to the customary international law analysis in the paradigmatic traditional customary international law decision examined in part 1, *The Paquete Habana* (1900). The essential difference is content: traditional customary international law focused on commercial, military, and diplomatic relationships between states; modern customary international law focuses more on human rights. But similarities overwhelm this difference. The fishing vessel exemption rule in *The Paquete Habana* did not reflect universal state practice. The rule lacked a pedigree in the consent of states. In reality, it was based on unrelated bilateral agreements scattered over centuries, the writings of scholars, pronouncements of international bodies, and the conclusory assertions of a U.S. court. The fishing vessel exemption was also vague; the line between the rule and its exception for fishing vessels of military or economic value was always unclear. Also like the new customary international law of human rights, the fishing vessel exemption was invoked opportunistically in accordance with states' different interests. The rule was even justified moralistically. Over a dozen times, the Court in *The Paquete Habana* claimed that the rule is a humanitarian measure designed to protect poor, industrious fishermen.

In short, the modern customary international law of human rights is structurally similar to traditional customary international law. Modern customary international law does not constrain states any more or less than traditional customary international law did. When a state declines to violate customary international law, this is usually because it has no reason to violate it. When modern customary international law does not reflect bilateral cooperation or coordination (as is usually the case in the modern human rights context), it is mostly aspirational, just as much of traditional customary international law was.

Conclusion

Liberal states that care about human rights in other states do not make a fetish of international law. When conditions are right, they will pressure human rights abusers regardless of whether they are signatories to a treaty or have violated customary international law. When conditions are not right, they will tolerate human rights abuses in other states regardless of whether they are signatories to a treaty or have violated customary international law. Thus, human rights law fades into the background. Some political scientists claim that human rights treaties have contributed to the formation and enforcement of transnational norms. And human rights lawyers who acknowledge the weakness of the existing legal regime nonetheless insist that the treaties are a necessary step in the future evolution of international human rights law, during which the law will become clearer and more precise, and states, losing the ability to claim adherence to vague norms while violating them in spirit, will gradually bring their practices into compliance with human rights ideals. But these claims obscure the reality, which consists of powerful states enforcing interests, including altruistic interests to be sure, and weak states yielding when sufficient pressure is brought to bear against them. The relationships are bilateral, and the degree of enforcement depends on the bargaining positions of the two states in each relationship. If human rights law becomes clearer and more specific, the likely outcome would not be greater compliance but rather more violations and perhaps withdrawal from the treaties as well (Helfer 2002). To be sure, there can be genuine bilateral cooperation in the human rights context, as the Peace of Westphalia and the slave trade treaties show. And multilateral treaties can clarify the expectations of those states willing to improve relations with states that respect human rights. But most human rights practices are explained by coercion or coincidence of interest.

CHAPTER 5

INTERNATIONAL TRADE

This chapter analyzes prominent treaty regimes governing international trade. We begin with the bilateral treaty regime that arose in the nineteenth century. We explain how this regime's distinctive features are best explained by our theory of international law and how its failures influenced the design of the great twentieth-century multilateral treaty regime, the General Agreement on Tariffs and Trade/World Trade Organization. GATT/WTO poses a challenge to our account of international law, for, according to conventional wisdom, it provides the basis for multilateral trade cooperation. As we shall see, however, the elements of GATT/WTO that have flourished generally solve coordination problems, not multilateral prisoner's dilemmas. The international trade rules that were designed to solve multilateral prisoner's dilemmas have failed. GATT/WTO might be best described as an effort to use bilateral means to solve a multilateral problem; its limitations can be traced to this mismatch between means and ends.

The Nineteenth-Century Trade Regime: Background

International trade has always been an important element of states' foreign policy. Before analyzing modern international trade law, we provide a little historical background, because one cannot understand the modern system without understanding how states would act in the absence of this international legal regime. Such a hypothetical trade regime would *not* necessarily be one of maximal trade barriers and economic autarky.

At the end of the Napoleonic Wars, the major trading states all had erected formidable trade barriers. Though Adam Smith had undermined the philosophical case for mercantilism, protectionism made sense on relative security grounds, and beyond this, tariffs were a major source of revenue for states. As peace took hold and the prospect of further war receded, relative security concerns diminished but did not disappear.

In Britain, the decline in trade barriers, which began in the 1820s and 1830s but were marked most famously by the Repeal of the Corn Laws in 1846, can be traced to diverse factors. The usual story is that manufacturers had obtained power relative to landowners, in part because of the economic changes brought on by the Industrial Revolution and in part because of political changes such as the Reform Bill of 1832. Manufacturers wanted to pay lower duties on imports of raw materials, and perhaps they also wanted their workers to have access to cheaper food. Landowners, of course, preferred to avoid foreign competition, but in the end they might not have been injured much by it because of subsequent developments in farming technology in Britain. Agriculture flourished even after the Repeal. Ideology, spiced with religion, also played a role in the decline of protectionism, as elites increasingly adopted Smith's position on the relationship between international trade and national wealth. The extreme view, which was by no means uncommon, was personified by Cobden, who believed that free trade would, by making states mutually dependent, promote international peace. The Repeal of the Corn Laws was also made possible by legal and financial innovation that began the shift from reliance on duties to other forms of taxation. Finally, some British believed that by opening the British market for farm products, the repeal of the Corn Laws would divert the continental economies from manufacturing to agriculture, thus keeping them weak relative to Britain (Kindleberger 1975, 27–36; Howe 1997).

However these factors may have combined against protectionism, the point is that Britain saw itself as having a unilateral interest in the reduction of trade barriers. Although many officials hoped that other states would follow Britain's lead and reduce their own trade barriers, few believed that reduction of trade barriers would be desirable only if other states followed suit. Indeed, unilateralism was borne out by subsequent events. Other states did not immediately follow Britain's example, at least not to as great a degree, but this failure did not lead to the reinvigoration of protectionism in Britain. On the contrary, protectionism was dead in mainstream politics for the next several decades. In early nineteenth-century Britain, then, we find evidence that the reduction of trade barriers is not necessarily a matter of international cooperation; it can occur as unilateral policy, just as in standard international trade economics, although the story was more complex.

Britain was the foremost commercial state during this period, but it was not the only state that was reducing trade barriers. Trade barriers in Prussia, and subsequently in the entire Prussia-dominated German customs union, were low at the beginning of the century, rose in the first half, and then declined in the second half.[1] Tariffs in France were high but gradually declined, only to rise again after the Franco-Prussian War in 1872. The other major European countries participated in the expansion of free trade after 1850, with some retrenchment in the 1870s, and then in another trend in favor of free trade in the 1890s, which petered out in the years leading up to World War I. Many of these movements can be explained by shifts in the balance of power between import-competing firms and farmers, and manufacturers that used imported supplies; shifting military alliances (for example, France lowering tariffs against British imports when it needed British support in Italy); and liberal ideology (Kindleberger 1975; C. Trebilcock 1981; Pahre 2001; Rogowski 1989).

Most interesting, for our purposes, is the increasing resort to trade treaties in the second half of the nineteenth century. Before then, trade barriers were mostly the result of unilateral action, and few trade treaties were in existence. This changed midcentury. France and Italy belonged to about a dozen trade treaties by the late 1860s. Britain entered fewer treaties, but these included important treaties with major trading partners such as France. Prussia was the one major state that entered a significant number of trade treaties in the first half of the century, but these were mainly with other German-speaking countries that joined the customs union; after 1865, and increasing significantly in the 1890s, Prussia and the customs union (which was unified into the single German state in 1871) entered numerous trade treaties with other powers (Pahre 2001, 35–37).

Nineteenth-Century Trade Treaties

State Interest

What interest is served by a treaty that reduces trade barriers? There are two conventional answers. First, the interest is state welfare. When state A enters a trade treaty with state B, state A's workers and investors benefit from access to state B's markets. Second, the interest is the welfare of export-oriented interest groups. When state A enters a trade treaty, state A's export industry benefits from access to state B's markets.

The first answer may contain some truth, but it does not provide good predictions of the behavior of states. If a state cares only about maximizing national welfare, then in most cases, it can achieve that aim by unilaterally eliminating trade barriers. States would not enter trade treaties because they would not have trade barriers to eliminate. An exception might be made for large states that dominate the world market for some goods; with respect to those goods, a state might have no incentive to eliminate trade barriers unilaterally (Bagwell and Staiger 2002). It can use its market power to extract some consumer surplus from foreign citizens. Trade treaties, then, would occur only between large states that dominate the world market in different goods: each state would reduce the barriers with respect to the goods in which it has an advantage as long as the other state did the same thing. Welfare is gained from the elimination of what are called terms-of-trade externalities. However, this is not an accurate description of the history of trade treaties; they are used more commonly than the theory predicts. Accordingly, we focus in this chapter on the second answer.

The second answer is the conventional wisdom, but it has problems of its own. A state's interest with respect to international trade will vary from good to good, depending on the relative political strength of exporters and import competers. If the domestic manufacturers of some good are weak, then the state will not be harmed by a reduction in trade barriers against that good. Indeed, a state might benefit from unilaterally reducing trade barriers, as it would if consumers or firms that use imports as inputs have a great deal of power. If the domestic industry is strong, then it will be harmed by a reduction in trade barriers against the good. If a state has a powerful export industry, then it will benefit from other countries reducing their trade barriers; otherwise, it will not (Schwartz and Sykes 1997).

On this view, states will unilaterally set zero, low, intermediate, or high trade barriers for different goods, depending on their internal political economy. Each state will sometimes benefit from other states reducing their trade barriers from the unilateral level, but sometimes not. When a state does benefit from other states reducing their trade barriers, then a trade treaty may be possible.

Cooperation through Bilateral Treaties

If all this is true, then states can sometimes produce mutual gains through bilateral treaties. The logic is familiar. At time o, each state has, say, intermediate tariffs for all goods. State A and state B both produce two goods: iron and rye. In state A, the iron industry has a great deal of political power; in state B, the rye farmers have dominant political power. A's iron industry would like greater access to B's market, and B's rye farmers would like greater access to A's market. The interest of each state reflects the relative influence of interest groups in that state: so in A, the state gains from a trade treaty only to the extent that the iron industry's gain exceeds, according to some political calculus, the rye industry's loss. If the reverse is true for B, then mutual reduction of tariff barriers could produce joint gains. Therefore, the states agree to reduce trade barriers.

The logic is that of the prisoner's dilemma: gains can be obtained as long as each state cares sufficiently about future payoffs and adopts an appropriate retaliatory strategy. Retaliation here is straightforward: if one state raises its trade barriers in violation of the agreement, then the other state responds by raising its own trade barriers. We don't need to rely on our other explanations of international law—coincidence of interest, coordination, and coercion—because the nineteenth-century treaties were, for the most part, straightforward exercises in bilateral cooperation. As mentioned in chapter 3, bilateral treaties do not usually reflect coincidence of interest because two states do not need a treaty to ratify unilaterally motivated behavior; coincidence of interest plays a role mainly in the explanation of compliance with multilateral treaties. Coercion did occur, but it usually involved relations between major states and undeveloped states that would become colonies. Trade treaties were mainly between major states, more or less equals, except when used for the purpose of unification: the German case, discussed below.

One example will suffice (Conybeare 1987, 183–88), though the history is complex. In 1881 Italy and France entered a trade treaty that reduced Italian trade barriers against French manufactured goods and French barriers against certain Italian agricultural products. The treaty was concluded during a period of rising protectionist agitation in both states and throughout Europe, apparently caused by farmers who had lost markets to cheap grain imports from Russia. In 1886 Italy denounced the treaty, and in 1887 it raised tariffs on French goods. At the same time, Italy denounced treaties with other trading partners. Italy apparently believed that because its trading partners were dependent on its agricultural exports, it could obtain better terms, and indeed it renegotiated trade treaties with many of its partners. But France refused to budge and insisted that the terms of the 1881 treaty be preserved in any new treaty. In 1889 Italy finally agreed to these terms, but France would not normalize trading relations until 1898. During this period, both Italy and France suffered economically from lack of bilateral trade, but Italy, the smaller and poorer country, suffered a great deal more.

A few observations are in order. First, France and Italy initially saw themselves in a prisoner's dilemma: it was in each state's interest to raise trade barriers in the absence of an agreement to fix them, but both states would do better through mutual restraint. The treaty provided for such mutual restraint. The legalization of the agreement, however, was not the source of restraint; although nineteenth-century trade treaties frequently had fixed terms, states often denounced them and then sought to renegotiate them. The treaty was just a device by which the states communicated expectations about their joint conduct (see Pahre 2001 for some of the history).

Second, Italy's denunciation of the treaty with France might have been a mistake, but might also have reflected domestic political changes. Evidence that the denunciation was a mistake is that France, unlike other treaty partners, refused to renegotiate the trade relationship on more favorable terms to Italy, and that some contemporary observers believed that the Italians thought that France was more dependent on Italian agriculture than it was in fact. This is possible, but it is also possible that Italian import competers obtained more power during the 1880s and that they drove the Italian government's trade policy. If so,

Italy did not cheat; it just experienced higher costs from complying with the 1881 agreement and rationally ended it.

Third, France's response looks like classic retaliation. It would be useful to understand why France did not agree to the 1881 terms when Italy gave up its demands. Theory does not tell us; mild and extreme retaliation strategies can both be used to solve a prisoner's dilemma. If France was farsighted enough, it might have incurred the high short-term losses of harsh retaliation in the expectation that this would deter Italy and other trading partners from denouncing treaties far into the future. Another possibility is that France's import competers obtained greater political power at the same time that Italy's did. On this view, neither state after 1886 would have benefited from a new trade agreement because in both states the import competers had political power and thus no interest in cooperating over trade.

Fourth, France's response to Italy's move might also have been constrained by most favored nation (MFN) terms in its treaties with other states. In the nineteenth century, many but not all trade treaties contained MFN clauses, which held that if one of the treaty parties enters a subsequent trade agreement with a third state, any more favorable trade terms granted to the third state would apply to the other treaty partner as well. Although MFNs are not well understood, the idea appears to have been to prevent the following situation from occurring (Bagwell and Staiger 2002). Suppose that Britain and France enter a trade agreement that reduces the tariffs on Britain's textiles to 5 percent and on France's wine to 5 percent. France then enters an agreement with Italy, under which France, in return for some concession from Italy, agrees to reduce tariffs on Italian textiles to 2 percent. Assuming that British and Italian textiles are of equal cost and quality, France will end up importing all its textiles from Italy and none from Britain, while Britain will be required to continue charging the low 5 percent tariff on French wine. In this way, Britain loses the benefit of its bargain as a result of France's subsequent action. The MFN clause prevents this from happening by requiring France to reduce the tariff on British textiles to 2 percent once it agrees to the 2 percent tariff on Italian textiles.

Returning to the Franco-Italian trade dispute, France's MFN treaties with other states implied that if France agreed to place low tariffs on Italian agricultural goods, then France would also have to lower tariffs on similar goods imported from other trading partners protected by MFN clauses. To be sure, France could have denounced or violated these treaties; but presumably if it had, it would have risked retaliation from these other countries, and it was more dependent on these other countries for imports than it was on Italy (Conybeare 1987, 187). Here we see that although trade relations were usually conducted on a bilateral basis, they frequently had third-party effects. If a state has an MFN treaty with a third party, then its ability to make concessions is constrained by that treaty. Even if a state does not have a related MFN treaty with a third party, granting concessions to one state may cause trade diversion from an earlier partner, leading that earlier partner to protest and threaten to denounce the earlier treaty. States understood that in this way every major bilateral trading relationship had important third-party effects, and when they negotiated with each other, they paid attention to the effect of the negotiations on the attitudes of other states. As a result, bilateral trade negotiations involving multiple states often clustered—during 1881–1884, 1890–1891, and 1904–1906, for example (Pahre 2003, chap. 12)—and in this way a system that was bilateral at its core created pressure in the direction of multilateralism.

A final point concerns why international trade expanded so rapidly during the second half of the nineteenth century. It is tempting to credit the increasing legalization of international relations during this period. With a more robust international legal order, firms had the confidence to invest abroad. However, there is no evidence that international law played such an important causal role. There was no international law that required states to liberalize trade policy, of course, and the treaties, including their MFN terms, merely ratified political arrangements that states believed were in their (temporary) interest. Pahre (2003) argues that MFN terms became a "norm," that is, a constraint on states' behavior, but he musters no more than a few pieces of anecdotal evidence for this argument. As we have seen, the most plausible explanation for MFN terms is that they enabled parties to a treaty to protect their gains from subsequent trade treaties between one of the original parties and a third party. MFN terms served the interests of the state parties, and that is all.

Technology, politics, and economics explain the growth of international trade in the nineteenth century. Industrialization, the revolution in transportation and communications, developments in international finance, and similar technological and economic factors significantly reduced the cost of shipping goods from one state to another and also reduced the cost of entering contracts and financing investments. Manufacturers thus saw new opportunities in foreign markets and lobbied their governments to negotiate reductions in foreign tariffs. Some governments also believed that cheap food imports would pacify hungry laborers. Peace and political stability were also important causal factors: when relative security concerns are low, states will focus on absolute gains. Although Kindleberger (1975) and others give credit to British power and the British interest in opening foreign markets, credit should probably be given to the balance of power system as a whole.

World War I through GATT

The golden age of international trade ended with World War I. Trade barriers erected during World War I persisted long after the war ended. There are many theories for the interwar breakdown of international trade, but we focus on a single strand of the complex explanation. After World War I, there were many more major trading states than before the war, when Germany, France, and Britain were the dominant trading powers and a handful of smaller European countries such as Italy played a minor role. Conybeare (1987) argues that the MFN "norm," by which he seems to mean a moral commitment of states, led to free-riding that was less manageable in a large group of states than it had been among a small group of states prior to the war. As we noted earlier, if state A and state B are parties to an MFN treaty, then state A (or B) benefits when state B (or A) negotiates lower tariffs with state C, and the state obtains this benefit without having to make any new concessions itself. But that means that each state will wait for the other state, holding back rather than aggressively seeking lower barriers with new or existing trading partners.

But the blame should not be put on an MFN norm so much as on the intrinsic third-party effects of international trade, to which the use of MFN terms in bilateral treaties was an imperfect response. If the states had solved the MFN problem by repudiating all MFN treaties and abandoning the use of that term, the problem would have remained that every bilateral agreement would be vulnerable to trade diversion caused by a subsequent trade deal between one of the original parties and a third party—indeed, this was the problem that the MFN term was intended to solve. As new states were created and old economies matured, the temptation to engage in trade diversion became extreme and unmanageable. To this must be added the usual factors: political instability, nationalist extremism, the threat of military conflict, the worldwide economic downturn starting in 1929, and perhaps U.S. trade policy, which, while traditionally protectionist, hit new levels of protectionism in the 1930s, which provoked retaliation by other countries.

By World War II, it was conventional wisdom, especially in the U.S. government, that the trade wars of the 1930s deepened the depression and contributed to the rise of fascism and the outbreak of a second war. The conviction that this should not happen again led to GATT. Thus, from the start, GATT was colored by concerns about security. By 1947, international trade had become a field of battle in the cold war.

Theory of GATT

The original 1947 GATT agreement set out a number of principles that reflected the practices of the nineteenth-century regime. Here we discuss five of these principles: that there would be periodic multinational trade negotiations; that protectionism would be embodied in tariffs rather than nontariff barriers; that states would not discriminate against other GATT members; that barriers would be reduced through a process of reciprocation; and that international panels would adjudicate GATT disputes, although enforcement would be left to the affected parties. We argue that all of these principles have straightforward explanations consistent with our theory. Many of the principles were designed to solve simple coordination problems. States benefited from a framework within which bilateral trade negotiations and enforcement could occur. The framework was like a language or set of standards, such as the rules governing the use of the radio spectrum, that facilitates communication; it was self-enforcing because once the framework was agreed on, no state had an incentive to deviate from it, lest it be misunderstood in a bilateral relationship and provoke retaliation against policy intended to be cooperative. But there were two complications. The coordination game, as is almost always the case, had asymmetric payoffs, and in such a repeated battle of the sexes game, some deviation will occur. More important, many of the designers of GATT aspired to do more than solve coordination problems: they also wanted to solve multilateral cooperation problems (the n-player prisoner's dilemma). As we will see, the rules that reflected these aspirations were not obeyed.

Periodic Multinational Trade Negotiations

Article XXVIII bis of GATT provides that contracting parties may sponsor periodic multilateral rounds of tariff negotiations. The article was an amendment of the initial GATT agreement but reflected understandings that developed earlier. There have been eight rounds since 1947— Geneva (1947), Annecy (1948), Torquay (1950), Geneva (1956), Dillon (1960–61), Kennedy (1964–67), Tokyo (1973–79), and Uruguay (1986–94) (the declaration launching the current Doha round was adopted by the WTO in 2001)—with the number of states involved rising from 23 in the first round to 125 by the end of the eighth.

Article XXVIII bis raises two questions: Why did states believe that multilateral bargaining would be superior to bilateral bargaining? and Why was this system self-enforcing? The answer to the first question is clear from the nineteenth-century history. Because states gain from trade agreements only if they obtain concessions in return for their concessions, every trade deal is vulnerable to a subsequent trade agreement that results in trade diversion. To prevent this from happening, states need to negotiate together. Thus, our assumptions about the interests of states—that they seek to promote the welfare of domestic import competers and exporters—leads to the conclusion that international trade is not a bilateral prisoner's dilemma between multiple pairs of states, but a collective action problem, that is, a large-n prisoner's dilemma. (There are other respects in which international trade is best understood as a collective action problem; for example, see Maggi 1999.) Bilateral trade agreements, then, cannot exploit the entire potential surplus from international trade.

There are two parts to this problem. The first is that of arranging multilateral negotiating rounds; the second is that of enforcing the agreements that are obtained during the rounds. Article XXVIII bis addresses only the first part; we discuss the second part later. As to the problem of arranging multilateral negotiating rounds, this is a problem of asymmetric coordination, or a multiplayer battle of the sexes game. Every state benefits from meeting with all other states during a specific time, at a specific place, rather than having to arrange a meeting with each of its dozens of trading partners. But each state will have a private optimum: a meeting next year rather than this year, in a convenient city rather than a faraway city. Still, these considerations, the time and place, are trivial compared to the amounts at stake, and it is no surprise that GATT members could reach agreement, no doubt under the leadership of the major powers, time and again. The logic is familiar: once all states agree that a trading round will occur in Geneva on a certain date, no single state can benefit by sending a delegate to New York City; although coalitions might form and cause trouble, the gains from doing so seem low. Indeed, the mutual benefits from multilateral negotiation are high enough that it can occur in a decentralized fashion. Thus did clustering occur with increasing frequency in the second half of the nineteenth century, and did so in the absence of any formal legal obligation. Clustering was endogenous, driven by concerns about the third-party effects of bilateral treaties.

There is a further point, which is that multilateral negotiations are not exclusive of bilateral negotiations, and bilateral negotiations occur both outside rounds and within rounds. During the rounds, states usually bargain over concessions in a bilateral exchange with each major trading partner; subsequently, the states adjust their concessions using the results of the bilateral negotiations as a baseline. In addition, much trade negotiation occurs outside the formal multilateral rounds; indeed, negotiation occurs nearly continuously. Side agreements also may be made during the rounds (see Dam 1970, 56–68; Long 1985, 21–28).

These strategic considerations led to behavior different from what the GATT legal system technically required. The GATT charter did not require a consensus for the launching of a round; only a majority was necessary. But it became clear that this majority rule meant nothing. If a majority consisting of small states sought to launch a round with an agenda unfavorable to the powerful states, the latter would simply have refused to participate. The large states never tried to launch a round without the participation of the small states because the large states wanted to trade with small states just as they wanted to trade with other large states. Thus, in practice, trade rounds have not been launched without the support of a consensus, but not because there is a consensus "rule."

In sum, all states have an interest in multilateral trade bargaining, and the only strategic problem is that of coordinating the time and place of bargaining. To the extent that states also have an interest in engaging in bilateral negotiations or other negotiations outside the formal trading rounds, they do so. Any effort to restrict such bargaining would be unenforceable.

Ban on Nontariff Barriers

Article XI bans quantitative restrictions, and Article III as well as other provisions in GATT and supplementary agreements require that foreign products be regulated in the same way that domestic products are. The purpose of these rules was to channel protectionism into tariffs. Although tariffs are generally superior to nontariff barriers—beyond the effect on trade, they raise revenue as well—this would not be a reason for an international agreement. Protectionist states ought to choose to rely on tariffs even if no international agreement tells them to. Indeed, foreign firms that export into protectionist states would often prefer protectionism to take the form of quotas rather than tariffs, for the quotas allow them to restrict supply and obtain consumers' surplus, whereas tariffs convert this surplus, or some of it, to revenue for the importing country. But presumably there are domestic political reasons for choosing quotas over tariffs, and many nontariff barriers are harder to detect than tariffs are.

The general GATT structure—to tolerate tariffs rather than to require their elimination—reflects the political economy assumption that states will often benefit from trade barriers regardless of how other states respond, as they will when import competers have dominant political power. The puzzle, then, is why GATT demands that protectionism occur through tariffs and prohibits the use of nontariff barriers. Why not permit states to achieve their ideal level of protectionism through any policy instrument?

The ban on nontariff barriers was probably designed to narrow the bargaining range and clarify what moves counted as cooperation and what moves counted as defection in a repeated prisoner's dilemma.[2] Tariff barriers are more easily measured and compared than nontariff barriers. If all states can agree not to use nontariff barriers, then it will be easier for them to determine (1) whether any other state's concessions compensate them for the cost of their own concessions, and (2) whether the other state has complied with its agreement. By contrast, some nontariff barriers, although not all, are opaque: a rule that regulates the processing of meat can have both health and trade protection benefits if domestic processors happen to use the approved system more frequently than foreign processors do. Empirical studies can help sort out the effects, but these are time-consuming and imperfect. Negotiation is easier if states need to think only about tariffs, which are relatively commensurable, and not about diverse, incommensurable nontariff barriers (Jackson 1969, 312). By limiting the set of instruments that states can use to create and divide trade surpluses, the ban on nontariff barriers serves a coordinating function.

The problem with the ban on nontariff barriers is that hard-to-monitor behavior cannot easily be banned precisely because it is hard to monitor. Consider this example. A state agrees to tariff T but also can implement nontariff barrier R. R will eventually be discovered, but in the meantime the state enjoys its first best outcome: an open market for its exporters and protection for its import competers. The affected state will retaliate after R is discovered, but delayed retaliation is not as effective as immediate retaliation, which can (more or less) occur if a state violates the tariff binding instead. Indeed, the incentive of each state is to cheat on the deal by inventing a nontariff barrier that is fiendishly obscure. These barriers might not be perfect substitutes for the ideal level of protection, but they become more and more attractive by a kind of hydraulic pressure as bound tariffs decline. As nontariff barriers rise, they eat away at the gains from trade both directly and by resulting in domestically inefficient regulation whose value is mainly the result of trade externalities.

The empirical evidence is not conclusive but suggests that the decline of tariffs among GATT members has been offset by an increase in nontariff barriers, so that protectionism has remained constant (Ray 1991; Mansfield and Busch 2000). In the 1960s and 1970s, for example, the United States imposed quotas on steel, textiles, and meat, albeit in the form of "voluntary quotas" extracted from states that the United States threatened with (illegal) trade barriers. More significant is the phenomenon of discriminatory regulation. States engage in discriminatory regulation when they adopt laws that have apparent health or safety rationales but that mainly keep out products from other countries. Europe's rules against genetically modified crops, for example, disproportionately harm American farmers, while having (at the time of this writing) no substantial scientific support.

Nondiscrimination

Article I (and provisions scattered elsewhere) prohibits states from granting concessions in a discriminatory manner. For example, if a state reduces its tariffs to T for certain goods originating from state X, then it also must reduce to T tariffs for such goods originating from all other GATT members. The nondiscrimination provision derives from the use of MFN terms in bilateral trade treaties. There are numerous exceptions to Article I, including the escape clause; another notable exception is for preferential trading areas (Article XXIV).

The nondiscrimination rule is a second-best rule that, in trying to solve one collective action problem, creates another one. As we have seen, two states that enter a trade deal have an incentive to externalize costs on a third state that was a party to an earlier trade treaty with one of the two current parties. States protected themselves with MFN terms, but MFN terms give states an incentive to delay entering negotiations to lower existing tariffs in the hope that the current treaty partner will first enter a treaty with a third party that results in unilateral reduction in tariffs vis-à-vis the original partner. In the nineteenth century, some treaties had MFNs but other treaties did not; presumably, the choice from treaty to treaty reflected each state's assumptions about how the trade-off worked in any particular case. The decision to create a general MFN rule in GATT may have reflected the judgment that delay caused by the nondiscrimination rule was less harmful than the uncertainty and economic distortion that occur in a system that allows discrimination; it also was driven by U.S. fears that trade discrimination would weaken the Western military alliance against the Soviet Union.[3]

In any event, the nondiscrimination rule can be understood only as an effort to solve a multilateral prisoner's dilemma, each state making a deal that diverts trade from a third state, and so our prediction is that it would likely fail. This prediction appears to be correct. Although states do not explicitly violate the rule, they circumvent it easily by creating preferential trading areas under Article XXIV, of which there are hundreds.[4] NAFTA is just one example. Although Article I prevents the United States from discriminating in favor of Canada and Mexico by lowering tariffs on goods originating from those countries, Article XXIV permits the United States to enter a preferential trading agreement (PTA) with those countries that has a similar effect.[5] Another example is the Treaty of Rome of 1957, which created the European

Economic Community. The problem was not just that the major trading states within the EEC discriminated against the rest of the world by creating a free trade zone in Europe. The problem was that the EEC insisted on maintaining France's colonial preferences, and then on negotiating new preferential agreements with numerous countries all over the world (Hudec 1990, 220–26; see also Srinivasan 1998, for a general discussion).

GATT provides specific rules regulating the conditions under which PTAs may be created, and it creates a body that evaluates PTAs; however, this body has rarely agreed that a particular PTA complies with or violates the rules and thus has not been able to prevent the formation of PTAs. Mansfield and Reinhardt (2003) show that PTAs routinely violate GATT rules and that their formation reflects simple strategic priorities. States enter PTAs so that they can obtain trade concessions from important trading partners without having to wait for GATT rounds and without having to make return concessions that will benefit all GATT members. This also increases their bargaining power when the GATT rounds occur.

In sum, the nondiscrimination rule was supposed to solve a collective action problem but it failed. A large group of states cannot easily force all members to refrain from discrimination.

Reciprocation

Article XXVIII bis says that negotiations will be held on a "reciprocal" basis, but this provision is clearly not a rule in the conventional sense and could easily be regarded as merely an aspiration. Nonetheless, many commentators assert that a reciprocity principle exists at the heart of GATT. According to this principle, when state X makes trade concessions, then other states should reciprocate by making equivalent trade concessions (Jackson 1969, 241). A state that refuses to do this violates the spirit, and possibly the letter, of GATT.

However, the idea of reciprocity is hard to understand in a political economy framework. State X is willing to lower tariffs only if exporters have gained influence at the expense of import competers. If the same thing has happened in state Y, a deal is possible. But there is no reason to think that the amount gained by X's exporters (or this amount minus the loss to X's import competers?) should equal the amount gained by Y's exporters. For one thing, the monetary gain to each group must be translated into political currency, and the political exchange rate will depend on domestic political institutions. Politicians in X might not stir themselves for less than a $100 gain for their exporters, whereas politicians in Y will act if as little as $10 is at stake. In addition, politicians will take account of the losses to import competers, which may be asymmetrical, and to consumers and others, not to mention other international political considerations. Deals might be possible and attractive, even though the gains and losses on each side (however measured) are not equivalent and an equivalence constraint (if equivalence could be measured) would not improve outcomes.

Bagwell and Staiger (2002, 64–68) latch onto the "equivalent concessions" language of Article XXVIII as another example of the reciprocation "norm" at work. This article provides that if, during a round of negotiations, a party withdraws previously granted concessions, an affected party may respond by withdrawing equivalent concessions. According to Bagwell and Staiger, this rule is a constraint, and indeed it favors small countries by preventing large countries from using their bargaining power to obtain gains in the terms of trade.

But this claim is doubtful. The more plausible explanation of the reciprocity norm, as it appears both in initial negotiations and in renegotiations, is that it is endogenous, albeit equivalence must be understood in the loosest possible sense. In every bargain, each side seeks to gain and will not come to agreement unless it gains. Thus, every bargain results in a gain on both sides. Gains are rarely equivalent; they reflect the relative bargaining power of the parties. But our intuitions about equivalence are extremely rough: we don't call bargains unfair if in a domestic sale the consumer and the seller fail to divide the surplus equally; on the contrary, in a competitive market we expect the seller to gain just enough to cover costs. Between states, each trade will result in greater or lesser gains on either side, and in this loose and banal sense there is reciprocation, but equivalence is far too strong a description.

The simplest explanation of reciprocity is that it reflects the commonplace that in trade negotiations, every state that consents to a deal will gain from it. For rhetorical purposes, states frequently argue that all gains should be equal, but there is no mechanism in GATT for ensuring that gains will be equal, if indeed equality could ever be determined, and one would normally expect gains to be divided according to bargaining power (Grieco 1990; Steinberg 2002).

GATT contains many clauses that urge violators and victims to engage in "consultations" to resolve disputes. But the prospect of consultation will not deter a state from violating a provision that is against its interest. The heart of the GATT enforcement regime is Article XXIII, which provides, in essence, that a party whose GATT benefits are "nullified or impaired" has the right to retaliate by withdrawing concessions.[6] As it evolved, the enforcement regime was understood to provide victims of trade violations the right to ask that a tribunal hear its complaint; if the tribunal found in favor of the complainant, it could retaliate. However, GATT's procedures require consensus among all members, including any member in the role of defendant in a particular case. Therefore, a defendant could always refuse to consent to the creation of the tribunal or adoption of its judgment. The veto power raises a puzzle: How can an enforcement regime succeed if violators can block enforcement?

There are two possible answers. The first, which is conventional wisdom among lawyers, economists, and political scientists, is that states complied with the spirit of GATT even if they could have undermined its goals by blocking all enforcement actions against them. The second, which we advance, is that GATT provided some useful administrative infrastructure for handling trade disputes between states and that tribunals could in theory provide a neutral resolution of a dispute. GATT's achievement was the replacement of regular diplomatic channels and ad hoc arbitration decisions[7] with a relatively continuously developing jurisprudence, though this replacement would not be complete until the creation of the WTO. As we will explain, the creation of such a system was a matter of multilateral coordination, not the solving of a prisoner's dilemma or collective action problem.

The GATT adjudication system is a puzzle for the traditional international lawyers' thinking because states that complied with GATT law to the letter could easily undermine the system. A rational state that has "complying with international law" in its utility function, but not any other reputational concerns, would always block a tribunal (or sanction) rather than permitting a judgment against it that it would not be willing to acquiesce in. Thus, the system would not work. The question, then, is Why bother creating the enforcement system, or why bother creating it with vetoes? The drafters of GATT apparently believed that states would demand vetoes so that they could protect themselves from adverse outcomes in politically sensitive trade disputes, but would not exercise the vetoes in "normal" cases. But at this point we need a theory about why states would use their veto only in this way, and, if states could be expected to act in good faith in their use of the veto, why they couldn't be expected to trust other states to operate the tribunal in good faith. We have not found an answer to these questions in the literature.

To understand the GATT adjudication system, one can usefully begin by conceiving of the trade system as a large number of bilateral relationships: U.S.-EU, U.S.-Japan, EU-Japan, Japan-Canada, and so forth. Each state pays attention to the behavior of a trading partner and complains and threatens retaliation if the partner violates its commitments. So far, this description could apply as well to the nineteenth century as it does today. What did the GATT adjudication system add? Nothing more than this: it created a protocol for requesting a tribunal that would have an institutional relationship with prior tribunals, including a collective memory or jurisprudence. If the tribunal is neutral, then it can provide information about the extent of the violation (if any), or it can choose an outcome that would serve as a focal point for coordination of the states. If both parties adopt a cooperative strategy—comply with my commitments unless a neutral tribunal says that the other party violated its commitments—then the tribunal will contribute to bilateral cooperation. In the absence of a neutral tribunal, the states might mistakenly interpret a cooperative move as a violation, resulting in the breakdown of a trading relationship. But there are two limits on the extent of cooperation. First, cooperation can occur only if the tribunal makes decisions that consistently divide the surplus rather than favoring one state to the extent that the other state receives higher payoffs by failing to cooperate. Second, cooperation can occur only as long as future payoffs and discount factors are high enough: a perfectly competent and neutral GATT tribunal cannot ensure compliance of a state that no longer values cooperation with a particular partner on existing terms. If either of these limits is crossed, then one state or the other will refuse to consent to tribunals or will ignore their judgments.

Understanding the achievement of GATT compared to the nineteenth-century system, then, requires a theory of how international tribunals function and how neutral tribunals can be possible (Guzman 2002b; Posner and Yoo 2004). Briefly, all that is required is for two states involved in a dispute to think that following the established GATT procedures for creating a tribunal is usually superior to normal diplomatic channels, the creation of an ad hoc tribunal, or termination of the relationship. These possibilities, except for the last, are alternative methods for achieving the same aim: the discovery of information, or the choosing of a focal point, such that a breakdown of bilateral cooperation is avoided when the parties otherwise have the right incentives for continuing such cooperation. This is essentially a problem of coordination, and initial U.S. leadership plus the relatively high quality of GATT decisions seems to have provided the focal point for resolution of trade disputes. But nothing could force states to use this system if they preferred not to cooperate over certain trade issues, as happened when payoffs changed as a result of shocks. European countries ignored the GATT adjudication system in the decade after the creation of the European Community; the United States circumvented the system in the 1980s, when it preferred to use unilateral methods of enforcement. The continued recourse to the GATT adjudication system occurs when the states seek to cooperate over the trade issue at stake and believe that the GATT system provides higher-quality decisions than alternative forums or institutions. The GATT adjudication system is less like a government than like the private arbitration systems that obtain business from firms by developing a reputation for impartiality, so that disputes between parties that seek to continue to cooperate can be resolved in a neutral fashion.

If our theory is correct, a defendant that loses a GATT adjudication will not necessarily bring its trade policy into compliance with GATT rules. It depends on the reason the defendant violated GATT. If the reason was that it "cheated," in the sense of gaining from the complainant's unreciprocated cooperation, then it will obey the GATT judgment, assuming that the judgment is roughly correct, for otherwise, the state will find itself in the lower-payoff noncooperative equilibrium, as the complainant would cheat in response rather than accept the "sucker" payoff. If the reason the defendant violated GATT was that circumstances changed, or the domestic political gains from noncompliance exceeded the costs even if the complainant retaliated and cheated as well, then the defendant will not bring its behavior into compliance, though in the latter case, the two states can be expected eventually to renegotiate their obligations toward each other.

Our first hypothesis, then, is that states will comply with GATT judgments when the joint gain from compliance exceeds the joint cost. (When new conditions create asymmetries in the gains, renegotiation or side payments may be necessary.) Compliance here means (1) not blocking an adjudication and (2) obeying the judgment once issued.[8] Thus, compliance means more than technical legal compliance; it means compliance with the general purposes of the GATT system. Unfortunately, this hypothesis cannot be easily tested: the gains and losses are political, not economic, and so cannot be straightforwardly measured. An extremely crude test looks at the stakes: one might think that cases involving large amounts of money (such as the dispute over U.S. tax subsidies for exporters) or political controversies (such as the beef hormones dispute) would more likely result in noncompliance with adverse judgments. There is indeed evidence from a study of U.S.-Europe disputes that noncompliance rises with the stakes of the dispute (Busch and Reinhardt 2003b). However, this evidence is not very strong, as high stakes for the complainant may mean high stakes for the defendant as well, in which case it is ambiguous whether the joint costs of compliance exceed the joint gains.

The first hypothesis seems most plausible when the trading partners are roughly the same size. But what happens when a large state's violation of trade concessions harms a small state? If the large state is a monopsonist of the small state's goods, then it will declare the terms of trade that gives it (the large state) the surplus from trade. Thus, when the large state violates a GATT concession or rule, it is, in essence, unilaterally renegotiating the exchange of concessions between the two states. The small state has no alternative but to yield and so will not bother to bring a GATT case against the large state. The evidence indicates that small states are less likely to file complaints against large states than other large states are, and that large states are more likely to fail to comply with GATT judgments than small states are (Hudec 1993; Busch and Reinhardt 2002; Busch and Reinhardt 2003a). Evidence also suggests that the best predictor of compliance is the economic power of the complainant (Bown forthcoming).

We have found only one rigorous empirical test of this view. Reinhardt (2001) observes that defendants are more likely to make concessions prior to a panel ruling than after a panel ruling. From 1948 to 1994, defendants made full concessions in 19 of 30 cases (63.3 percent) after a panel was established but before a ruling, but made full concessions in only 38 of 91 cases (41.8 percent) after a ruling in favor of the complainant. As we have seen, the compliance itself is not a puzzle for the rational choice assumption; Reinhardt claims that the fact that compliance is more likely before the judgment than after the judgment is a puzzle.

The alternative view is that states have internalized trade law (Kovenock and Thursby 1992). Reinhardt (2001) argues that the data show that in fact states, or some states, care about complying with GATT rulings. But his argument depends on some tricky premises. He makes two main assumptions about private information: (1) that the complainant has private information about its toughness, its willingness to retaliate against a defendant that does not bring its trade practices into compliance; and (2) that the defendant has private information about the utility cost it incurs when it violates a ruling (we call defendants who care about the law "law abiders"). At the same time, he claims that the adjudication does not reveal this information or any other kind of information. The adjudication only generates a decision that causes disutility to law abiders who violate it. To avoid this disutility, law abiders will settle prior to the adjudication. In addition, some non–law abiders will settle prior to adjudication to avoid the risk of retaliation coming after an adverse decision. These non–law abiders will have to offer a generous settlement because the complainant thinks, with some probability, that they are actually law abiders. Thus, there will be a relatively high rate of settlement in which the defendant agrees to bring its policy into full compliance. After adjudication, however, no new information is revealed. The remaining non–law abiders have no reason to comply, and so the degree of compliance with rulings will be lower.

There are several problems with this argument. First, it does not explain the role of the veto. If a defendant cares about avoiding an adverse GATT ruling, it can simply prevent such a ruling by blocking the panel or the implementation of the sanction. Reinhardt (2001) implicitly assumes that a law-abiding defendant incurs disutility by exercising the veto, but he does not justify this assumption. As we have seen, such an assumption is hard to reconcile with the establishment of the veto right in the first place. Second, Reinhardt's data show that the settlement rate is quite low prior to establishment of the panel. Full compliance occurs in 38 of 125 cases (30 percent); it then rises after the panel is established, and then falls again after the ruling. Reinhardt does not explain why establishment of a panel, a largely formal procedure, should make so much of a difference. Settlement, and therefore compliance, could occur before a panel is established, indeed before a complaint is filed. The relevant comparison is not the postpanel-prejudgment settlement rate and the postjudgment settlement rate, but the prejudgment and post-judgment settlement rates. These numbers are 57 out of 155 (37 percent) versus 38 out of 91 (41.8 percent). Compliance is higher after judgment, not before: the empirical puzzle that provides the basis of Reinhardt's argument does not exist.[9]

Third, it is implausible to think that major trading states have significant private information about their propensity to retaliate and their propensity to comply with GATT rulings. These variables reflect political culture, institutional structure, current politics, economic conditions, and so forth, all highly visible in democracies and easily inferred from prior trade behavior.

The data are too crude to provide much support for any theory of GATT adjudication that depends on predictions about compliance rates at different stages of litigation. The data show that states that violate their GATT obligations and are subsequently dragged before a tribunal are willing to return to compliance some of the time but not always. States return to compliance either because the temporary violation was sufficient to pay off import competers or there was a genuine ambiguity in law or fact that was resolved by the tribunal; they fail to return to compliance either because they believe that the tribunal made a bad decision or continuing violation is necessary to pay off import competers. There is no strong evidence that states comply with tribunals because of a sense of legal obligation (Bown forthcoming).

Summary

GATT is a solution to a series of coordination problems—when to meet, with whom to negotiate, whom to hire as arbitrator—that states partially obey. Within the GATT framework, states break and enforce trade deals in the same ways that they always have: bilaterally. Rules or aspirations within the GATT framework that were designed to generate collective goods—the ban on discrimination, for example, or multilateral punishment of states that break the rules—have failed. The successes and failures of GATT, in short, track our claim that international law can solve coordination problems and bilateral prisoner's dilemmas, but not collective action problems.

Then why did GATT's drafters include rules designed to solve collective action problems? They might have erred, or they might have thought that the United States could unilaterally enforce the entire system. But the more plausible explanation is that the GATT drafters did not have a clear idea of what GATT would and could accomplish. GATT was intended as a provisional statement of general principles that would guide trade negotiations only until the International Trade Organization came into existence. The ITO would then have the power to address problems of international trade as they arose, in the flexible way that the International Monetary Fund and the World Bank address problems of international finance and development. When the ITO was rejected by the U.S. Congress, GATT remained the framework within which international trade negotiations took place, and, as one would expect, states pragmatically ignored or violated those aspects of GATT that were not sustainable, while building on those aspects that were robust.

WTO Innovations

Many scholars who might accept our claim about the limited role of GATT in international trade will insist that all this changed with the creation of the World Trade Organization. The claims in the legal literature are optimistic. Critics and supporters alike believe that WTO will force states to adopt policies that are against their interests. No longer a framework within which states negotiate for trade concessions, GATT/WTO is a "constitution" that authorizes an independent body to dictate trade policy to states. (Representative articles include Stephan 2002; McGinnis and Movsesian 2000; and Guzman 2002c.) The concern now is to prevent WTO from overreaching; what are needed are legalistic procedural protections modeled on the political constitutions that constrain governments. If WTO is a government, rather than a forum in which trading partners hash out trading policy, then its watchwords are transparency, representativeness, fairness, and process (McGinnis and Movsesian 2000; Weiss 2000; Charnovitz 2001). The ineluctable scholarly process by which a useful device for diplomacy is transformed into an international legal regime has begun.

However, a look at the Dispute Settlement Understanding (DSU), the agreement that created WTO, reveals that it introduced only modest procedural reforms.[10] The main procedural innovations of WTO were its elimination of the veto power and the creation of a continuous appellate body. Under GATT rules, a defendant could block the formation of a panel and the implementation of its judgment. Under WTO rules, a defendant can do neither. Note what this says about the earlier practice of blocking. If blocking a panel or sanction produced the same kind of reputational cost that violation of the law did, then there would be no point in eliminating the veto. The state that refused to comply with any WTO ruling would incur the same sanction as the state that blocked a GATT ruling: the reputational cost.

In the GATT era, when a powerful state's effort to obtain a remedy was frustrated by blocking, the state would sometimes unilaterally retaliate by raising trade barriers against the offending party. This the United States did several times against Europe. Under WTO, this behavior is brought within international law. A defendant state that loses its case in the WTO system can still refuse to stop its offending behavior. WTO, under Article 22(1) of the DSU, now grants the complainant the right to "compensation." What is compensation? The right to raise its own trade barriers by an amount equal to the cost generated by the illegal behavior. In other words, WTO authorizes the retaliation that occurred illegally under GATT, but in addition it seeks to ensure that a panel will determine the extent of retaliation rather than leaving it to the discretion of the victim of the trade violation.

This raises the following question: If GATT could not prevent states from unilaterally retaliating against states that engage in trade violations, why should we expect the DSU to prevent states from retaliating at a level beyond whatever is authorized by a WTO panel? If states follow the law just because it is the law, then the DSU would not be necessary. If they do not, then it is hard to see why the DSU would change their behavior.

The evidence provides few clues. Although there are more disputes per year than under GATT, the increase is mainly due to the increase in the number of members and the greater scope of substantive trade law, which absorbed services and intellectual property, not the procedural reforms of WTO (Busch and Reinhardt 2002). In addition, there is not yet any evidence that the WTO procedures have enhanced compliance with international trade law, either in the sense of compliance with judgments or compliance with the law itself. Although one can point to some clear cases where states changed their laws in response to a WTO ruling, the Busch and Reinhardt study finds that although the full concession rate increased from 40 percent under GATT to 66 percent under WTO, this difference is due to the expansion of trade law to include intellectual property and services, where, one might assume, more tractable disputes are still being addressed. When these disputes are excluded, WTO produces concessions no more often than GATT panels did. Bown (forthcoming) similarly finds no evidence that WTO procedures have improved compliance; instead, he finds that compliance is a function of the power of the victim state to retaliate against the violator. If future data confirm these results, then it will be clear that the effect of GATT and WTO has not been to force states to adjudicate their disputes—that appears to be impossible—but to make available to them a continuous adjudicatory body that they will jointly prefer to alternatives. The elimination of the veto will turn out to have been of little importance.

But all of this is of little relevance to the question of whether the elimination of the veto matters. If compliance with WTO decisions turns out to be greater than compliance with GATT decisions, that could be due to the innovations in adjudicatory procedures rather than the elimination of the veto. The creation of the continuous appellate body, for example, might improve trade jurisprudence and thus produce better and more consistent decisions. On this view, states would comply with WTO decisions more enthusiastically than they comply with GATT decisions because WTO decisions are better: they provide more information, or they are more likely to result in outcomes that are within the tolerance of both sides. Unfortunately, we see no way to discriminate between these hypotheses using an empirical test.

Legalism and International Trade

GATT inspired a debate about the proper level of legalization of international trade law. The legalists pressed for more detailed substantive rules, more reliance on judicial procedures and decisions, and clearer sanctions (Davey 1987). The pragmatists argued that GATT should remain a loose framework within which states could negotiate trade policy. Where the legalists argued that legalism would strengthen the international trade system and limit the influence of protectionism, the pragmatists argued that legalism encourages advocacy, which leads to conflict rather than order.

The debate confuses separate issues. The first is the question of the proper level of detail at which international trade obligations should be negotiated. GATT's provisions are vague; the new WTO provisions are only slightly less so. By contrast, the tariff schedules are immensely detailed, going on for thousands of pages. We see no reason for thinking that the general procedural rules and substantive obligations are too vague (or that the tariff schedules are too specific). When states are coordinating policies but do not know what the future will bring, they will not agree to specific rules. It does not matter that, in the abstract, clear rules are better than vague aspirations because rules provide clearer guidance (Jackson 2000, 121; M. Trebilcock and Howse 1999). GATT/WTO rules are vague because states will not agree to anything more specific; indeed, the greater specificity of the ITO, the trade institution that was designed to come into existence shortly after GATT, may have doomed it (R. Gardner 1969, 383).

The second issue is the degree to which dispute resolution should be "judicialized," that is, subject to formal rules of evidence and procedure and administered by independent judges who employ the conventional tools of legal reasoning, rather than left to negotiations among the affected parties. Reliance on judges makes sense when issues are complex and require expertise, independence can be guaranteed, and states anticipate a continuing interest in the maintenance of the regime. The first and last conditions are met for trade; the second might be. But the point here is that the difference between a legal and a negotiated outcome in international law is subtle and often invisible. The violator of a trade commitment in a legalized regime does not have to submit to a legal outcome and can choose to incur the reputational cost (if any) instead. The violator in a nonlegalized regime can choose to pay compensation because it seeks to maintain a reputation for cooperativeness. The main difference is not in the nature of the reputational cost but in the involvement of third parties in resolution of the dispute. The involvement of third parties is justified if states can agree to and comply with procedures that ensure that individuals chosen as judges bring information and judgment but not bias to dispute resolution.

The third issue is the question of whether the GATT/WTO system should have the power to sanction states that break the rules. Of course, there is no "system" that has the power of agency: either states, individually or collectively, sanction other states that break the rules or they do not. Collective action problems put a limit on whether sanctions can work. Our view is that multilateral sanctions rarely work. Rules, such as those governing preferential trade agreements, that depend on multilateral enforcement have gone unenforced. GATT/WTO has worked as well as it has because states are willing to retaliate, even risking a trade war, if trading partners violate their obligations. The bilateralism of trade sanctions implies that weak states cannot credibly commit to sanction powerful states, and that powerful states will in general have more freedom of action than weaker states. The United States, the EU, and Japan can destroy the GATT/WTO system by leaving it; other states cannot. The heavy reliance in the literature on ill-defined reputational sanctions has not been justified by detailed empirical work.

There have been sporadic efforts to make GATT/WTO more legalistic; the DSU is the most impressive example. But these efforts can only run into trouble if the underlying interests of the states, their need to retain the flexibility to raise trade barriers when protectionist pressures surge, are not sufficiently precise and durable. If not, efforts to increase legalization will fail in two ways: (1) a few states violate the rules, absorbing reputational costs, if any, and then other states follow (presumably with no reputational costs by this time); or (2) states will yield to the hydraulic effect and switch to near substitutes (for example, PTAs rather than discrimination). This is one theory for the failure of the GATT dispute resolution process in the 1960s; it had become over-legalized in the 1950s as a result of the efforts of the United States, but international trading policy had to change when the EC entered the system (M. Trebilcock and Howse 1999, 52). There is a danger, often neglected by commentators (for example, the essays and commentary in M. Hart and Steger 1992; Kovenock and Thursby 1992), that increased legalization of international trade will either displace trade from illegal barriers to legal barriers without improving efficiency or, if the legal barriers are removed as well, put too much pressure on the system and cause it to collapse (see Reinhardt 2003; Bown forthcoming).

PART 3

RHETORIC, MORALITY, AND INTERNATIONAL LAW

Henkin's observation that "almost all nations observe almost all principles of international law and almost all their obligations almost all of the time" (1979, 47) has inspired a generation of international law scholars, who have assumed that this observation can be true only because international law, by exerting normative force, constrains the pursuit of state interest. The theory of international law set forth in parts 1 and 2 of this book has tried to show that Henkin's dictum is misleading. The behavioral features of international law—how it originates and changes, when and why states act consistently with and violate it, why it has such limited content—are better explained by a theory of state self-interest than by the various alternatives. While the pursuit of state self-interest can, as we have shown, generate cooperation or coordination in some circumstances, especially in bilateral relationships, such cooperation and coordination will last only as long as the conditions that made them possible in the first place.

In part 3, we address three external challenges to our theory and analyze the theory's normative implications. The first challenge comes from those who argue that the rhetorical practices of states cannot be reconciled with an instrumental theory of international law. Diplomatic and military disputes are frequently clothed in the language of international law. If states did not take seriously international legality, that is, if they did not treat law as a special reason for engaging in or refraining from certain acts, why would they so frequently use the language of international law? In chapter 6, we address this question and show how international moral and legal rhetoric fits with our theory.

A second challenge comes from traditionalists who claim that our positive theory of international law is no response to international law's normativity. Even if states comply with international law only when it is in their interest to do so, they nonetheless have a moral obligation to comply with it even when doing so is not in their interest. In chapter 7, we argue that states have no such moral obligation. Even morally sensitive leaders have no moral obligation to conform their states' behavior to the requirements of international law. This is not an argument for violating international law, but rather an argument for excluding international law from the set of moral reasons for compliance.

A third challenge comes from cosmopolitan theory, which argues that states should be more other-regarding and should enter treaties and provide aid that would increase global welfare, even though doing so would lower state welfare. In chapter 8, we show how this argument is inconsistent with another fundamental tenet of cosmopolitan theory, namely, that liberal democracy is the optimal form of domestic governance. The liberal democratic form of domestic government ensures that foreign policies, including aid, treaty making, and war, reflect the usually self-regarding interests of voters.

CHAPTER 6

A THEORY OF INTERNATIONAL RHETORIC

During the sixteenth year of the Peloponnesian War between Athens and Sparta, an Athenian force landed on the island of Melos, a Spartan colony and a neutral in the war. Thucydides recounts a dialogue between Athenian envoys and Melian leaders. In a famous passage, the Athenians demand that the Melians submit to their rule:

> For ourselves, we shall not trouble you with specious pretenses—either of how we might have a right to our empire because we overthrew the Mede, or are now attacking you because of wrong that you have done us—and make a long speech which would not be believed; and in return we hope that you, instead of thinking to influence us by saying that you did not join the Spartans, although their colonists, or that you have done us no wrong, will aim at what is feasible, holding in view the real sentiments of us both; since you know as well as we do that right, as the world goes, is only in question between equals in power, while the strong do what they will and the weak suffer what they must. (Thucydides 1982, 5.89)

This passage is striking because the Athenians make no attempt to mask their imperialistic aims behind "specious pretenses." They simply assert that they have an interest in ruling the Melians and will achieve this end because they are more powerful. As one historian has noted, if these and related passages in *The Peloponnesian War* are accurate, "the Athenians of the fifth century were . . . a very remarkable, if not unique, people in admitting openly that their policy was guided by purely selfish considerations and that they had no regard for political morality" (Jones 1957, 66).

In contrast to Thucydides' Athens, Nazi Germany paid extravagant respect to the forms of political morality. When Hitler established universal military service in March 1935, he claimed that this violation of the Versailles Treaty was justified by the allies' prior violations of the treaty. Similarly, he justified occupation of the Rhineland in March 1936, a violation of the Locarno Treaties (in which Germany agreed that the Rhineland would remain demilitarized), on the ground that the treaties had been nullified by a 1935 France-USSR mutual assistance pact. In November 1936, Germany and Japan signed the Anti-Comintern Pact, a mutual assistance treaty against the USSR. Germany renounced this treaty when it signed the Nazi-Soviet Pact in August 1939, claiming that Japan had breached the treaty first. Hitler also provided legal justifications for his invasions of Austria, Czechoslovakia, Poland, Denmark, Norway, Belgium, Holland, France, Yugoslavia, and Russia and for his declaration of war against the United States. He justified these and other international acts in moral terms as well, harping on the injustice of the Versailles Treaty and asserting the need for humanitarian intervention in other countries to halt mistreatment of German-speaking populations. Nazi documents captured by the allies make it clear that Hitler at all times sought to maximize his power and the power of Germany so that he could achieve his imperialistic dreams, and he self-consciously used moral and legal rhetoric to mislead his enemies, avoid alienating neutrals, and pacify domestic opposition (Weinberg 1980; Rich 1973).

Hitler's Germany, not Thucydides' Athens, typifies the use of moral and legal rhetoric in international affairs. Consider other examples:

- As we showed in chapter 2, before the Civil War, the United States, a traditional neutral power with a relatively weak navy, argued in diplomatic circles that international law gave neutral ships broad protection from belligerent attack. During the Civil War, when the United States was a belligerent with a relatively powerful navy for the first time, it reversed course. It asserted unprecedentedly broad belligerent rights, and it insisted in diplomatic correspondence that these actions were consistent with international law.
- The Soviet Union invaded eastern Poland on September 13, 1939, twelve days after Germany invaded western Poland. The invasion violated several international laws, including the 1921 Treaty of Peace between the Soviet Union and Poland (which established the

Poland-USSR borders), the 1928 Kellogg-Briand Pact (which renounced war as an instrument of national policy), and the 1932 Poland-USSR Nonaggression Pact. Nonetheless, beginning four days after the invasion and continuing throughout September and October 1939, the Soviet government, through diplomatic notes, radio broadcasts, and reports to the Supreme Soviet and *Pravda*, made a "comprehensive case in international law" in support of the invasion (Ginsburgs 1958, 69).

- In the treaty of 1907 in which Russia and Britain partitioned Persia, the two nations promised to "respect the integrity and independence of Persia" and claimed to be "sincerely desiring the preservation of order throughout the country" (Niebuhr 1932, 105). Similarly, as Niebuhr (id.) notes, Secretary of State Hughes rationalized U.S. imperialistic policy in Latin America as follows: "We are aiming not to exploit but to aid; not to subvert, but to help in laying the foundations for a sound, stable, and independent government. Our interest does not lie in controlling foreign peoples, [but] in having prosperous, peaceful, and law-abiding neighbors."

- China signed the International Covenant on Civil and Political Rights several years ago. Although it continues to violate the civil and political rights of its citizens, it claims that it acts consistently with international law. Many other countries, weak and powerful alike, sign or ratify human rights treaties and claim adherence to them even though they violate them.

- "Bismarck records the remark made to him by Walewski, the French Foreign Minister, in 1857, that it was the business of the diplomat to cloak the interests of his country in the language of universal justice" (Carr 1946, 72).

In sum, states provide legal or moral justifications for their actions, no matter how transparently self-interested their actions are. Their legal or moral justifications cleave to their interests, and so when interests change, so do the rationalizations. At the same time, states frequently accuse other states of violating international law and norms, as though to discredit them. One must ask, What do leaders who talk this way accomplish? Because the talk is obviously self-serving, why would anyone ever believe it? And if no one believes it, why would anyone bother engaging in it?

Yet not all international talk is deceitful. Consider these examples:

- Under international law, states traditionally "declared" war, and this declaration would notify belligerents and neutrals alike that the declaring state intended to follow certain rules of war.
- When a state recognizes other states or governments, the mere utterance of words alters numerous international relationships involving diplomatic rights and privileges, the capacity to make treaties, and more.
- States constantly talk about establishing military alliances, adjusting trade relations, modifying patterns of immigration, extraditing criminals, and so forth, and in a wide range of circumstances this talk seems to influence policy and behavior.

In these examples, talk straightforwardly produces gains. The point of the talk is thus clearer here than in the earlier examples. But the mechanism by which the talk influences behavior remains uncertain. Once again, the question arises: Why is the talk believed, and how does it influence action?

Conventional Wisdom

Discussions of international moral and legal rhetoric can be found in the major realist writings of the twentieth century: Niebuhr's *Moral Man and Immoral Society* (1932), Carr's *The Twenty Years' Crisis* (1946), and Morgenthau's *Politics among Nations* (1948a) and *In Defense of the National Interest* (1951). These classic texts were in part manifestos designed to warn people against the moral and legal rhetoric issuing from the leaders and propaganda offices of powerful states. They were thus not particularly concerned with providing a positive theoretical account for the rhetoric. But they did provide one in passing, and their account has been influential.

The realists argued that states' legal and moral rhetorics are "disguises" or "pretexts" for actions motivated by a desire for power (Morgenthau 1948a, 61–62; Morgenthau 1951, 35). The pretexts are aimed at domestic constituents, whom leaders persuade to support the state's foreign policy (Morgenthau 1951, 62; Niebuhr 1932, 95–96, 105). The rhetoric is also designed "to fool the outside world"—foreign leaders and foreign domestic audiences (Morgenthau 1951; Niebuhr 1932; but compare Carr 1946). At the same time, legal and moral rhetoric "heal[s] a moral breach in the inner life of the statesman, who find themselves [*sic*] torn between the necessities of statecraft and the sometimes sensitive promptings of an individual conscience" (Niebuhr 1932, 105). Regardless of the psychological cravings of leaders, realists believe that states are motivated primarily by power, not moral and legal precepts.

Critics of this argument point out that if legal and moral norms were not efficacious, the appeal to such norms would lack rhetorical power. As Carr (1946, 92) himself acknowledged: "The necessity recognized by all politicians, both in domestic and international affairs, for cloaking interests in the guise of moral principles is in itself a symptom of the inadequacy of realism." If political leaders never acted on the basis of international law or morality, their claims to the contrary would not be believed (Elster 1989). Citizens are not likely to be fooled by politicians who never tell the truth, and leaders adept at rationalizing their policies in moral terms will not be deceived by foreign leaders who have the identical skill. The prevalence of moral rhetoric in an amoral world is thus thought to be a rebuke and a challenge to realism.[1]

Building on these criticisms of realism, constructivist scholars in political science and many international law scholars view moral and legal rhetoric as evidence of the efficacy of international norms. For these scholars, international norms emerge through practice and debate and influence the policies of state leaders (Finnemore 1996; Risse and Sikkink 1999; Risse 2000; Kratochwil 1989; Chayes and Chayes 1995). International moral and legal rhetoric is not a puzzle for these scholars; it is just the working out of the norms of international behavior through deliberation. What this literature lacks, however, is a mechanism for *how* moral and legal talk influences national behavior, an explanation for the strategic uses of moral and legal rhetoric, and an account of the many instances in which there appears to be no relationship between this rhetoric and state behaviors.

Authors influenced by the institutionalist and strategic choice strands of international relations theory take yet a different view. They believe that international communication matters but think that it can be explained without abandoning the premise that states are fundamentally self-interested and rational (Keohane 1984; Lake and Powell 1999; Morrow 1994b). This literature, on which we draw, has explored the incentives to make promises, threats, and other communications and the effect of these communications on the beliefs and actions of other states (Garrett and Weingast 1993; Guisinger and Smith 2001; Mc-

Gillivray and Smith 1999; Sartori 1999; Martin 1993; Fearon 1994; Schultz 1998; Bueno de Mesquita and Lalman 1992; Keohane 1984). But it has not focused on international moral and legal rhetoric per se. It therefore has not reconciled the widespread use of such rhetoric and its rational choice assumptions. This is our aim in the remainder of this chapter.

Why States Talk

There are two conditions under which communications are not believable. The first is that of pure conflict. In a two-state zero-sum game, one state would not make a statement that would give another state an advantage over it, so the other state would always assume that a statement made by the speaker is intended to injure it. Because the recipient of the message would therefore not believe it, there would be no reason for the speaker to make that statement, at least for purposes of conveying information to this particular rival. Second, if international relations were a positive-sum game but states had full information about each other's characteristics and strategies, talk would also not make sense. All talk would either be rejected as inconsistent with known information or ignored as superfluous.

Thus, talk is possible only if international relations present opportunities for mutual gain and if states do not know other states' payoffs or (in some cases) strategies. Both of these premises are plausible, and they underlie models of communication that we use to analyze international communication.

Pooling Equilibria When States Seek Reputations for Cooperativeness

Suppose that state leaders have private information about the political stability of the state, which can be formalized as its discount rate or some other characteristic that makes the state attractive (as a partner) or unattractive (as a threat) to others. A state wants other states to know that it has a low discount rate, for that would make it an attractive partner in treaties and other cooperative relationships. States with high discount rates want to conceal this information. The same is true for private information about other characteristics, for example, the political influence of a particular ethnic minority, or the warlike tendencies of the people. But to keep the exposition simple, we will focus on discount rate or political stability.

To distinguish themselves, the cooperative states will try to send signals that the other states are unable to afford. Any action will serve as a signal as long as its cost exceeds the benefit that other states can obtain from imitating it. Costly actions might include paying a debt (Cole and Kehoe 1995), refraining from seizing alien property, respecting state borders, or resisting domestic discrimination against minorities.[2] These acts are costly in the sense that, holding the response of other states constant, a state does better by defaulting on debts, seizing property, and invading neighbors than by refraining from these behaviors. It is possible to construct a separating equilibrium in which some states send signals to show, for example, that they have low discount rates or the right kinds of interests, while other states do not.

In the analysis so far, talk is not necessary for the purpose of issuing a signal. Talk is unnecessary because the act of paying debts, protecting property, respecting borders, or enacting civil rights statutes is sufficient to provoke the desirable response. If talk is costless, a state that merely says that it is cooperative or politically stable will not be believed, for any state can say the same thing; if the talk is accompanied by appropriate actions, there is no need to persuade the audience that the speaking state belongs to the right type. Costless talk cannot by itself send a signal, and thus signaling cannot be a direct explanation of discursive practices.

Nonetheless, talk might play a weak role in signaling type. To see why, think of talk as not costless but as a signal whose cost is arbitrarily close to zero. There are games in which all players pool around a cheap signal. As an example, consider Spence's (1973) original discussion of job market signaling. He argued that an education can serve as a signal, because education is more costly for bad workers than for good workers. But education can serve as a signal only if it is sufficiently costly for the bad workers. If education is cheap enough, there can be an equilibrium in which both good and bad workers obtain the education. The reason the workers might pool in this way is that, given that the employer believes that people who fail to obtain the education are bad types, the workers can obtain the job only if they obtain the education. The employer reasons that given that the education is cheap, someone who fails to obtain the education cannot possibly belong to the good type, and the employer would rather hire someone who is a good type with probability equal to the representation of good types in the population than someone who is definitely not a good type. Both kinds of worker send the signal, but the signal does not reveal their types.

Suppose, now, that an employer is trying to decide between hiring two otherwise identical people, one of whom says, "I am a hard worker" and the other of whom says, "I am a no good, lazy worker." The employer is obviously more likely to hire the self-proclaimed hard worker even though the statement is cheap talk. The reason is that the statement "I am a hard worker," like the cheap education, is an arbitrarily cheap signal; so a worker who did not send this signal would clearly belong to the bad type. The employer will reason that someone who says that he or she is lazy cannot possibly be hard-working and so would rather hire someone who claims to be hard-working than someone who admits to being lazy. Observe that in equilibrium, no rational job applicant will admit to being lazy, and so the employer will not be able to discriminate on the basis of the applicants' types.

This analysis applies to international talk. Because the talk is cheap, no one will be influenced by a state's claim that it is cooperative; that is, no state would adjust its prior belief about the probability that the speaker is cooperative. But a state that failed to send this weak signal would reveal that it belongs to the bad type. In equilibrium, all states send the signal by engaging in the appropriate international chatter. In this pooling equilibrium, everyone sends the weak signal because no one gains from failing to send it. Talk does not have any effect on prior beliefs about the likelihood that the speaker is cooperative, but it is not meaningless, because failure to engage in the right form of talk would convey information that the speaker is not cooperative.

With the possible exception of fifth-century B.C. Athens, no state publicly admits that its foreign policy is driven solely by power and interest. Instead, states proclaim that their acts are consistent with, and often motivated by, international law or morality. Candor is off the equilibrium path, just as candor on the part of lazy job candidates is off the equilibrium path. This argument casts doubt on Thucydides' account of the Melian dialogue, about which there is in fact much historical doubt (Jones 1957, 66–67; Grundy 1948, 436–37). The clear historical record of Hitler's duplicity is more reliable evidence of what states do. Hitler did not acknowledge that Germany violated international law and morality because he could not gain by doing so.

To be sure, we have not yet explained why international talk has the content it has, that is, why states make moralistic and legalistic claims rather than simply saying that they are cooperative or something similar. The explanation is a bit more complex than the analogous explanation in the job market context: applicants say they are hard-working because employers want hard-working employees. The reason for the complexity is that the audience of international talk is more diverse than the audience of a job applicant. We discuss this issue below.

Coordination Games with Full Information

The information-conveying role played by cheap talk is easiest to see in pure coordination games. As we discussed in parts 1 and 2, in a coordination game all states benefit from engaging in the same action that other states engage in, but there are at least two sets of mutually beneficial actions and the states do not know which action the other players will take. When states face coordination problems, coordination can occur spontaneously, through repeated interaction, conflict, and adjustment. But it can be achieved more quickly through talk. For in a pure coordination situation, one player has an incentive to announce his move (and take the move announced), and the other player has an incentive to believe him and make the same move. The second player does not improve her payoff by disbelieving the first player and acting on the resulting belief.

This is a simple but important point. When states are in coordination games (as opposed to, say, a one-shot prisoner's dilemma), they have an incentive to talk and to believe the talk of the other state (Crawford and Sobel 1982). Cheap talk solves a coordination problem by picking out one of the multiple equilibria.

There are, of course, numerous complications. Pure coordination games, in which all parties prefer the same equilibrium or are indifferent to multiple equilibria, are rare. More common are battle of the sexes games, in which there is some conflict over the equilibrium. Still, it is clear that when there is not too much conflict of interest, players will believe each other's talk, and even when there is some conflict of interest, players will simply discount somewhat the value of talk rather than disbelieving it completely (Morrow 1994b).

Cooperation in a Repeated Bilateral Prisoner's Dilemma

Imagine that two states face a prisoner's dilemma in which they can obtain mutual gains by refraining from predatory behavior such as an invasion across a border or prosecution of a foreign diplomat. If they have low enough discount rates, enjoy a continuing relationship, and satisfy the other conditions outlined in chapter 1, they can cooperate to achieve the outcome of mutual restraint. But this cooperation might be hindered by an unforeseen contingency that creates ambiguity about what counts as a cooperative action. For example, one state might believe that pursuing criminals across the border is not an invasion, whereas the other assumes that it is. And one state might believe that prosecuting a diplomat for espionage does not violate rules of diplomatic immunity, but the other believes that it does. Such disagreements in the interpretation of the cooperative move might lead to retaliation and thus to a breakdown in cooperation.

Such situations are, as we explained in chapter 1, nothing more than a coordination problem over what counts as a cooperative move. Talk clarifies which actions count as cooperative moves and which count as defections that will provoke retaliation (Garrett and Weingast 1993). By disambiguating actions, cheap talk facilitates cooperation, although the reservations made in the prior section concerning distributive consequences and dynamic considerations apply here as well.

Consider the example we have used throughout this book: the nineteenth-century rule of customary international law that prohibited a belligerent from seizing an enemy's coastal fishing vessels. As we discussed in chapter 2, in some cases, the behavioral regularity might have reflected a bilateral repeated prisoner's dilemma in which states A and B refrained from seizing each other's fishing vessels because each recognizes that it is better off than it would be if each state preyed on the other's fishing vessels.

Cooperation is possible here, but it depends on each state having the same understanding of what counts as a seizure of a *coastal fishing vessel*. If A thinks a fishing vessel could be a giant fishing trawler, and B thinks that a fishing vessel is a small vessel manned by a few sailors, then when A seizes a giant fishing trawler under B's flag, B will interpret A's innocent act as a violation of the implicit deal not to seize fishing vessels. B might retaliate by seizing one of A's small vessels. A will interpret this act not as justified retaliation but as an unprovoked instance of cheating. Cooperation can break down. But there is another possibility: A and B realize that they might not have the same understanding of the game that they have been playing. Rather than retaliating against B immediately, A lodges an objection and threatens retaliation unless B provides an explanation. By talking, by exchanging information about what counts as a coastal fishing vessel, both before and after incidents, the states can avoid breakdowns of cooperation. The talk is credible because each state receives higher payoffs from cooperation than from defection.

Cheap Talk with Information Asymmetries

Another useful model is that of cheap talk with two audiences (see Farrell and Gibbons 1989; Austen-Smith 1992). Suppose a cold war–era revolution brings a new government to power in the Third World. The government can align itself with the Soviet Union or with the United States; each alignment brings different sorts of aid, but let us suppose of equal cash value. The state rendering aid expects to be able to use the territory of the state in question for military bases and to exclude its enemy from that same territory. Aid is conditional on fulfillment of these expectations. Members of the new government have private information about their own ideological or pragmatic leanings or those of the groups that support them. The payoff matrix might look like Table 6.1. The payoffs are to the new government and assume that the new government obtains a payoff of 2 when it receives aid (regardless of the source) but incurs a cost of -2 when it gives bases to, and submits to the political interests of, a state whose ideology is inconsistent with the new government's ideological or political leanings.

Table 6.1

	New government's ideology	
	Pro-West	Pro-East
Announce "capitalism"	2	0
Announce "socialism"	0	2

Holding constant the level of aid, the pro-West government prefers dealing with the United States, and the pro-East government prefers dealing with the Soviet Union. Cheap talk consisting of an announcement of alignment reveals information about the government's orientation. To see why meaningful cheap talk can exist in equilibrium, observe that if the state announces capitalism, the United States by hypothesis gains more by rendering aid and receiving strategic advantages than by declining to do so, given the Soviet Union's strategy to stay out in this eventuality. If the state announces socialism, the United States gains more by declining aid, as it will not have access to the territory. Analogous reasoning applies to the Soviet Union. As to the new government, given these strategies by the United States and the Soviet Union, it can do no better than truthfully announce its inclination toward capitalism or socialism.

International Talk and Domestic Audiences

When a leader talks publicly to other leaders, he or she often intends the talk for the consumption of the domestic audience. Two cheap talk models can explain why such talk occurs.

First, some domestic audiences might be poorly misinformed (or, if you want, "rationally ignorant"). President Kennedy talked tough to the Soviet Union while withdrawing missiles from Turkey. The relevant domestic audience might believe the talk and be unaware of the concession or be unable to evaluate the significance of the concession. Because it fears the Soviet Union, it is pleased to hear the talk. Meanwhile, the leader achieves foreign policy goals that are inconsistent with the interests of the audience he or she fears offending. Foreign leaders, by contrast, invest heavily in understanding the motives of other states and are unlikely to be deceived. There is a similar view in the public choice literature, which holds that politicians must disguise interest group transfers because the public pays some attention to policy and will not vote for politicians who make the wrong transfers. Thus, transfers to farmers must take the form of price supports or ethanol initiatives rather than piles of cash. Similarly, concessions to the Soviet Union or Cuba are concealed by rhetorical posturing. Both theories raise the question of why the public does not eventually catch on and implicitly assume that politicians adopt mixed strategies and occasionally act consistently with their words.

Second, leaders have constituents who demand evidence of loyalty. Even cheap talk can commit a leader to a particular audience by alienating competing audiences (Fearon 1994; Schultz 1998; Bueno de Mesquita and Lalman 1992). A Republican politician might alienate some moderate supporters by complaining about the civil rights record of China (even without taking any action) but also obtain offsetting political returns from the far right. Multiple audiences can discipline speakers, forcing them to tell the truth when they would rather dissemble (Farrell and Gibbons 1989).

International Talk and Audiences of Foreign Citizens

When a leader talks publicly, he or she sometimes intends the talk for the consumption of citizens in foreign states. Shortly before World War II, different segments of the British public disagreed about Hitler's motives. One segment believed that he sought to take over Europe; another segment believed that he sought merely to annex territory occupied by German-speaking populations. We now know that the first group was correct, but Hitler's main foreign policy achievements prior to 1939—the military occupation of the Rhineland, the Anschluss with Austria, and the occupation of the Sudetenland—were consistent with both theories. Britain could confront Germany aggressively, through heavy investment in armaments and mobilization, only with the support of both segments of the public, so Hitler's goal before the invasion of Poland was to prevent the second group from realizing the truth. Hitler did so by making moral and legal claims: he argued that the Versailles Treaty was invalid because it was unjust; by implication, he left open the possibility that Germany would comply with valid treaties, including the Munich Agreement. He used moral and legal rhetoric to obscure his intentions, thus exploiting divisions among his enemies. If he had openly admitted his intentions in response to the many diplomatic challenges, his foreign adventures would have met with more opposition.

Formally, this model is the same as the asymmetric information model involving the nonaligned state's announcement of capitalism or socialism. Suppose that British citizens have identical preferences. They believe that Britain should mobilize for war if Germany wants to take over Europe with probability greater than 0.8. Initially, suppose that prior to Munich, among the British, the appeasers believe that the probability is currently only 0.3, whereas the militarists believe that the probability is 0.9. After the Germans march into the Sudetenland, neither group has any reason to update its beliefs: they have no new information about whether the Germans seek to control territory that is not already occupied by German-speaking populations. Hitler's strategy was to avoid invading non-German states as long as possible, and in the meantime conceal his intentions behind a haze of ambiguous rhetoric. If, instead, he admitted that he intended to take over Europe, the appeasers would update their beliefs and Britain would mobilize, to the disadvantage of Hitler (compare Sartori 1999).

Our claim that Hitler's rhetoric concealed his intentions is similar to the realists' claim that moral and legal rhetoric is a ruse. The problem with the realists' view is that it lacked a mechanism to explain how the ruse would work. We have shown how states' verbal adherence to moral and legal norms can have a point even if state behaviors are not guided by these norms in a meaningful way. Hitler's moral and legal rhetoric was rational for two reasons. First, he did not want to send the wrong signal; if he had admitted that Germany had every intention of violating international law, people would have realized that Germany was an unreliable state, not to be trusted in cooperative dealings, and that Germany's interests (in more territory) were in direct conflict with their own, so appeasement would be self-defeating. Second, he wanted to divide his enemies (both domestic and foreign), and he could do so as long as his talk and behavior were consistent with the more benign interpretation of German intentions, held by many in Europe until the outbreak of the war.

Whether leaders address their rhetoric to foreign leaders, domestic citizens, or foreign citizens, their communications are often but not always credible, and the communications can serve strategic purposes. First, a kind of empty happy talk is common in the international arena just as it is in other areas of life; it is largely a ceremonial usage designed to enable the speaker to assert policies and goals without overtly admitting that he or she is acting for a purpose to which others might object. Second, talk is used to coordinate actions when states are indifferent among multiple equilibria; this talk is often found in bilateral relations when states must differentiate between cooperative and noncooperative actions. Third, talk can reveal private information when states have sufficiently similar interests or are disciplined by the presence of multiple audiences.

These are all conjectures. With so many possible things going on with talk, we cannot say precisely what is going on in every case, at least not without a detailed examination of each case. Our aim is simply to show that the existence of talk about international law cannot be taken as evidence against our rational choice premises, as is so often claimed.

On the Content of Talk: Legalism and Moralism

The models discussed so far imply that states find it in their interest to talk, and sometimes will update their beliefs after hearing talk. But the models say little about the content of the talk. The first model implies that the talk is anything but an admission that the action was influenced by a high discount rate or by other characteristics of a state that make it unstable, hostile, or unreliable. The other models imply that talk will reflect efforts to coordinate but not that states use moralistic and legalistic rhetoric. They show why Hitler might threaten war and why other states might believe him, but not why he appeals to the injustice of the Versailles Treaty or the rights of German-speaking minorities. Why, then, do states engage in moral and legal talk?

This question raises the problem of multiple equilibria. Many different messages are consistent with the models that we have discussed. In narrowing down this universe of possible messages to the handful that we observe, we rely on psychological intuitions, which has been the convention among scholars since Schelling (1963) suggested that focal points enable players to choose among multiple equilibria. This concession to the limits of rationality, however, is not a concession to the view that the messages have intrinsic moral force.

The first model shows that states want to deny that they have a high discount rate. One way to make these denials is to be explicit, to say, for example, "Our actions are motivated by our long-term state interest, not short-term political gain for existing officeholders." In fact, the practice is more subtle: states invoke ideals.

These ideals could in principle be anything. A state might justify a violation of a border by saying that the border reflects historical injustices, or that the other nation, by persecuting minorities, forfeited its sovereign rights under international ethical norms. It could say that the border was the result of a treaty that is invalid because it violates an international legal formality. It could say that it was commanded by God to strike down the infidels. It could say that non-Christian states forfeit certain international entitlements. But among all these possibilities, what determines what a state will say?

We conjecture that the appeal to the basis of obligation will occur at the lowest level of abstraction consistent with the characteristics of the intended audience. If a given state cares only about cooperating with Christian nations because only Christian states have military and economic power or non-Christian states are uncompromisingly hostile, then an appeal to Christianity is a way of saying that predatory behavior directed at a non-Christian state does not imply predatory behavior toward a Christian state. In other words, the predation is not the result of a high discount rate or an aspiration to rule the world; it is the result of a policy of engaging in predation only against non-Christian states. The reference to the Christianity of states is an economical method for designating the set of "in-group" states, the states with which the speaker seeks to have cooperative relations because of similar interests.

Why shouldn't talk be more general? Why would a Christian state appeal to common Christian beliefs rather than to common humanity or to common moral or legal ideals, as would happen later? The answer probably lies in the two-audience game. Suppose the Ottoman Turks generally do not cooperate with Christians but that the possibility of a military alliance between one Christian state and the Turks against another Christian state cannot be discounted altogether. The two-audience game shows that by appealing to Christian values in ordinary disputes, a Christian state can reveal that it would receive low payoffs from dealing with Turks, for otherwise it would not alienate the Turks by excluding them from the audience of potential cooperators. But if, as time passes, Christian and non-Christian states begin to derive returns from cooperation, moralistic appeals will be watered down so that non-Christian states do not infer that they are being repudiated.

Our conjecture implies that the history of international discursive practices reflects shifts in payoffs from cooperating with different states. When returns from cooperation are maximized by dealing with a small number of states with similar traditions and values, talk will appeal to relatively specific values: religious (Christian), regional (Europe), and so forth. When returns are maximized by dealing with a larger number of diverse states, talk will be watered down and reference will be to thin moral values (friendship, loyalty, trust) and, at the extreme, purely formal values such as law or political interests that are already shared. In outline, this historical development looks like this:

1. Christian states (seventh century–eighteenth century)
2. European states (eighteenth century–nineteenth century)
3. Civilized states (nineteenth century–second half of twentieth century)
4. Human rights–respecting states (second half of twentieth century–present) (Fisch 2000; Gong 1984; Frey and Frey 1999; Fidler 2001)

As we turn from the use of language to support a general reputation of cooperativeness to its use in specific international relationships, we also observe moral and legal rhetoric.

Two states in a repeated prisoner's dilemma coordinate on what move counts as cooperation, say, not searching neutral ships. Then one state deviates "by mistake." That state's navy employs captains who must exercise judgment in difficult circumstances; some might opportunistically search vessels in violation of orders, others might search the vessels for suspected spies. At this point, the state will want to reassure the other state that this was an aberration and will not be repeated, if in fact that is the case. Alternatively, the states may recognize that payoffs have changed—spying had not been a problem, now it is—and cooperative gains are no longer available.

The states have an interest in distinguishing the two cases: the case of continuing cooperation, and the case of cooperative failure. There is a conventional way of doing so. As Britain did in the nineteenth century, one argues that the treatment of neutral ships is a matter of customary law in the first case and mere comity in the second case. This argument could be made using amoral language, in which reference is made to expectations and the potential surplus that can be obtained through cooperation. But this would be artificial. The language of cooperation is the language of obligation: in both cases, one engages in (short-term) sacrifice for the sake of a greater (joint) good. In distinguishing actions that contribute to a surplus (custom) and actions that do not (comity), it is a natural use of language to claim that the first is a matter of moral obligation and the second is not.

If this explanation is correct, it shows why some observers of international relations mistake strategic behavior for moral behavior, and thus attribute moral goals to amoral polities. When states cooperate in their self-interest, they naturally use the moralistic language of obligation rather than the strategic language of interest. But saying that the former is evidence of moral motivation is like saying that when states talk of friendship or brotherhood they use these terms, which are meant to reflect aspirations for closer relations, in a literal sense.

Conclusion

Moralistic and legalistic rhetoric can be important under two conditions. First, states acting aggressively need some convenient rhetoric with which to influence speculation about their preferences. They do so by describing their motives in universalistic or semiuniversalistic terms. Moral or religious rhetoric will sometimes suffice, but the idea of law, because it is purely formal, is particularly convenient. The appeal to law is simply the denial of self-interest. Even as ruthlessly power-hungry a state as Nazi Germany always cloaked its behavior in the garb of international law and political morality.

Second, states seeking to coordinate in complex interactions appeal to past statements and practices to clarify their own actions or to protest the actions of other states. This negotiation over what actions count as proper, usually but not always in bilateral cooperative relationships or multilateral coordination, is familiar and is illustrated by the examples provided in the introduction. When states argue about whether certain export practices count as dumping, whether the targeting of neutral vessels is implied by a declaration of war, whether undersea mining may extend over the continental shelf, and whether certain diplomatic privileges follow from recognition of a sovereign state, they are attempting to establish the meaning of the words they use in international discourse, and thus to control the consequences of their announcements.

CHAPTER 7

INTERNATIONAL LAW AND
MORAL OBLIGATION

The instrumental theory of international law outlined in parts 1 and 2 was offered as an alternative to the conventional wisdom that international law has a normative component that pulls states toward compliance, contrary to their interests. Some traditionalists will claim that our purely positive, or explanatory, analysis is not responsive. Even if international law is best explained by states acting in their self-interest, states *should* obey international law's moral command. On this view, our preoccupation with the conditions under which states in fact comply with international law is of little interest. The important issue is what states should do; international law scholarship should press states to live up their obligations, regardless of whether it is in their interest to do so.

This argument's assumption, an assumption that permeates modern international law scholarship, is that states have a moral obligation to comply with international law. In this chapter, we argue that this assumption is wrong. Our claim is not that states should not follow international law, but that they have no moral obligation to do so. A state's instrumental calculus will usually counsel in favor of international law compliance, at least with respect to treaties that the state entered into self-consciously. But when the instrumental calculus suggests a departure from international law, international law imposes no moral obligation that requires contrary action. (For a discussion of the literature, see Buchanan and Golove 2002.)

Can a State Have Obligations?

I n common speech and the speech of politicians and diplomats, states
are corporate agents that have intentions, interests, and obligations;
they can declare war, make promises, and form alliances; they can grow,
shrink, divide, and merge. For some scholars, the use of anthropomor-
phic language to refer to collectivities like states and corporations is a
convenience only (Lewis 1991). According to these scholars, only individuals can have obligations, and references to state obligations are
metaphors for the duties of rulers or citizens.

One could imagine an international law theory that started from
these individualistic premises. An old version is that princes recognize
that they owe one another moral obligations, and these obligations form
the basis of international law. Hume (1978) took this position, quali-
fying it with the claim that because states depend less on each other
for aid than individuals do, the obligations among princes have less
force than the obligations among ordinary citizens. But with the rise
of the nation-state, this view could no longer be sustained. For Morgenthau (1948b), nationalism spelled the end of international ethics because it destroyed the transnational social ties of aristocratic elites; it
made leaders beholden to the masses of a single state and thus left them
without any sense of obligation toward the masses of another state. The
masses of one state will also not tolerate leaders who have ethical scru-
ples; on the contrary, each state identifies its own values with the truth
and seeks to impose them on others, through violent means if necessary.
Under such circumstances there can be no international law that exerts
influence on the behavior of states.

Morgenthau's (1948b) argument relies on a pessimistic empirical
claim about citizens' sense of obligation. If one adopted a more optimistic view, could an individualistic theory of international law be created? Suppose that the government serves as an agent of the citizens,
and when the government makes promises, the citizens inherit the obligation to keep the promises. They discharge this obligation by pres-
suring governments to keep their promises and removing governments
that do not. Citizens also pressure the government to comply with other
obligations under international law. When one government takes the
place of another, citizens must pressure the new government to comply
with obligations created by the old government.

The problem with this view for the international law theorist is that it contradicts the fundamental premise of international law theory, namely, that states—not individuals or governments—bear legal obligations. If international legal obligations were borne by individuals or governments, rather than by states, then an international obligation would end whenever a government was replaced or generations of citizens turned over. Treaties would constantly expire on their own; customary international law could not persist for more than a few years. In addition, nondemocratic governments would not be able to bind citizens to international law, and even in a liberal democracy, the problem of aggregating preferences through voting procedures and representative institutions would sometimes break the agency relationship. Because the state drops out of the picture, every international obligation would be vulnerable to the claim that citizens, or discrete groups of citizens, did not acquire the obligation through consent or some other acceptable procedure. For these reasons, international law is not built on the obligations of individuals.

The more common view is that a state, like other corporate bodies, can bear obligations. States have obligations to protect the rights of citizens. They have obligations to keep their promises, respect the sovereignty of other states, and help their allies (Maxwell 1990). It cannot be denied that people speak this way and that this way of speaking is meaningful. Similar language is used for corporations, religious associations, and other collective bodies, and it gives us no trouble in these contexts. Still, states do not act by themselves; they must be made to act by leaders and citizens. Even if states can be said to have obligations, the leaders and citizens must believe that they have a duty to guide the state in a way that is consistent with those obligations. If they do not, the obligations of the states are idle and of no importance.

A useful analogy comes from the corporate world. Corporations have legal and moral obligations that are independent of the obligations of shareholders and other stakeholders. When a corporation violates a legal obligation, it must pay fines and other penalties. To pay these fines and penalties, the corporation diverts revenues that would otherwise go into the pockets of shareholders. These shareholders have no basis for complaining that they are being made to pay for legal violations that they did not commit, did not know about, or could not have stopped, such as illegal acts secretly committed before current shareholders bought their shares. The reason they have no basis for complaint is that they voluntarily accepted these obligations when they purchased the shares (Kutz 2000, 253). The price they paid reflected a discount for the market's estimate of existing corporate liabilities, however incurred, given that the shareholders' right to the corporation's revenue stream is, as a matter of law, secondary to the rights of holders of fixed obligations on account of the corporation's legal violations. Citizens, by contrast, do not purchase their citizenship. If a prior government made a bad promise, one cannot tell current citizens that their price of admission already reflects that obligation. If citizens have a moral obligation to cause the state to comply with its obligations, the reason cannot be similar to the reason that shareholders must accept the corporation's obligations.

The problem with the corporatist approach to international law is that it depends on citizens and rulers feeling that they have an obligation to live up to the state's obligations. The citizens and rulers are the people who decide what the state does, and they are free to disregard a state's obligations if they believe they are spurious. Citizens and rulers might believe that they inherit the state's obligations only if the state is a liberal democracy, or only if it is coextensive with the people or the *Volk,* or only if these obligations were acquired in recent memory. By contrast, we can demand that corporations comply with legal obligations, penalize managers and shareholders of corporations that do not comply, and justify the penalty by virtue of these individuals' freedom not to join the corporation if they prefer to avoid the corporation's liabilities. We can similarly blame the corporation for its wrongful behavior, holding shareholders responsible for this behavior and blaming them for not taking remedial action even if they cannot be blamed for the original act.

Thus, international law finds itself in a dilemma. On the one hand, if international law takes the state as the primary obligation-bearing agent, then it can have no direct moral force for the individuals or groups who control the state. There could be, by definition, state obligations under international law, but these obligations would have no influence over the behavior of states except when citizens (or, in autocratic states, autocrats) happen to identify closely with the state or have independent grounds for supporting international law. On the other hand, if international law takes the individual or nonstate group as the primary moral agent, then it can claim the agent's loyalty but it must give up its claim to regulate the relationships between states. It becomes vulnerable to the births and deaths of individuals, migrations, the dissolution and redefinition of groups, and ambiguity about the representativeness of political institutions. States would flicker, and so would their obligations to treaties and rules of customary international law.

International law grasps the first horn of the dilemma: It purports to bind states, not individuals. Although individuals sometimes have obligations under international law, these obligations are derived from the actions of states. But if we grant international law the power to bind states—and we henceforth make this assumption—we still must ask why individuals and governments should feel obligated to cause the state to comply with its legal obligations.

Consent

The most common explanation for why states have a moral obligation to comply with international law is that they have consented to it. This theory is reflected both in the *pacta sunt servanda* principle for treaty compliance and the *opinio juris* requirement for customary international law.

The first thing that must be said about the consent theory is that it has a narrower compass than its advocates pretend. Much of international law does not rest on consent. New states, for example, are expected (by old states) to comply with most, if not all, of international law at the moment of their emergence. Kazakhstan, for example, did not, as a region of the Soviet Union, consent to the international law commitments that bound it at the moment of its birth as a state. But even old states are bound by customary international law that they played no role in creating. International lawyers say that a state can be bound by failing to object to an emerging customary norm, and although this is true, it has nothing to do with consent. Silence rarely implies consent in morality or domestic law; it does at the international level only because consent is not a real requirement. Finally, as frequently noted, a state cannot eliminate its international law obligations simply by withdrawing consent. A state that acts inconsistently with a treaty cannot deny that it has violated international law just by saying that it no longer consents to the treaty (Brierly 1958). Although states often do consent to a particular obligation, including a treaty, consent is neither a necessary nor a sufficient basis for creating an international legal obligation.

These points mirror arguments made about the role of consent in domestic political obligation. Against an old view that consent is the basis of political obligation, scholars have pointed out that people do not really have the option to consent to their own domestic political system: they are born into it, and the choice not to emigrate to another country is not the same thing as consent to the domestic political system. In addition, the normal ways one expresses consent to a political system (voting, tax paying) are themselves not based on consent but on decisions made by other people in the past. Consent cannot by itself ground political obligation (Hume 1978; Raz 1987). The most one can say is that citizens who enthusiastically express consent for the political system may have some kind of special moral obligation growing out of it (Raz 1987; Greenawalt 1987). But few citizens do this.

So states frequently fail to consent to international law, just as citizens rarely consent to their particular domestic political arrangement. Still, states consent to some aspects of international law—most notably, treaties—and so one might want to argue at least that states have a moral obligation to comply with treaties, just as ordinary individuals have a moral obligation to keep contracts as well as ordinary promises. However, the argument from consent at the international level is weaker than the argument from consent at the domestic level.

To see why, one must understand that a state, like a corporation, is not an agent whose well-being demands moral consideration. Although states make promises and enter treaties and so can be said to consent to certain courses of action, one must distinguish between the words that states use and the practices to which these words refer. States are not individuals, and what is true for individuals is not necessarily true for states. John can promise that he will perform some act in the future; but John cannot in the same way commit a third person, Mary, to perform an act. When a state at time 1 promises that it will act in a certain way at time 2, the state at time 1 is committing a different entity, the state at time 2, which might be as different from the state at time 1 as Mary is from John. The state at time 2 might be a liberal democracy, whereas the state at time 1 was a corrupt dictatorship, or the state at time 2 might have a different population, or a population with different interests. The relationship between the state at time 2 and the state at time 1 is different from the relationship between John at time 2 and John at time 1.

One might argue that the state is like a corporation, and corporations make promises in contracts and are obligated to keep them. But, as we saw earlier, states and corporations differ in one crucial respect: the shareholders of a corporation voluntarily take on the obligations of the corporation when they purchase shares; indeed, the corporation's obligations are reflected as a discount in the price of a share. People who are born into citizenship of a state do not consent in a similar manner to take on the obligations that others have acquired in the name of the state.

Another way to stress the disanalogy between states and individuals is to focus on one reason consent is held to create a moral obligation for an individual. Consider an individual's promise to perform an action. On one view, the individual's duty to keep his or her promise derives from the relationship between promising and autonomy. Individuals should have the power to control their lives, to draft and execute "life plans," as it is often put, and an important part of this power is the ability to make binding promises. Those individuals who can make binding promises have more opportunities than those who cannot, for they can obtain the cooperation of others in projects that they cannot accomplish on their own.

States, however, do not have life plans. The power to make binding treaties might extend the range of opportunities that a state has, but a state's power to choose among opportunities is not a good in itself. Similarly, we don't say that a corporation should have the power to make binding contracts because corporations should enjoy autonomy. The reason for holding that the state or another corporate body should be able to make binding contracts or treaties cannot be that these entities should have freedom or autonomy in the way that human beings do; the reason can only be that human beings enjoy an enhancement in their autonomy if these institutions are able to make binding contracts or treaties.

But when a state enters a treaty, it binds a large number of people to policies to which they do not consent: people who are not yet born, people who have not yet immigrated, people who have no power under the existing political system. If states comply with their treaties, some people might enjoy greater autonomy—those people whose opportunities are closely tied to the state's foreign policy or the benefits that the state obtains through cooperation with other states—but many others will not. The question is empirical, and it seems doubtful—keeping in mind the ambiguity of the concept of autonomy, the many ways that people exercise autonomy in their ordinary local activities, and neglect by many states of the interests of their citizens as well as those of third parties who might be affected by the promise—that there is a relationship between the autonomy of individual citizens and a state's power to enter treaties.

Perhaps it is sufficient to observe that most states throughout history, and even during recent history, have not been liberal democracies and have not placed any special weight on the autonomy of their citizens. The ability of these states to enter treaties is not likely to have an impact on the autonomy of their citizens. It would be odd to say that these states have an obligation to comply with international law, but whatever one's view on that issue, it would be odder still to say that other states, including liberal democracies, should expect these states to comply with international law against their interest. In such a nonideal world, it would be hard to say that liberal democracies' consent to treaties with these states should create any moral obligations. Perhaps liberal democracies ought to keep promises they make to each other, but we have seen that international law does not require this; international law requires all states to keep their treaties, regardless of the domestic political arrangements of the promisor or the promisee.

Take the case concerning the *Gabcikovo-Nagymaros* (1997), a casebook favorite that involved a treaty between Hungary and Czechoslovakia (subsequently, Slovakia) for the construction of a dam and hydroelectric power plants on the Danube River. The treaty was ratified in 1977, when both states were under communist rule; the project was widely seen as an environmental disaster. After Hungary made the transition to democracy, its government, bowing to public pressure, sought to withdraw from the treaty. Do members of the public really have an obligation to pressure their government to maintain adherence to a treaty that could only have disastrous effects for the state and its citizens and that never had any democratic legitimacy?

None of this is to say that a state should not comply with its treaties. Outside of coincidence of interest situations, states frequently comply with their international obligations, especially treaties, because it is in their interest, or their citizens' interests, to do so. The state's obligation to keep promises is a prudential decision, not a moral decision. The decision to keep a promise turns on its effect on the good of the state. (This is hardly a new idea; see Spinoza 1958.)

Well-Being

Consent is not the only source of obligations. Another theory for why individuals have the duty to obey the law appeals to the capacity of governments to do good for their citizens (Raz 1987). Governments have authority because a centralized, powerful institution is needed to coordinate the behavior of individuals, to enable them to pursue projects, and to protect them from one another. An institution that benefits people, and that is just, is owed a duty of allegiance by those who are so benefited. But then the legitimacy of the government and the individual's obligation to obey any law extend only as far as the government's success in enacting good laws.

Transferring this theory to the international context creates puzzles. Who is the international authority to which states owe allegiance? When we look for such an authority, we find none: no world government and no authoritative international institution. All we can find are rules of customary international law that have evolved gradually over hundreds of years, their provenance mysterious except that we know that current governments representing living individuals did not create them. Still, we might say loosely that this institution, or maybe "international society" (Bull 1977), has authority and can create obligations as long as it is good.

Domestic laws are good because they respect and promote the autonomy of citizens, or because they promote the welfare of citizens. But, as argued earlier, states do not have autonomy in the way that individuals do. States do not have projects and life plans; nor do states experience welfare or utility. States are vehicles through which citizens pursue their goals, and although we can talk meaningfully about whether the citizens of a state in the aggregate enjoy a high level of welfare or enjoy a great deal of autonomy, the state itself does not experience these things. The state's own autonomy (in the moral, not political, sense) or welfare cannot be a reason for complying with international law. When people argue that states should comply with international law, they always appeal to the rights or welfare of individuals. Individuals would be better off in a world in which states had an obligation to comply with international law. *That* is why states should obey international law.

The first thing to see about this argument is that it is based on an empirical judgment. There are many reasons for thinking that this judgment is dubious. The main source of doubt arises from the fact that states do not always act in the interest of their own citizens, and even more rarely act in the interest of citizens of other states. States without representative political institutions, or with bad institutions, or with highly heterogeneous populations frequently do not serve the interests of their citizens or respect their autonomy. If states do not choose good domestic laws and policies, they will not enter good treaties either. In a world populated by bad states, it is doubtful that people are better off with international legal obligations.

One might argue that international legal obligations can be created only when the states involved are liberal democracies (Tesón 1998), or when the obligations themselves are good. But this is just an argument that international law, which does not limit its obligations in this way, must be changed. Perhaps such a legal system would be better, but it would not be current international law, which derives its power from its insistence that all states are equally subject to the law and that international obligations are not vulnerable to ambiguity about the quality of domestic political institutions, in which case many existing treaties and rules of customary international law would be thrown into doubt.

Even when states are liberal democracies, they never attach as much weight to the well-being of foreigners as they do to the well-being of their own citizens. (See chapter 8 for an elaboration of this view.) As a result, treaties and rules of customary international law will often advance the interest of the involved states at the expense of third parties. Two powerful states, for example, might enter a treaty that lowers tariffs between themselves but raises tariffs for imports from a third, competing state, which might be weaker and poorer and the home of a population greater than the combined population of the first two states. The democratic institutions of the first two states drive them toward these results as long as the interest groups or publics in those states care more about their own well-being than that of the population of the third state. The rules of international law facilitate cooperation, but do not necessarily facilitate cooperation benefiting the world.

The same can be said about domestic law, and for this reason philosophers tend to believe that individuals have a moral obligation to obey only good laws. If this is true for states as well, then states have no general moral obligation to obey international law and should obey only good international laws, a conclusion that, of course, would deprive international law of its authority (A. Simmons 1979). For Raz (1987), domestic law can have authority on epistemic grounds: the law might incorporate knowledge not available to citizens. But, however plausible this argument may be for domestic law, it is unlikely to be true for international law.

Despite the absence of a strong philosophical basis, commonsense thinking suggests that individuals have a prima facie moral duty to obey laws with a democratic pedigree, and we will assume for now that this view is correct. There are in this respect two important differences between domestic and international law. The first difference concerns the question of presumption. We presume that domestic laws are good in a liberal democracy, where citizens have influence over the political process. The same cannot be said about international law. Much of the foundational rules of international law evolved long before liberal democracy became a common mode of political organization; more recent international law, it is generally agreed, almost always reflects the interests of the powerful (and not always liberal) states rather than the interests of the world at large. The law reflects the interests of states, not of individuals; that is why apparent humanitarian interventions like the war in Kosovo can be illegal (Henkin 1999). For these reasons, it seems unwarranted to presume that international laws are good.

The second difference concerns compliance and enforcement. Domestic law is enforced in well-ordered societies. Thus, people's sense of moral commitment works hand-in-hand with the state's monopoly on force to ensure that law is usually complied with. This is important because people do not have an obligation to obey a law that everyone else violates (Rawls 1971); indeed, domestic laws that are not enforced (speed limits, drug laws in some places, certain kinds of tax laws) exert little normative force. What is the anomaly for domestic law is the norm for international law. Except when states construct self-enforcing treaties and when customary international law reflects stable equilibria, international law is not reliably enforced and depends entirely on states voluntarily setting aside their immediate interests. There is no reason to expect the powerful states to take the role of a police force responding to every violation: that job would be an impossible burden and would provide few benefits to the citizens of the states that take it on.

As a further illustration of this point, compare a domestic contract that harms third parties and a treaty that harms third parties. At the domestic level, we can clearly distinguish the parties' legal and moral obligations. If the contract violates the law and is thus void, then the parties have neither a moral nor a legal obligation to keep their promises. This is true for a contract to fix prices. If the contract does not violate the law, then the parties have a legal obligation but might not have a moral obligation to keep their promises. Think of a contract between an owner and a builder that requires the latter to build a house that neighbors will think ugly. The owner and the builder learn the neighbors' opinions after they enter the contract but before either party has sunk any cost in the project, and they could cheaply switch to a different plan that would be less objectionable. Now, many people might argue that the parties do have a moral obligation to keep their promises (or, at least, that the contractor should build the house if the owner does not release him from the obligation) and should not worry too much about the neighbors. If building ugly houses is a public bad, then there will be a law against it; if not, it must not be a public bad. Perhaps the view is that modern architecture always meets resistance but should be encouraged on cultural grounds. The contractor who feels bad about offending the neighbors could say, with some justice, that he or she assumes that the contract is morally inoffensive because the government does not discourage it. If the contractor were to violate the contract merely on the basis of some protests, he or she would wrong his or her contracting partner without producing any offsetting benefit. This argument depends on the government having superior information and the contractor being justified in relying on the government's action (or inaction).

Whatever one thinks of this domestic case, it is hard to see how it would work at the international level. Suppose that two states enter a treaty under which they agree to impose economic sanctions on a third state. These sanctions are intended to coerce this third state to open its markets to products that citizens of the third state sincerely believe threaten their culture and values. One of the original pair of states then decides whether to violate the treaty or comply with it. In making this decision, it cannot appeal to a higher government's judgment, in the way that the contractor could. It cannot, like the contractor, assume that, roughly, the law will release it if the treaty is bad and not otherwise. For there is no reason to think that international law will track moral right or the public interest, as there is a reason to think that domestic law in a well-ordered democracy will. Thus, the state must make its own moral judgment and (if it is inclined to be guided by morality) comply with the treaty only if compliance is the right thing to do. International law has no moral authority.

International law scholars tend to confuse two separate ideas: (1) a moral obligation on the part of states to promote the good of all individuals in the world, regardless of their citizenship; and (2) a moral obligation to comply with international law. The two are not the same; indeed, as we explore in detail in the next chapter, they are in tension as long as governments focus their efforts on helping their own citizens (or their own supporters or officers). If all states did have the first obligation (which is an attractive but utopian idea), and they did comply with that obligation, then they would agree to treaties that implement, and would engage in customary practices that reflect, the world good; then they might have an obligation to comply with international law in the same rough sense that individuals have an obligation to comply with laws, or most of them, issued by a good government. But this is not our world. In our world, we cannot say that if a particular state complies with international law—regardless of the normative value of the law, regardless of what other states do, and maybe regardless of the interests of its own citizens—or even treated compliance as a presumptive duty, the world would be a better place.

Morality and International Legal Change

The morality or immorality of international law is exhausted by its content; international legality does not impose any moral obligations. The truth of this proposition is revealed most clearly in the phenomenon of international legal change. Every state act that is inconsistent with existing international law is open to two interpretations. First, the act might be said to be a violation of international law by a state that intends only to take advantage of other, compliant states. Second, the act might be said to be a proposal for revision of existing international law; the state acts inconsistently with international law in an effort to change it, to stimulate a new equilibrium that better serves its interests and, in the usual case, the interests of other states that have sufficient power and influence.

Usually, the interpretation is made after the fact. At the time of the inconsistent act, many states will protest and take steps to reassert the status quo international rule. Other states that see an advantage in the proposed law will support the alleged violator. As an example, consider the military intervention in Kosovo. The intervention clearly violated the UN Charter, but many states and international lawyers who supported the intervention quickly claimed that the intervention reflected an evolving international law norm that provided that force can be used for humanitarian purposes. Again, we see how an act that is inconsistent with international law can be interpreted either as a violation of it or as a first step in its revision. If we had perfect information about the interests and capacities of all the states involved, we would know immediately whether the inconsistent act will later be considered a violation or instead the first step in a new legal regime. Because we do not, we will not be able to choose between these interpretations until many years have passed and it has become clear either that states routinely go to war for humanitarian reasons or do not.

This phenomenon—illegality leading to a new order—is not unique to international law. The ratification of the U.S. Constitution was a violation of the Articles of Confederation, whose amendment provision required unanimity. The formal illegality of the U.S. Constitution was of no importance because the citizens of the new state acquiesced in it and paid no more attention to the Articles of Confederation. Subsequent generations have, in turn, violated the formal amendment provision of the U.S. Constitution by recognizing constitutional rights and powers that were not originally in the document. Rather than saying that these new rights and powers are illegal, courts and others understand that when new rights and powers obtain sufficient acceptance among the public and the political class, they become real constitutional changes. Looking backward, we can identify new actions, say, the congressional-executive agreement, that had no clear constitutional warrant and thus might have been thought a violation of the Constitution, but that have been validated by practice rather than subsequently rejected.

But if both international law change and constitutional law change occur through actions that formally violate the law but subsequently receive support or acquiescence, the phenomenon is far more common at the international level than at the domestic level. The reason is that international law is more decentralized, and there is no generally accepted mechanism for changing international law. The closest thing to such a mechanism is the multilateral convention. But such conventions are cumbersome. Unless all states, or all major states, agree to the new rules—and this almost never happens, and when it does only with reservations, understandings, and declarations that hollow out the consensus—then the result of a convention will be ambiguous, and we do not know whether the convention really changes the law until we observe the subsequent behavior of states. Thus, many states bypass conventions and press for new legal changes by violating the old law.

This should make clear that we cannot condemn a state merely for violating international law. The question is whether by violating international law a state is likely to change international law for the better from a moral perspective. This is why so much international legal argument seems indistinguishable from moral argument. When people criticize the United States for intervening in Kosovo or Iraq, their argument should be interpreted as a claim that the status quo international rules are good and that they should not be changed. When they support these interventions, they are arguing that the use of force rules are outmoded and that they should be changed: to allow for humanitarian intervention in the first case, to allow for preemptive self-defense in the second case. As the debate between the two sides develops, international law, as an institution that exerts its own moral force independent of its content, falls away. The reason that it can exert no moral force comparable to the moral force of domestic law is that it has no democratic pedigree or epistemic authority; it reflects what states have been doing in the recent past and does not necessarily reflect the moral judgments or interests or needs of individuals. It can have no democratic pedigree because there are no international institutions that reliably convert the world public's needs and interests into international law and that can change existing international law when the world public's needs and interests change.

Does It Matter?

We have not given the philosophical accounts of political obligation the detailed treatments that they deserve. Nor have we discussed, except in passing, various other theories of domestic political obligation, including the "fair play" theory, the "natural justice" theory, and the "gratitude" theory.[1] Conceivably, one of these theories might provide the appropriate analogical basis for international moral-legal obligation, but, given their controversy even for explaining domestic political obligation, this seems highly unlikely. The weakness of existing accounts of political obligation has led many philosophers to believe that individuals have no moral obligation to obey domestic law, and others to hold that such an obligation, if it exists, is quite narrow. If there is little reason to believe that citizens have moral obligations to their governments, there should be no strong expectation that states have moral obligations to the "international system." Indeed, the claim that states, or the citizens that control them, have moral obligations to other states faces formidable additional difficulties. International law is the product of agreements and practices of democratic governments that favor their own citizens over the rest of the world and authoritarian governments that favor some subset of their own citizens; of powerful governments imposing their will on others and weak governments submitting because they have no alternative; of governments pursuing time-bound interests with little concern for future generations. There is little reason to believe that the resulting system as a whole is just, though particular regimes or arrangements within the international system may be, and that individuals throughout the world, or their governments, owe any duty to it.

One might ask, Does it matter whether states have a moral obligation to obey international law? States do what they do; they might violate a moral obligation even if they have it, or they might comply with international law even if they do not have a moral obligation to comply with it. H. L. A. Hart (1961) denied that it matters whether states have a moral obligation to obey international law or feel that they have such a conviction; all that matters is that states have a reason to comply with international law. But Hart's philosophical concerns are different from those of international lawyers, for whom the question does matter.

It will become clear why after a short discussion of the methodological assumptions of international law scholarship.

International law scholars have long grappled with the question of whether international law is law. Some express impatience with this question as merely a matter of definition, but the question never goes away. The question does not go away because it reflects a puzzle about the purpose of international law scholarship and whether it has a distinctive role in the academy. One possible answer to the question is that international law is not law but politics. It reflects patterns of behavior that emerge in international relations. But if international law is just politics, understanding international law does not depend on any special legal expertise and should be the province of the political scientist.

Another possible answer is that international law is not law but morality. International law reflects the moral obligations that states owe to one another. Domestic law, by contrast, is not a pure reflection of moral principles, but instead limits them as is necessary to accommodate the need for clear guidelines, the time and expense of judges, the distribution of political power, and other constraints. The problem with international law as morality is not just that this view leaves the field in the possession of moral philosophers with nothing for international lawyers to do. The problem is that morality is so indeterminate and so contested, especially among states and peoples, that it can provide little guidance for international relations.

The mostly implicit methodological consensus among international lawyers threads a needle. The norms of international law are different from morality: they are more precise and reflect positions where moral principles run out. The norms reflect institutional constraints just as domestic laws do. But norms of international law are distinguished from agreements, customs, and other political accommodations by virtue of their moral specialness. A third category, between politics and morality, is separated out and made the subject of a special discipline, that of international law.

But as the domestic analogy shows, this third category is vexed. The (domestic) lawyer's task is easily distinguished from the moralist's and the political scientist's: laws, though influenced by politics and morality, can be distinguished as the rules created by special institutions like legislatures and courts. As there are no special world legislatures or courts, at least, none from which all international law can be traced, the subject matter of the international lawyer is trickier to distinguish. The international law community has declared that some agreements and customs are law because the states say so or treat them that way, but they do not explain why these agreements and customs should be treated as the subject of a special discipline rather than as just a part of international politics that states call law. Instead, international lawyers raise the law part of international politics to a higher plane by claiming that states are more likely to comply with what they call "law" than with other agreements and customs.

Pressed for an explanation for why states would do this, international law scholars typically argue (as we have seen) that law is internalized, is given special status, or is obeyed because that is the right thing to do. But if states do not, in fact, have a moral obligation to obey international law, then this attempt to save international law from politics or morality must fail.

This is not to say that the international lawyer's view could not be given a different defense. States could have an intrinsic desire to comply with international law for reasons other than moral obligation. It is possible that even if states did not have a moral obligation to comply with international law, citizens and leaders might think that the state has an obligation to comply with international law. They might make this mistake for several reasons: they are under the spell of a legalistic ideology; they make unrealistic assumptions about the enforceability of international law; or they make some other error in moral reasoning. But none of this seems plausible and is certainly not a firm foundation for international law.

The more plausible view is that efficacious international law is built up out of rational self-interest of the type described in parts 1 and 2. It is politics, but a special kind of politics, one that relies heavily on precedent, tradition, interpretation, and other practices and concepts familiar from domestic law. On this view, international law can be binding and robust, but only when it is rational for states to comply with it.

This prudential view does not imply that international law scholarship is unimportant. The scholarship retains its task of interpreting treaties, past practices, and other documents or behaviors. When states coordinate with one another, or cooperate, they need to establish a point of coordination. For this purpose, interpretive techniques are helpful. The international lawyer's task is like that of a lawyer called in to interpret a letter of intent or nonbinding employment manual: the lawyer can use his or her knowledge of business or employment norms, other documents, and so forth to shed light on the meaning of the documents, but the documents themselves do not create legal obligations even though they contain promissory or quasi-promissory language.

There is a practical reason why it matters whether states have a moral obligation to comply with international law. International law scholars who believe that states have such an obligation are, as a result, optimistic about the ability of international law to solve problems of international relations, and they attribute failures to the poor design of international treaties and organizations. They argue that if states entered treaties with more precise and stronger obligations, gave up more sovereign powers to independent international institutions, used transparent and fair procedures when negotiating treaties, and eschewed unilateralism and bilateralism for multilateralism, then a greater level of international cooperation would be achieved than is currently observed. All of these normative recommendations flow from the premise that states want to comply with international law. If that premise is wrong, then these recommendations have no merit, or else must be defended on other grounds.

The prudential view, by contrast, suggests that stricter international law could lead to greater international lawlessness. If treaties were stricter, then compliance with them would be more costly. But then states would be more likely to violate international law or not enter international agreements in the first place. Efforts to improve international cooperation must bow to the logic of state self-interest and state power, and although good procedures and other sensible strategies might yield better outcomes, states cannot bootstrap cooperation by creating rules and calling them "law."

CHAPTER 8

LIBERAL DEMOCRACY AND COSMOPOLITAN DUTY

Chapter 7 analyzed a state's moral duty to comply with international law. This chapter analyzes the state's moral duty to enter into treaties and to take other related forms of international action in the first place. Mainstream international law scholarship contends that states, especially liberal democratic ones, should be more other-regarding. They should enter into more treaties that would benefit third-party states, give up sovereignty to justice-promoting institutions like the International Criminal Court (ICC), and, in general, act internationally on the basis of global welfare rather than state welfare.

This chapter argues that this commitment to strong state cosmopolitanism cannot easily be reconciled with mainstream international law scholarship's equally strong commitment to liberal democracy itself as the optimal form of domestic governance (Fox and Roth 2000; Doyle 1983; Slaughter 1995; Tesón 1998; compare Fox 1992; Franck 1992). The institutions needed to make liberal democracy work make it difficult to engage in strong cosmopolitan action. The problem is not just the absence of democratic support for cosmopolitan policies, although that is a problem. Constitutional and collective action hurdles constrain cosmopolitan action as well. Cosmopolitan argument, we argue, must be bounded by institutional and moral constraints that arise in the domestic-democratic sphere. A coherent ideal of liberal democracies' cosmopolitan duties must accommodate these realistic limits on what liberal democracies can do.

In arguing for these points, we focus primarily on the United States, the world's richest, most powerful, and, in some respects, most vigorous liberal democracy and also a frequent target of cosmopolitan criticism. This criticism comes in two forms. The first focuses on *U.S. national interest* and maintains that *the welfare of U.S. citizens would be enhanced* in the fairer, safer, and more prosperous world that would result from increasing assistance to others. The basic claim here is that the United States harms itself and its citizens by not ratifying certain treaties and by failing to give aid and to intervene more frequently and with greater intensity. We have no quibble with this argument, which focuses on what is best for U.S. citizens, on leaders' information errors, on means-ends rationality (and related issues like unintended consequences), and on democratic-process pathologies such as time inconsistency and interest group capture.

The second form of criticism focuses on *U.S. cosmopolitan duties.* It maintains that the United States should ratify global treaties and intervene more vigorously to stop human rights abuses, *even if doing so would lower net U.S. welfare.* This argument emphasizes that the United States should act to help peoples and states outside the United States, even when the actions would not survive a U.S.-focused cost-benefit analysis. The argument does not try to clarify the U.S. national interest. It maintains that the United States should focus less on the interests of its own people and more on the interests of all humanity. This chapter argues that this second form of criticism is misplaced.

The Institutional Turn in Cosmopolitan Theory

International law scholarship is full of claims that the United States should act with greater cosmopolitan regard by joining more treaties (such as the ICC and the Kyoto Protocol) and by giving more foreign aid of various sorts. This literature rarely examines or defends the ascription of strong cosmopolitan duties to the United States and other liberal democracies. The philosophical literature does, however, and so we begin with its arguments.

From Individual to Institutional Duties

Cosmopolitan theory begins with the premise that every human being's life is equally valuable, regardless of group or national membership. Cosmopolitanism seeks to enhance attachments and duties to the community of all human beings, regardless of national or local affiliation, and to attenuate attachments and duties to the nation-state, fellow citizens, and local culture.

Some believe that cosmopolitan premises require relatively well-off *individuals* to assist relatively non-well-off individuals, including noncompatriots (Singer 1972). In recent years, however, cosmopolitan theorists have begun to reject the ascription of strong cosmopolitan duties to individuals. They have begun to argue instead that these duties are best viewed as attaching to *domestic institutions* (for example, governments) and, derivatively, to international institutions. The main reasons for this institutional turn are that cosmopolitan duties are too demanding for individuals and that institutions can better achieve international social justice. In short, cosmopolitan theorists use "plausibility limitations" on individual duties as a basis for ascribing cosmopolitan duties to political institutions.

Michael Green's work (2002) provides an example. Green contends that we cannot properly attribute cosmopolitan duties to individuals. He reaches this conclusion on the basis that "commonsense morality" in the global context is impeded by the "phenomenological features of [individual] agency." Three important features of commonsense morality are that individuals, and not groups, are the "primary bearers of responsibility"; that individuals have greater duties with respect to acts than omissions; and that individuals have "special obligations" and thus give priority to the near over the remote. The commonsense conception of morality is a restrictive one that precludes the ascription of responsibility to individuals for the problems of global injustice. Green thinks that "institutional agents do not face the same limitations as individual agents"; institutions are better at collecting and processing information. They have "power" and efficacy and thus "can alter mass behavior" (id., 85–86). And they can better spread the costs of action. These differences between the capacities of individuals and those of institutions justify attributing greater responsibilities to institutions. For example, because "institutional agents are better able to perceive and act on the consequences of their omissions than individuals are," it makes sense to attribute less significance to the distinction between action and omission when we are attributing responsibility to institutions. Among other things, this means that "there is more room to hold government responsible for taking steps to regulate harm, even though it does not cause the harm itself" (id., 87).

Iris Young (2000) also argues that obligations of social justice are primarily owed by institutions rather than by individuals. The reasons she gives are similar: "Individuals usually cannot act alone to promote justice; they must act collectively to adjust the terms of their relationships and rectify the unjust consequences of past and present social structures, whether intended or not" (id., 250). Young proposes "a global system of regulatory regimes to which locales and regions relate in a federated system," and she suggests that "reform of the United Nations System is one reasonable goal" toward this end (id., 267, 272). Other cosmopolitan theorists make similar arguments (Barry 1999; Pogge 1992; Beitz 1979; Lichtenberg 1981).

The Relevance of Plausibility Constraints

These cosmopolitan theories invoke five types of limitations on individual capacities as bases for ascribing duties to institutions. The first is based on commonsense intuition: in rejecting the ascription of strong cosmopolitan duties to individuals, appeal is made to conceptions of human agency that are informed by our ordinary practices and intuitions. The second concerns limits grounded in human biology or psychology: certain types of cosmopolitan duties, such as, for example, Peter Singer's (1972) version of utilitarianism, make superhuman demands of calculation and concern. The third type of limitation is moral: certain cosmopolitan duties are inconsistent with any reasonable conception of a good life, which must allow space for individuals to flourish without regard to the demands of morality, and especially without regard to the extraordinary demands of some cosmopolitan moral claims. A fourth concern is the problem of noncompliance: people cannot be expected to comply with obligations that are so strong that others will not do their fair share (L. Murphy 2000). Fifth, and relatedly, individuals often face severe collective action hurdles.

Why is it appropriate to invoke such limits in cosmopolitan argument? The main answer is that political theory, in Thomas Nagel's (1991, 21) words, must be "motivationally reasonable." As Nagel puts it: "If real people find it psychologically very difficult or even impossible to live as the theory requires, or to adopt relevant institutions, that should carry some weight against the ideal." For similar reasons, John Rawls (1971) imposes plausibility constraints on the ideal (or full compliance) theory of justice that emerges from the original position. As Rawls puts it, an important consideration for ideal theory is "men's capacity to act on the various conceptions of justice," a consideration that includes "general facts of human psychology and the principles of moral learning" (id., 145). These principles are relevant because, in the original position, "if a conception of justice is unlikely to generate its own support, or lacks stability, this fact must not be overlooked," for parties in the original position must suppose that other parties "will adhere to the principles eventually chosen" (id., 145). Even when we consider nonideal (or partial compliance) theory, human frailty remains relevant.

Something like this reasoning underlies the invocation of human frailty as a basis for ascription of institutional responsibility. Any theory that aims to be realistic and consequentialist in the senses described must be motivationally reasonable. It must be capable of assent without making extraordinary psychological or physical or moral demands, and it must set forth plausible mechanisms for achieving these ends.

There are at least two significant difficulties in capturing which duties are motivationally reasonable. The first is the danger of thinking that "any radical departure from accustomed patterns is psychologically unrealistic" (Nagel 1991, 22). This is the danger of confounding the familiar with the necessary, with viewing as unalterable that which is merely inconvenient to change. Often, change is not impossible, but simply very costly. A second and related difficulty concerns how we identify plausibility limits. Philosophers speak of certain duties as inconsistent with a morally attractive conception of human life; they rely a great deal on intuitions about "commonsense morality," and they often appeal to human biological and psychological limits.

Liberal Democracy and Cosmopolitan Duty

Here we describe the theoretical, practical, and moral limitations on the ascription of strong cosmopolitan duties to liberal democratic governments. Our claim is that these limitations are akin to the biological, moral, and psychological "plausibility constraints" on individual action that cosmopolitan theorists invoke as a justification for ascribing cosmopolitan duties to political institutions.

Individuals act altruistically if they have the goal of benefiting another person, they benefit that person, and they could have done better for themselves had they chosen to ignore the effect of their action on the other person (Piliavin and Chang 1990). Individuals often act altruistically. But if individuals are altruistic, why aren't the liberal states that represent them?

A similar puzzle arises in the corporate context. Individual shareholders may be altruistic, but corporations generally are not. The standard explanation is that a corporation furthers the purpose for which its members incorporated, which generally has to do with advancing member welfare, not nonmember welfare. Individuals can donate their dividends to charity, if they wish; they rarely want the corporation's managers to do this for them. The same logic might apply to the state.

This argument is open to the objection that a corporation (or any group) may consist of cosmopolitan-minded individuals who have organized to pursue cosmopolitan ends. The theories sketched earlier in this chapter correctly argue that institutions can (in theory) engage in cosmopolitan action and that cosmopolitan individuals can act through such institutions more effectively than acting alone. There is power in numbers. Institutions can efficiently gather and transmit the information needed for collective action; they can exploit economies of scale; they can monitor individual contributions and punish free-riding; they can provide norms and focal points to motivate and coordinate individual participation in group action; and they can solve psychological collective action problems. Cosmopolitan-minded individuals might lack motivation for cosmopolitan action because of a perceived inability to make a difference through individual action alone. An institution with power to effectuate change can motivate such individuals to action by clarifying the causal pathway between individual action and global change and by helping the individual to envision his or her action as part of an undertaking involving many others.

These are the basic mechanisms that allow churches, charities, and other nongovernmental organizations to achieve greater collective cosmopolitan ends than group members could achieve acting on their own. But it does not follow that states can commit similar acts of cosmopolitan charity. There are many differences between these institutions and states. First, states are larger and more diverse. Their membership does not consist of self-selected members with relatively homogeneous and intense cosmopolitan sentiments. Rather, members of pluralistic societies vary significantly in their commitments to charity. Many citizens have no cosmopolitan sentiments, or have anticosmopolitan sentiments; others have weak cosmopolitan sentiments. Even strongly cosmopolitan-minded citizens can differ sharply about the appropriate focus of cosmopolitan charity. Supporters of aid for Israel and supporters of aid for the Palestinians, for example, might cancel one another out.

Heterogeneity of individual preferences related to cosmopolitan action, taken alone, is a reason to be skeptical of the claim that states can perform strong cosmopolitan duties. A major justification for the move to cosmopolitan duties for states is that individuals face collective action problems in performing cosmopolitan duties. If citizens possessed intense and homogeneous cosmopolitan sentiments, this argument might, for reasons just canvassed, make sense. But if the bulk of individuals do not have an interest in cosmopolitan charity, or if their interests are wildly varied and uneven, there is no collective action problem at the state level to overcome, and the move to political institutions achieves little.

Another crucial difference between a liberal democratic state and, say, Oxfam International is that the state does not organize itself for the purpose of engaging in acts of cosmopolitan charity. The dominant purpose of any state is to create a community of mutual benefit for citizens and other members, and more generally to preserve and enhance the welfare of compatriots. The U.S. Constitution, for example, was designed to create a more perfect *domestic* order, and its foreign relations mechanisms were crafted to enhance U.S. welfare (Marks 1973). The same is true of liberal democracies generally. In this sense, a liberal democracy is more like IBM than Médecins sans Frontières, and skepticism about corporate or institutional altruism makes more sense.

A third obstacle is that even when individuals are altruistic, their capacity for other-regarding action is not unbounded. Individuals tend to focus their attention, energies, and altruism on members of their community (friends, family, and compatriots) with whom they identify and share a common bond. Many view local attachments, and their cultivation, as central to human flourishing (Miller 1995; Tamir 1993). Others see patriotism and related local-regarding community-building mechanisms as necessary prerequisites to a flourishing state, especially a flourishing democracy (Post 2000; C. Taylor 1996). Whatever the merits of these normative claims, the underlying positive assumption is indisputable: solidarity and altruism depend to some degree on (physical, cultural, or familial) proximity. Viewing community from the state level, most citizens are more likely to sacrifice for a compatriot than a noncompatriot, especially when giving to noncompatriots comes at the expense of needy compatriots. Even within the state community, altruism does not come close to ensuring that the well-off adequately care for those who are not well-off; state coercion is needed for most in-state welfare transfers. Given this relatively weak altruism toward compatriots, we should not expect individual altruism to extend to people who are physically and culturally more distant.

None of this is to deny that solidarity is not perfectly coextensive with borders, or that some individuals have strong cosmopolitan commitments, or that many citizens have some regard for and are willing to sacrifice a little for noncompatriots. The point is simply that, as some cosmopolitans realize, widespread and intense cosmopolitan sentiments do not exist.

To the extent that citizens do in fact have weak or nonexistent cosmopolitan sentiments, political institutions in liberal democracies cannot easily engage in cosmopolitan action. In a liberal democracy, foreign policy must be justified on terms acceptable to voters. The theory of democratic foreign policy is that voters will throw out politicians who deviate too far from their foreign policy preferences. This means that political leaders who care about reelection cannot easily engage in acts of international altruism much beyond what voters or interest groups will support. Because the matter is so important, the U.S. Constitution imposes limits, over and above electoral recall, that reinforce the principals' (that is, voters') control over the agent (that is, leaders).

Consider the war power. War is among the most serious and fateful acts a state can undertake. This is one reason the framers gave Congress the power to declare war. The meaning and scope of this power is contested, especially in modern times when presidents have asserted independent war powers more aggressively. But at least one idea behind the War Powers Clause was to place an "effectual check to the Dog of war by transferring the power of letting him loose from the executive to the Legislative body" (Jefferson 1958, 392). The framers aimed to limit the president to wars fought in the interests of, and thus supported by, the people most affected by war: the voters. This agency-cost-reducing justification for a legislative check on the war power is the one that Kant (1795/1983) offered as the basis for his predicted democratic peace. And it has become one of the normative cornerstones of the democratic peace thesis (Russett 1993).

A similar justification explains the Constitution's involvement of the legislature in the process of legally binding international agreements. The legislative consent requirement in this context, like congressional control over the decision to go to war, reduces the agency costs of executive action. The legislature ensures that the agreement negotiated by the executive is aligned with the principal whose interests he purports to represent: U.S. voters. Of course, the executive might, in some contexts, more accurately represent voter preferences than legislators do, especially when one considers the aggregation and related collective action difficulties that attend the legislative process. But this just shows that the U.S. Constitution is biased against international agreements, just as it is biased against war. The requirement of dual executive-legislative consent promotes compliance by increasing the likelihood that the state enters into only those agreements that increase state welfare. But this benefit comes at a cost of interfering with some agreements that would have enhanced state welfare, either because the executive failed to negotiate or because the legislature failed to consent. This is a defensible trade-off because treaty compliance depends on both executive and legislative support (Milner and Rosendorff 1997).

In these and other ways, the U.S. Constitution—and, with different mechanisms, every liberal democracy—ties foreign policy action to voter preferences. Realists have long decried this tie, for they view the democratic process as an obstacle to a rational and coherent foreign policy (Morgenthau 1948a; Kennan 1996). The realist criticism overlooks the many countervailing foreign relations benefits of democratic foreign policy, some of which are outlined in this chapter and chapter 3. The important point for now, however, is not the normative issue, but the institutional fact that liberal democratic institutions cannot easily engage in cosmopolitan action unsupported by the people.

Humanitarian intervention provides the best example. Intellectual and policy elites have increasingly urged liberal democratic governments to intervene to prevent human rights atrocities in other states. But despite millions of lives lost as a result of these atrocities in the twentieth century, and despite recent CNN-covered atrocities in Rwanda, Bosnia,

Kosovo, East Timor, and the Sudan (among other places), Americans are not willing to spend blood and treasure on humanitarian interventions that are not in the national interest.

To be sure, U.S. political leaders and voters sometimes support humanitarian interventions to relieve human suffering, especially starvation. But they do not support these interventions if they are expensive or threaten nontrivial losses of American lives. Politicians understand this and act accordingly. This explains the first Bush and Clinton administrations' long delay in intervening to stop the atrocities in Bosnia and the eventual decision to do so with "pinprick" air attacks rather than ground troops (Power 2002). This is why the otherwise internationalist Clinton administration pulled out of Somalia when Americans began to suffer casualties. It is one reason the United States declined to intervene in Rwanda. And it is the lesson of the Kosovo intervention: even with a mixed strategic-humanitarian justification for intervention, U.S. fighter pilots flew at high altitudes and took other casualty-avoiding steps, and the Clinton administration precommitted not to use high-casualty ground troop operations (Power 2002; Luban 2002; Burk 1999).

The absence of democratic support is a fundamental check on humanitarian intervention. As David Luban (2002, 85–86) notes:

> In a democracy, the political support of citizens is a morally necessary condition for humanitarian intervention, not just a regrettable fact of life. If the folks back home reject the idea of altruistic wars, and think that wars should be fought only to promote a nation's own self-interest, rather narrowly conceived, then an otherwise-moral intervention may be politically illegitimate. If the folks back home will not tolerate even a single casualty in an altruistic war, then avoiding all casualties becomes a moral necessity.

These points are overlooked by those who, with increasing fervor, call for humanitarian intervention without regard to its lack of popular support. For example, Samantha Power's (2002) prominent critique of the U.S. failure to intervene to stop various genocides devotes little attention to the absence of popular support for costly humanitarian interventions. The little attention she does give the issue is devoted to criticizing leaders for deferring to popular opinion. The democratic deficit for humanitarian intervention is also missed by those who appear to oppose wars that lack congressional authorization *except* when those wars are fought for humanitarian ends (see Yoo 2000). The requirement for democratic support does not distinguish between wars fought on humanitarian grounds and those fought for national security reasons. If any distinction emerges in practice, it is one that favors wars fought for national security reasons and disfavors humanitarian interventions that lack a national security justification.

The democratic hurdles to cosmopolitan action should give pause to those who believe that individuals possess limited cosmopolitan sentiments but who nonetheless ascribe strong cosmopolitan duties to liberal democratic governments. Individuals act through and limit liberal democratic institutions. If there is reason to doubt that individuals lack powerful cosmopolitan motivations, there is reason to believe that this paucity of motivation will be reflected in the output of liberal democratic institutions.

A More Realistic View of the Democratic Process

Our analysis is incomplete in at least two important respects. It ignores evidence that U.S. voters might in fact be cosmopolitan-minded, and it assumes that leaders are perfect agents of the voters, which they are not. Even taking into consideration these points, however, it remains doubtful that liberal democracies can engage in strong cosmopolitan action.

We have two ways to tell whether and to what extent voters have cosmopolitan sentiments: how their representatives vote, and what opinion polls say. Neither method is foolproof, and tricky issues arise when polls say one thing and representatives act otherwise. Consider the ICC treaty and the Kyoto Accord, both of which (many believe) might require cosmopolitan action if ratified by the United States. Opinion polls consistently find that a majority of U.S. voters support these treaties (Chicago Council on Foreign Relations 2002). But just as consistently, political representatives from both parties oppose these treaties. By a vote of 97–0, the Senate in 1997 resolved that the United States should not sign a Kyoto-related treaty that (as Kyoto contemplated) did not extend greenhouse gas reduction requirements to developing nations or that would "result in serious harm to the economy of the United States" (Byrd-Hagel Resolution 1997). Similarly, in 2002 Congress enacted a statute by overwhelming majorities that opposed

U.S. participation in the ICC. To make the puzzle more complex, political leaders and other elites are significantly more committed to internationalism than are U.S. voters (Chicago Council on Foreign Relations 2002).

Why would leaders more committed to international engagement than voters oppose ambitious international treaties that voters appear to support? There are several possible explanations. The first is that voter support for the ICC and Kyoto treaties is not by itself evidence of cosmopolitan sentiment. Internationalism is not the same as cosmopolitanism, because in many situations, international acts enhance domestic welfare. Some Americans support the treaties on welfare-enhancement grounds, and the surveys do not distinguish the two possibilities.

Moreover, the most comprehensive survey of voter attitudes toward U.S. foreign relations confirms what casual empiricism and other evidence (such as paltry U.S. foreign aid as a percentage of GNP) suggests: "Most altruistic goals of U.S. foreign policy, those primarily concerned with the welfare of people in other countries other than the United States, are not given very high priority by the U.S. public" (Chicago Council on Foreign Relations 2002, 20). U.S. citizens rank "strengthening international law" below protecting American jobs and promoting American business (id., 19). And U.S. citizens "much more than foreign policy leaders tend to put a high priority on devoting resources to domestic spending programs rather than to foreign affairs," a tendency that has "grown stronger after the end of the cold war" (Page and Barabas 2000, 347). In this light, cosmopolitan sentiment for the ICC and Kyoto treaties is probably not deep or intense. This in turn means that well-organized groups with more intense anticosmopolitan preferences, such as business interests that would suffer the main burden of Kyoto's costs, can be more successful in the democratic process. Environmentalists decry such interest group domination of U.S. international environmental policy as a perversion of the democratic process and the national interest. But whether or not interest group politics is desirable in a democratic polity, it is an inherent feature of democratic process.

Another explanation for the puzzle is that politicians are more informed than voters about the treaties and in particular about their costs. In many polls finding support for the Kyoto Accord and the ICC, most respondents had never heard of these treaties before being asked about them (RoperASW 2002). Moreover, poll questions are rarely framed in ways that discuss noncompliance by other states, or the costs of enforcement and noncompliance. When the rare poll asks how much voters would be willing to pay for a treaty regime, support for the regime drops dramatically as the costs increase (Goldsmith 2003, 1684 nn. 72–73). As suggested earlier, polls also show similar cost sensitivity with respect to humanitarian intervention. Political leaders have powerful reelection incentives to learn about the costs of international action and the resources to do so. They base their judgments on these facts rather than polling data, for they know they will be accountable to voters when the costs of international action become apparent. Leaders recognize that constituents do not generally support international regimes that are not cost-justified, and they act accordingly.

A related cost of treaty regimes is international noncompliance. State leaders are always uncertain about the information, preferences, and motivations of other states. As a result, they worry about other nations' noncompliance with norms and agreements. The noncompliance consideration, which takes us from ideal to nonideal theory on the international stage, counsels caution in embracing international regimes that involve national sacrifices *and* that depend for their efficacy on compliance by other states. Precisely this concern underlies political opposition in the United States not only to the Kyoto Accord, but also to the Test Ban Treaty, the Landmines Convention, and the Bio-Weapons Convention.

This last point is overlooked by the institutionalist strand in cosmopolitan theory. Even if individual citizens did face a collective action problem in acting on their cosmopolitan sentiments, national institutions cannot necessarily solve the collective action problem. Rather, their existence changes the level and nature of the collective action problem. Many cosmopolitan proposals require international cooperation. Information and power asymmetries, as well as the absence of a centralized enforcement mechanism, make international collective action problems difficult to overcome even when there is a plausible argument that the international regime, if successful, would enhance the welfare of every participating state.

These latter considerations—about intensity of preferences, interest group politics, voter misinformation, aggregation difficulties, and international collective action hurdles—require qualification of the earlier assumption that liberal democratic leaders are simply agents for voters.

When voters' anticosmopolitan preferences are clear, informed, intense, and unopposed, and when international collective action problems can be overcome, leaders can act as faithful agents. But often, the connection between voter preference and international political action is skewed and complicated. For the reasons already canvassed, these complexities can further raise the bar to cosmopolitan action.

The opposite may be true as well. Agency slack permits leaders to act with cosmopolitan charity beyond what constituents support. An important strand of democratic theory has always held that elected representatives should not be yoked to constituent preferences, especially when constituents are relatively uninformed. Leaders should exercise wisdom and judgment in deciding, subject to electoral recall, what is best for their constituents. They should lead, not follow. They should shape constituent preferences, perhaps to reflect their more cosmopolitan outlook. And their capacity to do so is enhanced by the fact that the public pays relatively little attention to foreign affairs.

This conception of the democratic process does not mean that the U.S. government could plausibly engage in more generous acts of cosmopolitan charity. Even political leaders with powerful cosmopolitan sentiments who are unworried about reelection hesitate to engage in costly altruistic acts abroad.

One reason leaders hesitate is that, whatever their personal sentiments, they have (and perceive themselves to have) a moral duty, in virtue of their election, their oath, and their identity, to promote the welfare of the state and its citizens. The more fluid conception of democracy described earlier gives leaders discretion to identify what furthers constituents' interests. It does not permit leaders to impose significant local sacrifices for the sake of nonnationals beyond what can be justified in terms of local welfare enhancement.

Persistent domestic institutional constraints also hinder attempts by leaders to commit acts of cosmopolitan charity that exceed constituent preferences. In the U.S. system, it is really the president, and not legislators, who has the discretion to skirt short-term constituent pressures in this way. The president has broad independent foreign relations powers and is not burdened by collective action problems to nearly the same degree as Congress is. And yet, the president cannot act too far beyond the wishes of Congress (or the voters). The president's unilateral discretion is probably at its height with respect to war. But in this context, the president is unambiguously accountable to the people, and, in any event, an uncooperative legislature can still retaliate via legislation, hearings, appointment hold-ups, defunding, and the like. With respect to international agreements, foreign aid, and most other international initiatives, the president's room for unilateral action is more limited because legislative participation, support, and funding are more directly relevant. In addition, any short-term, unilateral, non-welfare-enhancing action the president takes is reversible by the people and their representatives in the medium term.

This conclusion is consistent with political leaders having wide discretion to emphasize and act on what they believe enhances U.S. welfare, especially in the short term. For example, the Clinton and second Bush administrations interpreted and reacted differently to the Iraqi threat and took different attitudes toward the importance of particular treaty regimes. More broadly, current events are full of examples of liberal democratic leaders departing from apparent constituent foreign policy preferences in the name of promoting a state interest that leaders believe constituents do not fully appreciate. Nothing in our analysis suggests that these departures are illegitimate; only time and election returns will tell whether the leaders' assessment of voters' interests was correct. Our point is simply that the various mechanisms described earlier ensure that, at least in the medium term and often in the short term, cosmopolitan action by a liberal democracy is bounded by constituent preferences.

On Education and World Government

If there are strict plausibility constraints on cosmopolitan action by liberal democracies, one should hesitate before claiming that states have duties to engage in strong cosmopolitan action. "Can" limits "should." Just as morality can be too demanding of individuals, it can be too demanding of institutions. At the very least, the attribution of cosmopolitan duties to liberal democratic states requires careful consideration of voter sentiment and institutional reality.

Below we address two possible objections to this argument. The first is that voters could be educated to be more cosmopolitan, thereby making liberal democratic states more cosmopolitan. The second is that liberal democracy is not sacrosanct; alternative forms of governance may better serve the ends of international justice.

Education

One response to our argument is that individuals' uneven cosmopolitan sentiments are not sacrosanct. Through cosmopolitan education, citizens in democratic states could become more cosmopolitan-minded. Cosmopolitan education can teach individuals to be troubled by world inequality, to understand what is local and nonessential, and to have a greater sense of other cultures and peoples (Nussbaum 1996). Enhanced cosmopolitan sentiments among individuals will translate into enhanced cosmopolitan actions by their governments.

Similar education arguments, and related assumptions about human perfectibility, have characterized cosmopolitan thinking for centuries. Modern mass communication is the greatest possible educator about distant states, their cultures, and the suffering of their peoples. But despite daily reminders of human suffering around the globe, the peoples and states of the world have not acted in ways that are progressively more altruistic. In the midst of the global communication transformations during the post–cold war period (that is, CNN, the Internet, and the like), foreign aid as a percentage of GDP among the wealthiest states dropped precipitously even though these states enjoyed a "peace dividend" amounting to approximately $450 billion per year (Pogge 2002). Similarly, increased knowledge about suffering abroad during this period has not led to increased humanitarian interventions.

There are many reasons, in addition to the institutional points already made, why this might be so. Mass communication can in theory enhance sympathy for noncompatriots by increasing knowledge of their suffering. But this effect can be counteracted by increased knowledge of difference or of countervailing interests abroad (Niebuhr 1932). In addition, the spread of democracy during the past two hundred years may have weakened cosmopolitan sentiment among citizens in democratic states (compare Morgenthau 1948b). Many have argued that successful democracies demand a high degree of mutual commitment and solidarity that is inconsistent with strong cosmopolitan sentiment (Post 2000; Taylor 1996). The types of education appropriate for a liberal democratic culture thus may be in deep tension with Nussbaum's (1996) proposed cosmopolitan educational reforms.

One rejoinder to our skepticism about the transformative potential of education is that other liberal democracies are more cosmopolitan than the United States. To take a frequently invoked example, Sweden is held out as a state with a cosmopolitan citizenry that supports cosmopolitan action by its government. Sweden is among the world's leaders in foreign aid, and it actively supports international institutions. U.S. citizens, properly educated, might become more like the Swedes, and the U.S. government, in turn, might become more other-regarding in its actions. Implicit in this argument is the claim that we have confused the characteristics of liberal democracy in the United States with the characteristics of liberal democracy generally.

Swedes may well be more cosmopolitan than Americans; they certainly are a more homogeneous population and are traditionally more committed to social democracy. But there is little reason to believe that the Swedish government engages in greater cosmopolitan action than the U.S. government. Our earlier arguments suggest that the hurdles to cosmopolitan action in a liberal democracy are structural: that too much cosmopolitan sentiment among a citizenry is inconsistent with democratic statehood; that liberal democratic governments cannot act much beyond what citizens will support; and that liberal democratic processes create multiple hurdles to cosmopolitan action, even assuming individual cosmopolitan sentiments. The evidence from Sweden is consistent with these claims and suggests broader structural constraints on the transformative potential of cosmopolitan education.

Begin with humanitarian intervention. This is perhaps the best test, for, unlike foreign aid and certain treaty regimes, we can identify and eliminate mixed-motive cases. If anything, the traditionally neutral Swedes, and Europeans generally, are less cosmopolitan than Americans when it comes to humanitarian intervention. Since World War II, European voters have consistently demanded increases in spending on *domestic* social programs and decreases in spending on military programs. One result is that Europe's military capacity to intervene for humanitarian reasons has diminished significantly. Even when humanitarian interventions are militarily feasible and close to home, as in Bosnia and Kosovo in the 1990s, Europeans remained skittish and were disinclined to intervene (Kagan 2003).

As for foreign aid: Sweden is described as the "darling of the Third World" because of its generous foreign aid program (Schraeder, Hook, and Taylor 1998, 295). Sweden traditionally gives more aid than the United States as a percentage of GNP. But there is significant evidence that Swedish aid should not be interpreted as cosmopolitan action. First, although more extensive than most other countries, Swedish foreign aid is still less than 1 percent of its GNP. Moreover, this aid was cut in the decade following the end of the cold war, even though the era was marked by a general peace and a large peace dividend (United Nations Development Programme 2002). Taken alone, this suggests that aid was at least in part related to broader national security aims during this period.

In addition, Swedish foreign aid is limited to ideologically similar states that have significant trade relations with Sweden and where heavy Swedish political and business interests predominate (Laatikainen 1996). Although Swedish governments long repudiated any link between aid and economic self-interest, following the cold war (when the security element of aid had diminished), Sweden began to tie its aid explicitly to the purchase of Swedish goods and services or to favorable financing arrangements (Schraeder et al. 1998). Swedish foreign aid looks even less charitable when one considers that the country's domestic agricultural and textile subsidies and other nontariff barriers harm the welfare of poor agricultural states to a significant degree, possibly enough to offset the effect of its foreign aid (ActionAid 2002; see also Blomstrom 1990). None of this is to deny that many Swedes are motivated by humanitarianism (Lumsdaine 1993). It is just to point out the reasons why aid by the Swedish government should not be viewed as cosmopolitan action as we have used the term.

Sweden's foreign aid and other cosmopolitan-seeming actions must be viewed in the context of Sweden's status as a "middle power" (Pratt 1990). The label refers to states that exercise political and diplomatic power on the international stage through "soft" mechanisms like food aid, participation in international institutions, international civil service, and similar internationalist mechanisms. Middle powers show a greater devotion to international law and institutions than do more powerful nations, because they can exercise power abroad most effectively in this fashion. But here, as before, it is important not to confuse internationalism with cosmopolitanism. Middle powers by definition have relatively little unilateral influence in politico-military issues. They focus their diplomatic and related foreign affairs resources where they can exert the most influence, especially against the major powers (Keohane 1969). Their commitments to international institutions associated with cosmopolitan charity thus have a structural explanation wholly apart from cosmopolitan sentiment. The more general point is that the welfare of a state's citizens, and thus the structure of the state's foreign policy, varies depending on the power and stature of each state on the international stage. Sweden's internationalism is not the same as cosmopolitanism, in that it has a structural explanation consistent with the claim that democratic foreign policy must serve the welfare of local constituents.

Alternatives to Liberal Democracy

A second objection is that liberal democracy at the level of the state should not be viewed as sacrosanct. Cosmopolitan theorists are usually quick to deny any desire for "world government"; many are firmly committed to decentralized liberal democratic governance. But some cosmopolitan theorists propose an array of global democratic institutions to alleviate international social injustice (Pogge 1992; I. Young, 2000). These proposals share many common features, including a reverence for the United Nations and the aim of shifting sovereignty upward toward international institutions. Many believe that the proliferation of international institutions and the rise of the European Union evidence moves in the globalist direction.

There are obvious objections to these quasi–world government or global democracy proposals. First are the well-known normative difficulties with global governance schemes. The most obvious difficulty concerns the democratic deficit associated with ever-broadening governmental institutions. A related concern is that large-scale uniformity inherent in global governance schemes comes at the expense of too many unsatisfied individual preferences. Finally, there is the difficulty of human motivation and loyalty with respect to large, impersonal organizations (Nagel 1991).

Second is the practical problem of how to construct such institutions, assuming they are normatively desirable. We know of no global democracy approach that spells out how or why states, especially powerful states like the United States (or, for that matter, the EU), would submit to a broader form of genuine global governance. States enter into international institutions because they gain more than they lose from doing so. Most important and effective international institutions (most prominently, the World Trade Organization, the World Bank, and the International Monetary Fund) serve the interests of powerful nations, especially powerful Western nations, most especially the United States. Powerful states do not join institutions that do not serve their interests.

Successful governance in the domestic realm works differently from this purely instrumental conception of international governance. There are two distinguishing factors in the domestic realm: genuine communal sacrifices (whereby some members sacrifice interests for others) and centralized coercion (compare Carr 1946). Neither of these factors can work on a global scale. The standard proposal for international coercion is to strengthen the United Nations (for example, I. Young 2000). But the United Nations failed in its original ambition of having a freestanding police force, and it has failed to transcend the problem of enforcement ever since. Like all collective security schemes, the United Nations depends wholly on member states' self-interested (and thus uneven) acts for coercion. It is hard to see how or why militarily powerful states would ever agree to any other scheme.

As for community, there are natural limitations on the size of democratic government. The larger and more ambitious the government becomes, the more varied the governed population becomes (in endowment, culture, language, preferences, and the like) and the more difficult it becomes to maintain social harmony (Walzer 2000). The EU is often invoked as a counterexample, but the EU is more like the United States in the eighteenth century and Italy and Germany in the nineteenth: it reflects state building by smaller units with a common heritage and common interests. The EU example shows the difficulties that inhere in such a process even among subunit states that in many respects share a common culture and that have been unified in various ways over two millennia (for example, the Roman Empire, the Catholic Church, the Holy Roman Empire, and the Concert of Europe). It does not provide a map for global government of peoples of radically different cultures, histories, and endowments.

CONCLUSION

I nternational law is a real phenomenon, but international law scholars exaggerate its power and significance. We have argued that the best explanation for when and why states comply with international law is not that states have internalized international law, or have a habit of complying with it, or are drawn by its moral pull, but simply that states act out of self-interest.

Part 1 argued that customary international law can reflect genuine cooperation or coordination, though only between pairs of states or among small groups of states. Other times, customary international law may reflect self-interested state behavior that, through coercion, produces gains for one state and losses for another. Much of customary international law is simply coincidence of interest.

Cooperation and coordination by custom have natural limits. We showed in part 2 how treaties can help overcome some of these limits. They do so by clarifying the nature of the moves that will count as cooperative actions in repeated prisoner's dilemmas and as coordination in coordination games. Institutions associated with treaties—domestic ratification processes and the default rules of treaty interpretation—can also provide valuable information that promotes cooperation and coordination. Treaties can also reflect coercion and coincidence of interest, although in these contexts the presence of the treaty suggests that an apparent coercion or coincidence of interest situation has some cooperative element. Although treaties can foster cooperation and coordination more effectively than customary international law, there are still limits to what treaties can achieve—limits determined by the configuration of state interests, the distribution of state power, the logic of collective action, and asymmetric information. It follows that some global problems may simply be unsolvable. This is a depressing conclusion, but is consistent with all we know of human history.

International law rhetoric pervades international relations. For the same reasons that treaties can improve cooperation and coordination by clarifying what counts as cooperation and coordination, international law talk can as well. More often, international legal rhetoric is used to mask or rationalize behavior driven by self-interested factors that have nothing to do with international law. In part 3, we explained why states speak the language of obligation while following the logic of self-interest. We bolstered this claim by arguing that moral citizens would not hold that international law creates moral obligations, and that liberal democracies are unlikely to support a cosmopolitan foreign policy.

We have not exhausted the subject of international law. Some of our descriptive and empirical claims about customary international law and treaties are controversial and might turn out to be wrong or incomplete. It might turn out that there are robust customary international laws that solve multistate collective action problems; we have not found any, but other scholars might. Other scholars might also discover areas of treaty law that reflect significant multilateral cooperation; we have not, for example, studied environmental law or the laws of war, two of the most significant areas of international law. The empirical literature in these fields provides little evidence that treaties enable robust cooperation (see Barrett 2003 on environmental law, Glennon 2001 on the laws of war). But a firm conclusion must await more research.

While we thus have not written a comprehensive treatise on international law, we do hope that this book will help put international law and international law scholarship on a more solid foundation.

ACKNOWLEDGMENTS

This book has benefited from comments from many friends and colleagues, including Curtis Bradley, Rachel Brewster, Einer Elhauge, Ryan Goodman, Derek Jinks, Ehud Kamar, Daryl Levinson, Jide Nzelibe, Kal Raustiala, Paul Stephan, Lior Strahilevitz, Alan Sykes, Eric Talley, Ben Wittes, Tim Wu, John Yoo, and numerous anonymous readers. We also thank participants at workshops at the University of Chicago, the University of Southern California, Yale, and Harvard. We received helpful research assistance from Nicole Eitmann, Brian Fletcher, Wayne Hsiung, Brian Killian, Bill Martin, Michael Vermylen, and Lora Viola. Many other people, too numerous to mention, commented on drafts of articles that were subsequently incorporated in revised form into this book. These earlier articles are "A Theory of Customary International Law," 66 *University of Chicago Law Review* 1113 (1999); "Understanding the Resemblance between Modern and Traditional Customary International Law," 40 *Virginia Journal of International Law* 639 (2000); "Sovereignty, International Relations Theory, and International Law," 52 *Stanford Law Review* 959 (2000); "Moral and Legal Rhetoric in International Relations: A Rational Choice Perspective," 31 *Journal of Legal Studies* S115 (2002); "Liberal Democracy and Cosmopolitan Duty," 55 *Stanford Law Review* 1667 (2003); "Do States Have a Moral Obligation to Comply with International Law?" 55 *Stanford Law Review* 1901 (2003); and "International Agreements: A Rational Choice Approach," 44 *Virginia Journal of International Law* 113 (2003). These articles have been shortened for the book and have been revised in response to criticism and in light of the evolution of our thinking about international law. In addition, the book contains much new material.

We also thank deans John Jeffries, Elena Kagan, and Saul Levmore, as well as Chris Demuth at the American Enterprise Institute, and the Russell Baker Scholars Fund, for their generous support. Finally, we thank our editor, Dedi Felman, for her patience, good sense, and encouragement.

NOTES

Chapter 1

1. As we explain in chapter 3, treaties, unlike customary international law, can never reflect pure coincidence of interest.

2. Swaine (2002) argues that these factors can be overcome because states care about their reputation for complying with international law. We address this and other reputation-based arguments for compliance in part 2.

3. The model for such an argument would come from evolutionary game theory (see H. Young 1998, 25–90). This model shows that as long as parties either experiment or occasionally make errors, and as long as they interact frequently, they will eventually coordinate on Pareto-optimal actions. "Eventually," however, may be a very long time, and the games the model uses rely on institutional structure that is lacking with respect to customary international law. For an evolutionary approach to customary international law, see Chinen (2001).

4. For criticisms of our argument, see Swaine (2002), Chinen (2001), Guzman (2002a), and Norman and Trachtman (2004). Swaine, Guzman, and Norman and Trachtman offer rational choice theories of customary international law that could explain a more robust degree of cooperation; however, their stronger theories are not supported by the evidence of customary international law that we discuss in chapter 2.

Chapter 2

1. Some prize courts stated during and just after the war that free ships, free goods was a rule of customary international law. See, for example, *The Marie Glaeser* (1914, 53–54, dicta). But most of these cases read free ships, free goods

so narrowly as to render it practically a nullity. For example, the principle was limited to private enemy property; a belligerent could recover public enemy property on a neutral ship (see Colombos 1940, 170). Similarly, free ships, free goods did not prevent a belligerent from capturing enemy property on one of its own merchant ships (see id., 179), or from capturing enemy cargo loaded from an enemy to a neutral ship (see id., 162), or unloaded from a neutral ship (see *The Batavier II* 1917, 434). In addition, prize courts did not make captors liable for the destruction of goods on board neutral ships (Colombos and Higgins 1926, 106). By the middle of the war, even the pretense of judicial adherence to free ships, free goods had evaporated (see Jessup 1928, 44–47).

2. A perhaps more accurate game theoretic representation of diplomatic immunity is the battle of the sexes game. If state X knows that state Y will harm X's diplomat, X will want to protect Y's diplomat to keep communications open. If state Y knows that state X will harm Y's diplomat, Y will want to protect X's diplomat to keep communications open. Both of these outcomes are equilibria, but the more plausible outcome is a mixed-strategy equilibrium in which each state harms foreign diplomats with some probability p, and protects them with probability 1−p. In other words, one would observe occasional but not constant violations of diplomatic immunity, depending on the relative payoffs from violation and protection. To keep our analysis simple, we ignore these complications (without, we think, sacrificing much accuracy).

Chapter 3

1. The legalized approach can, of course, be preferred when one or even two of these conditions are not met. For example, when potential trading partners demand that the president be given fast-track authority prior to negotiations, they are in effect forgoing receipt of the information that a full-blown consent process would bring in order to more readily reach an agreement in a context where the executive and legislature often have divergent policy interests.

2. As we noted earlier, domestic constitutions sometimes provide for legalized international agreements to be made without legislative participation. In the United States, this happens with "sole" executive agreements, which are treaties (in the international sense) made on the president's authority alone. While sole executive agreements do not require legislative participation, they must be reported to Congress and thus made public, under the Case-Zablocki Act. If the president wants to keep the agreement with the other head of state as a secret, or wants to minimize publicity, he will prefer to

call it a nonlegal agreement. Also, because executive agreements are governed by international law, they benefit from the Vienna Convention default rules and from the convention concerning seriousness of commitment.

Chapter 4

1. This table was derived from four sources: (1) the most recent RUDs collection for the ICCPR that we could find, see www.hri.ca/fortherecord2003/documentation/reservations/ccpr.htm; (2) a United Nations collection of RUDs to the Covenant on Economic, Social and Cultural Rights, which also contains necessary information on RUDs to the ICCPR for some states, see www.unhchr.ch/html/menu3/b/treaty4_asp.htm; (3) the latest United Nations information we could find on ratification of the ICCPR, see www.unhchr.ch/pdf/report.pdf; and (4) a source indicating Swaziland's status as an ICCPR party, see web.amnesty.org/web/wire.nsf/June2004/Swaziland. All of these sources were last visited on August 16, 2004.

Counting reservations, understandings, and declarations (RUDs) is difficult and requires judgment calls. For this table, we counted only those RUDs that actually qualify state consent to the ICCPR. This means, for example, that we did not count the United States declaration that the ICCPR is nonself-executing. A more vexing problem is how to count a RUD that qualifies consent to two parts of one article in a treaty. Where the two references within the same article are closely related, or where qualifications to several articles are closely related, we conservatively count this as a single RUD. For example, Finland, Iceland, and other states reserve the right to ignore the juvenile segregation provisions in articles 10(2) and 10(3); we counted this as a single RUD. Similarly, many EU states qualify their acceptance of articles 19, 21, and 22 by stating that they accept only those portions that are not in conflict with European human rights treaties; again, this is treated as one RUD. In addition, when a state qualifies its consent without specific reference to a provision in the treaty, this is counted as a single RUD. This occurs, for example, when countries declare that ratification does not entail recognition of the state of Israel. Even with these guiding principles, some of our interpretations were, at the margins, difficult. Any disagreements at the margins, however, do not affect the overall pattern of the table, which clearly demonstrates that liberal states are much more inclined than nonliberal states to condition consent to the ICCPR with RUDs.

1. Measurement of nineteenth-century trade barriers founders on data limitations; in some cases, figures for trade openness are used as a proxy for trade barriers (see Pahre 2001, 32–35).

2. According to R. Gardner (1969, 20), U.S. policy opposed nontariff barriers because they lent themselves to discrimination; discrimination was regarded as the real evil, on which see below.

3. Schwartz and Sykes (1997) argue that the nondiscrimination rules reflect the desire to protect the gains from bargaining, while the various loopholes allow discrimination when the political power of domestic constituents makes it unavoidable. But, as they acknowledge, there is little reason to think the GATT rules strike the right balance among the multiple considerations.

4. There have been a little more than a hundred PTAs that were notified under Article XXIV, but there are many other bilateral agreements that arguably create a PTA but have not been notified.

5. As is well known, preferential trading areas cause trade diversion. State X imports goods from fellow PTA state Y rather than lower-cost goods from non-PTA state Z. The gains in trade among PTA members can in theory be less than the efficiency loss (Viner 1950). And as each PTA is created, the states that are excluded from the market have a stronger incentive to create their own PTAs, resulting in the discriminatory regime that the MFN provision of the GATT was intended to prohibit (Bhagwati 2002, 106–20).

6. At least, as originally conceived. Subsequently, states would unilaterally retaliate for violations of specific clauses (Hudec 1990, 199).

7. According to Robert Pahre's database on trade treaties, these treaties rarely included arbitration clauses, and it appears that the usual practice in the nineteenth century was not to arbitrate treaty violations but to renegotiate treaties through diplomatic channels. We thank him for letting us see his data, which are available at www.staff.uiuc.edu/~pahre.

8. There is a further question why a state would allow a tribunal to be created but then block enforcement. The most likely answer is that the tribunal's decision was significantly more adverse than what the state predicted, or else that protectionist pressures increased between the creation of the panel and the rendering of its judgment.

9. Indeed, his own regressions show no such anomaly once controls are introduced (his model II). Our own manipulations of the data, which he helpfully provides at his Web site (userwww.service.emory.edu/~erein/data/index .html), show that not all of his controls are necessary to make the anomaly disappear.

10. The agreement creating the WTO also greatly expanded substantive trade law to include intellectual property and certain services, but we are focusing on procedural innovations.

Chapter 6

1. Stephen Krasner is a modern realist who has a somewhat different account for moral and legal rhetoric. Krasner (1999) argues that in the international environment characterized by multiple, contradictory norms (such as human rights and state sovereignty) and no authoritative decison maker, leaders are driven by purely instrumental concerns but nonetheless pay lip service to international norms to appease their many different domestic and international constituents. Krasner believes that nations receive small instrumental benefits from rhetorical bows to international law and morality. But he fails to explain how or why such talk brings benefits, or why this talk would ever be believed (Goldsmith 2000). Nonetheless, we agree with Krasner that the gap between talk and action on the international plane demands explanation, and we seek to build on his work.

2. A loose example comes from the difficulties that the United States had during the cold war persuading black African nations that it would be a reliable ally. African nations, informed in part by the various humiliations endured by their diplomats on U.S. soil, probably believed that the United States would never be as loyal to them as to European nations, just because many U.S. citizens were obviously racist. The State Department spent a lot of time trying to persuade the African states that U.S. intentions were good, but the states regarded this as so much cheap talk. By contrast, the Civil Rights Act would have been regarded as a substantial signal, at least if foreign observers understood how U.S. institutions worked: a deeply racist nation does not give equal rights to minorities. It is striking that one of the main proponents of the Civil Rights Act in the executive branch was the State Department (see Layton 2000).

Chapter 7

1. On the fair play argument, see Rawls (1964). Rawls argues that individuals who are part of a common enterprise that produces benefits for all, and who accept their share of the benefits, have a duty to do their part in contributing to the enterprise. But it seems doubtful that the international system can be called such an enterprise. For criticisms in the domestic context, see A. Simmons (1979, 110–18), who argues that it is wrong to say that citizens in a

meaningful sense "accept" benefits from governments; a similar point can be made about states and the international order. A similar problem afflicts the effort to apply Rawls's (1971) natural duty of justice argument to the international sphere, where it is doubtful that one can say that international law is just when most people live in unjust states that are supported by that system. It is also hard to explain, as it is for domestic political obligation, why a person or state would have this duty.

REFERENCES

Abbott, Kenneth W. 1989. Modern International Relations Theory: A Prospectus for International Lawyers. *Yale Journal of International Law* 14: 335.

Abbott, Kenneth W., and Duncan Snidal. 1998. Why States Act through Formal International Organizations. *Journal of Conflict Resolution* 42: 3.

———. 2000. Hard and Soft Law in International Governance. *International Organization* 54: 421.

Abbott, Kenneth W., Robert O. Keohane, Andrew Moravcsik, Anne-Marie Slaughter, and Duncan Snidal. 2000. The Concept of Legalization. *International Organization* 54: 401.

ActionAid. 2002. *Farmgate: The Developmental Impact of Agricultural Subsidies.* London: ActionAid.

Akram, Tanweer. 2003. The International Foreign Aid Regime: Who Gets Foreign Aid and How Much? *Applied Economics* 35: 1351.

Arnold-Forster, W. 1942. *The New Freedom of the Seas.* London: Methuen.

Austen-Smith, David. 1992. Strategic Models of Talk in Political Decision Making. *International Political Science Review* 13: 45.

Ayres, Ian, and Robert Gertner. 1989. Filling Gaps in Incomplete Contracts: An Economic Theory of Default Rules. *Yale Law Journal* 99: 87.

Bagwell, Kyle, and Robert W. Staiger. 2002. *The Economics of the World Trading System.* Cambridge, Mass.: MIT Press.

Baird, Douglas G., Robert H. Gertner, and Randal C. Picker. 1992. *Game Theory and the Law.* Cambridge, Mass.: Harvard University Press.

Barrett, Scott. 2003. *Environment and Statecraft: The Strategy of Environmental Treaty-making.* New York: Oxford University Press.

Barry, Brian. 1999. Statism and Nationalism: A Cosmopolitan Critique. *Nomos* 41: 12.

Baty, Thomas. 1900. *International Law in South Africa.* London: Stevens and Haynes.

Baxter, James. 1928. The British Government and Neutral Rights, 1861–1865. *American Historical Review* 34: 9.

———. 1929. Some British Opinions as to Neutral Rights, 1861–1865. *American Journal of International Law* 23: 517.

Baxter, Richard R. 1980. International Law in "Her Infinite Variety." *International and Comparative Law Quarterly* 29: 549.

Bayefsky, Anne F. 2001. *The UN Human Rights Treaty System: Universality at the Crossroads.* Ardsley, N.Y.: Transnational Publishers.

Beitz, Charles R. 1979. *Political Theory and International Relations.* Princeton, N.J.: Princeton University Press.

Benton, Elbert J. 1908. *International Law and Diplomacy of the Spanish-American War.* Baltimore: Johns Hopkins University Press.

Bernath, Stuart L. 1970. *Squall across the Atlantic: American Civil War Prize Cases and Diplomacy.* Berkeley: University of California Press.

Bhagwati, Jagdish N. 2002. *Free Trade Today.* Princeton, N.J.: Princeton University Press.

Birkenhead, F. E., and N. W. Sibley. 1905. *International Law as Interpreted during the Russo-Japanese War.* Boston: Boston Book.

Blomstrom, Magnus. 1990. Sweden's Trade and Investment Policies vis-à-vis the Third World. In *The Other Side of International Development: Non-Aid Economic Relations with Developing Countries of Canada, Denmark, The Netherlands, Norway, and Sweden,* ed. Gerald K. Helleiner, 167. Toronto: University of Toronto Press.

Bowles, Thomas Gibson. 1900. *The Declaration of Paris of 1856.* London: Sampson Low.

Bown, Chad P. Forthcoming. On the Economic Success of GATT/WTO Dispute Settlement. *Review of Economics and Statistics.*

Bradley, Curtis A., and Jack L. Goldsmith. 1997a. The Current Illegitimacy of International Human Rights Litigation. *Fordham Law Review* 66: 319.

———. 1997b. Customary International Law as Federal Common Law: A Critique of the Modern Position. *Harvard Law Review* 110: 815.

Bray, F. E., and C. J. B. Hurst. 1913. *Russian and Japanese Prize Cases.* Buffalo, N.Y.: W. S. Hein.

Brierly, James Leslie. 1958. The Basis of Obligation in International Law. In *The Basis of Obligation in International Law,* ed. Sir Hersch Lauterpacht and C. H. M. Waldock, 1. Oxford: Clarendon Press.

———. 1963. *The Law of Nations: An Introduction to the International Law of Peace.* Oxford: Clarendon Press.

Brown, E. D. 1994. *The International Law of the Sea.* Volume 1. Brookfield, Vt.: Dartmouth University Press.

Brownlie, Ian. 1960. *Principles of Public International Law.* 4th edition. New York: Oxford University Press.

Buchanan, Allen, and David Golove. 2002. Philosophy of International Law. In *The Oxford Handbook of Jurisprudence and Philosophy of Law,* ed. Jules Coleman and Scott Shapiro, 838. New York: Oxford University Press.

Bueno de Mesquita, Bruce, and David Lalman. 1992. *War and Reason: Domestic and International Imperatives.* New Haven: Yale University Press.

Bull, Hedley. 1977. *The Anarchical Society: A Study of Order in World Politics.* New York: Columbia University Press.

Burk, James. 1999. Public Support for Peacekeeping in Lebanon and Somalia: Assessing the Casualties Hypothesis. *Political Science Quarterly* 114: 53.

Burley, Anne-Marie Slaughter. 1993. International Law and International Relations Theory: A Dual Agenda. *American Journal of International Law* 87: 205.

Busch, Marc L., and Eric Reinhardt. 2002. Testing International Trade Law: Empirical Studies of GATT/WTO Dispute Settlement. In *The Political Economy of International Trade Law: Essays in Honor of Robert E. Hudec,* ed. Daniel L. M. Kennedy and James D. Southwick, 457. Cambridge, England: Cambridge University Press.

———. 2003a. The Evolution of GATT/WTO Dispute Settlement. In *Trade Policy Research 2003,* ed. John M. Curtis and Dan Ciuriak, 143. Ottawa, Canada: Minister of Public Works and Government Services.

———. 2003b. Transatlantic Trade Conflicts and GATT/WTO Dispute Settlement. In *Transatlantic Trade Disputes: The EU, the US, and the WTO,* ed. Ernst-Ulrich Petersmann and Mark A. Pollack, 465. New York: Oxford University Press.

Bynkershoek, Cornelis van. 1923. *De Dominio Maris Dissertatio.* Trans. Ralph Van Deman Magoffin. Translation of 1744 edition. London: Oxford University Press.

Byrd-Hagel Resolution. 1997. S. Res. 98, 105th Cong.

Calvo, M. Charles. 1896. *Le Droit International Theoretique et Pratique.* Volume 1. 5th edition. Paris: A. Rousseau.

Campbell, Robert Granville. 1908. Neutral Rights and Obligations in the Anglo-Boer War. *Johns Hopkins University Studies in Historical and Political Science* 26: 153.

Carr, Edward Hallett. 1946. *The Twenty Years' Crisis 1919–1939: An Introduction to the Study of International Relations.* 2nd edition. London: Macmillan.

Carter, Barry E., Philip R. Trimble, and Curtis A. Bradley. 2003. *International Law.* 4th edition. New York: Aspen Law and Business.

Chalk, Frank, and Kurt Jonassohn. 1990. *The History and Sociology of Genocide: Analyses and Case Studies.* New Haven: Yale University Press.

Charney, Jonathan I. 1993. Universal International Law. *American Journal of International Law* 87: 529.

Charnovitz, Steve. 1997. Two Centuries of Participation: NGOs and International Governance. *Michigan Journal of International Law* 18: 183.

————. 2001. Rethinking WTO Trade Sanctions. *American Journal of International Law* 95: 792.

Chayes, Abram, and Antonia Handler Chayes. 1995. *The New Sovereignty: Compliance with International Regulatory Agreements.* Cambridge, Mass.: Harvard University Press.

Chicago Council on Foreign Relations. 2002. *Worldview 2002: American Public Opinion and Foreign Policy.* Chicago: Chicago Council on Foreign Relations.

Chinen, Mark A. 2001. Special Feature: Game Theory and Customary International Law: A Response to Professors Goldsmith and Posner. *Michigan Journal of International Law* 23: 143.

Churchill, Robin R., and Alan V. Lowe. 1983. *The Law of the Sea.* Dover, N.H.: Manchester University Press.

Clark, Bruce A. 1973. Recent Evolutionary Trends Concerning Naval Interdiction of Seaborne Commerce as a Viable Sanctioning Device. *JAG Journal* 27:160.

Cole, Harold L., and Patrick Kehoe. 1995. Default, Settlement and Signalling: Lending Resumption in a Reputational Model of Sovereign Debt. *International Economic Review* 36: 365.

Colombos, C. John. 1940. *A Treatise on the Law of Prize.* 2nd edition. London: Longmans.

————. 1962. *The International Law of the Sea.* 5th edition. London: Longmans.

Colombos, C. John, and Alexander Higgins. 1926. *A Treatise on the Law of Prize.* London: Sweet and Maxwell.

Conybeare, John A. C. 1987. *Trade Wars: The Theory and Practice of International Commercial Rivalry.* New York: Columbia University Press.

Coogan, John W. 1981. *The End of Neutrality: The United States, Britain and Maritime Rights 1899–1915.* Ithaca, N.Y.: Cornell University Press.

Crawford, Vincent, and Joel Sobel. 1982. Strategic Information Transmission. *Econometrica* 50: 1431.

Dam, Kenneth W. 1970. *The GATT: Law and International Economic Organization.* Chicago: University of Chicago Press.

D'Amato, Anthony A. 1971. *The Concept of Custom in International Law.* Ithaca, N.Y.: Cornell University Press.

Damrosch, Lori F., Louis Henkin, Richard Crawford Pugh, Oscar Schachter, and Hans Smith. 2001. *International Law: Cases and Materials.* 4th edition. St. Paul, Minn.: West.

Davey, William. 1987. Dispute Settlement in GATT. *Fordham International Law Journal* 11: 51.

Downs, George W., and Michael A. Jones. 2002. Reputation, Compliance, and International Law. *Journal of Legal Studies* 31: S95.

Downs, George W., and David M. Rocke. 1995. *Optimal Imperfection? Domestic Uncertainty and Institutions in International Relations.* Princeton, N.J.: Princeton University Press.

Downs, George W., David Rocke, and Peter N. Barsoom. 1996. Is the Good News about Compliance Good News for Cooperation? *International Organization* 50: 379.

Doyle, Michael W. 1983. Kant, Liberal Legacies, and Foreign Affairs. *Philosophy and Public Affairs* 12: 205.

Dunhoff, Jeffrey L., and Joel Trachtman. 1999. Economic Analysis of International Law: Microanalysis of Macro-Institutions. *Yale Journal of International Law* 24: 1.

Economist. 1980a. How to Be a Good Ally without Putting Oneself Out. April 19.

―――. 1980b. Iranian Sanctions: Scarcely Worth Bothering to Bust. June 7.

Elster, Jon. 1989. Social Norms and Economic Theory. *Journal of Economic Perspectives* 3: 99.

Farrell, Joseph, and Robert Gibbons. 1989. Cheap Talk with Two Audiences. *American Economic Review* 79: 1214.

Fearon, James D. 1994. Domestic Political Audiences and the Escalation of International Disputes. *American Political Science Review* 88: 577.

Fenwick, Charles G. 1948. *International Law.* 3rd edition. New York: Appleton.

Fidler, David P. 1996. Challenging the Classical Concept of Custom: Perspectives on the Future of Customary International Law. *German Year Book of International Law* 39: 198.

―――. 2001. International Human Rights Law in Practice: The Return of the Standard of Civilization. *Chicago Journal of International Law* 2: 137.

Filartiga v. Pena-Irala. 1980. 630 F2d 876. 2d Cir.

Finnemore, Martha. 1996. *National Interests in International Society.* Ithaca, N.Y.: Cornell University Press.

First National City Bank v. Banca Para El Comericio Exterior de Cuba. 1983. 462 U.S. 611.

Fisch, Jörg. 2000. The Role of International Law in the Territorial Expansion of Europe, 16th–20th Centuries. *ICCLP Review* 3: 5.

Fox, Gregory H. 1992. The Right to Political Participation in International Law. *Yale Journal of International Law* 17: 539.

Fox, Gregory H., and Brad R. Roth. 2000. Introduction: The Spread of Liberal Democracy and Its Implications for International Law. In *Democratic Governance and International Law,* ed. Gregory H. Fox and Brad R. Roth, 1. Cambridge, England: Cambridge University Press.

Franck, Thomas M. 1990. *The Power of Legitimacy among Nations.* New York: Oxford University Press.

―――. 1992. The Emerging Right to Democratic Governance. *American Journal of International Law* 86: 46.

―――. 1995. *Fairness in International Law and Institutions.* New York: Oxford University Press.

Frey, Linda S., and Marsha L. Frey. 1999. *The History of Diplomatic Immunity.* Columbus: Ohio State University Press.

Fuller, Lon. 1944. Consideration and Form. *Columbia Law Review* 41: 799.

Fulton, Thomas Wemyss. 1911. *The Sovereignty of the Sea.* London: Blackwood.

Gabcikovo-Nagymaros (Hungary v. Slovakia). 1997. I.C.J. 1 (Sept. 25).

Gardner, James. 1920. *International Law and the World War.* New York: Longman, Green.

————. 1927. *Prize Law during the World War.* New York: Macmillan.

Gardner, Richard N. 1969. *Sterling-Dollar Diplomacy.* Oxford: Clarendon Press.

Garrett, Geoffrey, and Barry R. Weingast. 1993. Ideas, Interests, and Institutions: Constructing the European Community's Internal Market. In *Ideas and Foreign Policy: Beliefs, Institutions, and Political Change,* ed. Judith Goldstein and Robert O. Keohane, 173. Ithaca, N.Y.: Cornell University Press.

Gibbons, Robert. 1992. *Game Theory for Applied Economists.* Princeton, N.J.: Princeton University Press.

Ginsburgs, George. 1958. A Case Study in the Soviet Use of International Law: Eastern Poland. *American Journal of International Law* 52: 69.

Glennon, Michael J. 2001. *Limits of War, Prerogatives of Power: Interventionism after Kosovo.* New York: Palgrave.

Goldsmith, Jack L. 2000. Sovereignty, International Relations Theory, and International Law. *Stanford Law Review* 52: 959.

————. 2003. Liberal Democracy and Cosmopolitan Duty. *Stanford Law Review* 55: 1667.

Goldstein, Judith, Miles Kahler, Robert O. Keohane, and Anne-Marie Slaughter. 2000. Legalization and World Politics. *International Organization* 54: 3.

Gong, Gerrit W. 1984. *The Standard of "Civilization" in International Society.* Oxford: Clarendon Press.

Goodman, Ryan, and Derek Jinks. 2003. Measuring the Effects of Human Rights Treaties. *European Journal of International Law* 14: 171.

————. 2004. How to Influence States: Socialization and International Human Rights Law. Unpublished manuscript.

Green, Michael J. 2002. Institutional Responsibility for Global Problems. *Philosophical Topics* 30: 79.

Greenawalt, Kent. 1987. *Conflicts of Law and Morality.* New York: Oxford University Press.

Grewe, Wilhelm Georg. 2000. *The Epochs of International Law.* Trans. Michael Byers. Berlin: Walter de Gruyter.

Grieco, Joseph M. 1990. *Cooperation among Nations: Europe, America, and Nontariff Barriers.* Ithaca, N.Y.: Cornell University Press.

Gruber, Lloyd. 2000. *Ruling the World: Power Politics and the Rise of Supranational Institutions.* Princeton, N.J.: Princeton University Press.

Grundy, G. B. 1948. *Thucydides and the History of His Age*. Oxford: B. Blackwell.

Guisinger, Alexander, and Alastair Smith. 2001. Honest Threats: The Interaction of Reputation and Political Institutions in International Crises. Unpublished manuscript.

Guzman, Andrew. 2002a. A Compliance-Based Theory of International Law. *California Law Review* 90: 1823.

———. 2002b. The Cost of Credibility: Explaining Resistance to Interstate Dispute Resolution Mechanisms. *Journal of Legal Studies* 31: 303.

———. 2002c. Global Governance and the WTO. *UC Berkeley Public Law and Legal Theory Research Paper* No. 89.

Hall, William Edward. 1924. *A Treatise on International Law*. 8th edition. Oxford: Clarendon Press.

Hart, H. L. A. 1961. *The Concept of Law*. Oxford: Clarendon Press.

Hart, Michael M., and Debra P. Steger, eds. 1992. *In Whose Interest? Due Process and Transparency in International Trade*. Ottawa, Canada: Centre for Trade Policy and Law.

Hathaway, Oona. 2002. Do Human Rights Treaties Make a Difference? *Yale Law Journal* 111: 1935.

———. 2003a. Testing Conventional Wisdom. *European Journal of International Law* 14: 185.

———. 2003b. The Cost of Commitment. *Stanford Law Review* 55: 1821.

Hattendorf, John B. 1994. Maritime Conflict. In *The Laws of War: Constraints on Warfare in the Western World*, ed. Michael Howard et al., 98. New Haven: Yale University Press.

Heinzen, Bernard G. 1959. The Three-Mile Limit: Preserving the Freedom of the Seas. *Stanford Law Review* 11: 597.

Helfer, Laurence R. 2002. Overlegalizing Human Rights: International Relations Theory and the Commonwealth Caribbean Backlash against Human Rights Regimes. *Columbia Law Review* 102: 1832.

Helfer, Laurence R., and Anne-Marie Slaughter. 1997. Toward a Theory of Effective Supranational Adjudication. *Yale Law Journal* 107: 273.

Henkin, Louis. 1979. *How Nations Behave*. 2nd edition. New York: Columbia University Press.

———. 1995. *International Law: Politics and Values*. Dordrecht, The Netherlands: M. Nijhoff.

———. 1999. Kosovo and the Law of "Humanitarian Intervention." *American Journal of International Law* 93: 824.

Hochschild, Adam. 1999. *King Leopold's Ghost: A Story of Greed, Terror, and Heroism in Colonial Africa*. Boston: Houghton Mifflin.

Howard, Michael. 1962. *The Franco-Prussian War: The German Invasion of France 1870–71*. New York: Macmillan.

————. 1976. *War in European History*. New York: Oxford University Press.

Howe, Anthony. 1997. *Free Trade and Liberal England, 1846–1946*. Oxford: Clarendon Press.

Hudec, Robert E. 1990. *The GATT Legal System and World Trade Diplomacy*. 2nd edition. Salem, N.H.: Butterworth Legal Publishers.

————. 1993. *Enforcing International Trade Law: The Evolution of the Modern GATT Legal System*. Salem, N.H.: Butterworth Legal Publishers.

Hume, David. 1978. *A Treatise of Human Nature*. New York: Oxford University Press.

Hyde, Charles Cheney. 1922. *International Law, Chiefly as Interpreted and Applied by the United States*. Volume 1. Boston: Little, Brown.

Iida, Keisuke. 1993. When and How Do Domestic Constraints Matter? *Journal of Conflict Resolution* 37: 403.

Jackson, John H. 1969. *World Trade and the Law of GATT*. Indianapolis: Bobbs-Merrill.

————. 2000. *The Jurisprudence of GATT and the WTO: Insights on Treaty Law and Economic Relations*. Cambridge, England: Cambridge University Press, 2000.

Janis, Mark W. 2003. *An Introduction to International Law*. 4th edition. New York: Aspen.

Janis, Mark W., and John G. Noyes. 1997. *Cases and Commentary on International Law*. St. Paul, Minn.: West.

Jefferson, Thomas. 1958. Letter of Sept. 6, 1789, to James Madison. In *The Papers of Thomas Jefferson*, ed. Julian Boyd, volume 15, 392. Princeton, N.J.: Princeton University Press.

Jessup, Philip C. 1927. *The Law of Territorial Waters and Maritime Jurisdiction*. New York: G. A. Jennings.

————. 1928. *American Neutrality and International Police*. Boston: World Peace Foundation.

Jones, A. H. M. 1957. *Athenian Democracy*. Baltimore: Johns Hopkins University Press.

Kagan, Robert. 2003. *Of Paradise and Power: America and Europe in the New World Order*. New York: Knopf.

Kandori, Michihiro. 1992. Social Norms and Community Enforcement. *Review of Economic Studies* 59: 63.

Kant, Immanuel. [1795] 1983. To Perpetual Peace. In *Perpetual Peace and Other Essays on Politics, History, and Morals*. Trans. Ted Humphrey, 341. Indianapolis: Hackett.

Kaufmann, Chaim D., and Robert A. Pape. 1999. Explaining Costly International Moral Acts: Britain's Sixty-Year Campaign against the Atlantic Slave Trade. *International Organization* 53: 631.

Keith, Linda Camp. 1999. The United Nations International Covenant on Civil and Political Rights: Does It Make a Difference in Human Rights Behavior? *Journal of Peace Research* 36: 95.

Kennan, George F. 1996. American Democracy and Foreign Policy. In *At a Century's Ending: Reflections 1982–1995*, 127. New York: Norton.

Kennedy, Paul. 1989. *The Rise and Fall of the Great Powers.* New York: Vintage Books.

Keohane, Robert O. 1969. Lilliputians' Dilemmas: Small States in International Politics. *International Organization* 23: 291.

———. 1984. *After Hegemony.* Princeton, N.J.: Princeton University Press.

———. 1997. International Relations and International Law: Two Optics. *Harvard International Law Journal* 38: 487.

Kindleberger, C. P. 1975. The Rise of Free Trade in Western Europe, 1820–1875. *Journal of Economic History* 35: 20.

Koh, Harald Hongju. 1997. Why Do Nations Obey International Law? *Yale Law Journal* 106: 2599.

Koremenos, Barbara, Charles Lipson, and Duncan Snidal. 2001. The Rational Design of International Institutions. *International Organization* 55: 761.

Kovenock, Daniel, and Marie Thursby. 1992. GATT, Dispute Settlement, and Cooperation. *Economics and Politics* 4: 151.

Krasner, Stephen, ed. 1983. *International Regimes.* Ithaca, N.Y.: Cornell University Press.

———. 1991. Global Communications and National Power: Life on the Pareto Frontier. *World Politics* 43: 336.

———. 1999. *Sovereignty: Organized Hypocrisy.* Princeton, N.J.: Princeton University Press.

Kratochwil, Friedrich. 1989. *Rules, Norms and Decisions: On the Conditions of Practical and Legal Reasoning in International Relations and Domestic Affairs.* Cambridge, England: Cambridge University Press.

Kreps, David, and Robert Wilson. 1982. Reputation and Imperfect Information. *Journal of Economic Theory* 27: 253.

Kutz, Christopher. 2000. *Complicity: Ethics and Law for a Collective Age.* Cambridge, England: Cambridge University Press.

La Nostra Señora de la Piedad. 1801. 25 Merlin, Jurisprudence, Prise Maritime § 3, arts. 1, 3 (5th ed. 1827).

Laatikainen, Katie. 1996. The Disillusionment of Nordic Aid. In *Foreign Aid toward the Millennium*, ed. Steven W. Hook, 109. Boulder, Colo.: Lynne Rienner.

Lake, David A., and Robert Powell. 1999. *Strategic Choice and International Relations.* Princeton, N.J.: Princeton University Press.

Law Journal. 1929. Diplomatic Immunity and the Criminal Law. 68: 226.

Layton, Azza Alama. 2000. *International Politics and Civil Rights Policies in the United States, 1941–1960.* New York: Cambridge University Press.

Letter from Senator Jesse Helms, Ranking Member, and Joseph R. Biden Jr., Chairman, Senate Committee on Foreign Relations, to The Honorable Colin L. Powell, Secretary of State. 2002. (Mar. 15). Available at www.arms controlcenter.org/2002summit/a7.html.

Levy, Jack S. 1997. Prospect Theory, Rational Choice, and International Relations. *International Studies Quarterly* 41: 87.

Lewis, H. D. 1991. Collective Responsibility (A Critique). In *Collective Responsibility: Five Decades of Debate in Theoretical and Applied Ethics,* ed. Larry May and Stacey Hoffman, 17. Savage, Md.: Rowman and Littlefield.

Lichtenberg, Judith. 1981. National Boundaries and Moral Boundaries: A Cosmopolitan View. In *Boundaries: National Autonomy and Its Limits,* ed. Peter G. Brown and Henry Shue, 79. Towtowa, N.J.: Rowman and Littlefield.

Lipson, Charles. 1991. Why Are Some International Agreements Informal? *International Organization* 45: 495.

———. 2003. *Reliable Partners: How Democracies Have Made a Separate Peace.* Princeton, N.J.: Princeton University Press.

Lloyd, C. C. 1975. Armed Forces and the Art of War: Navies. In *The New Cambridge Modern History: War and Peace in an Age of Upheaval, 1793–1830,* ed. C. W. Crawley, 76. Cambridge, England: Cambridge University Press.

Long, Olivier. 1985. *Law and Its Limitations in the GATT Multilateral Trade System.* Boston: M. Nijhoff.

Luban, David. 2002. Intervention and Civilization: Some Unhappy Lessons of the Kosovo War. In *Global Justice and Transnational Politics: Essays on the Moral and Political Challenges of Globalization,* ed. Pablo De Greiff and Ciaran Cronin, 79. Cambridge, Mass.: MIT Press.

Lumsdaine, David Halloran. 1993. *Moral Vision in International Politics: The Foreign Aid Regime, 1949–1989.* Princeton, N.J.: Princeton University Press.

Lutz, Ellen L., and Kathryn Sikkink. 2000. International Human Rights Law and Practice in Latin America. *International Organization* 54: 633.

Maggi, Giovanni. 1999. The Role of Multilateral Institutions in International Trade Cooperation. *American Economic Review* 89: 190.

Mansfield, Edward D., and Marc L. Busch. 2000. The Political Economy of Nontariff Barriers: A Cross-national Analysis. In *International Political Economy: Perspectives on Global Power and Wealth,* ed. Jeffry A. Frieden and David A. Lake, 353. Boston, Mass.: Bedford/St. Martin's.

Mansfield, Edward, and Eric Reinhardt. 2003. Multilateral Determinants of Regionalism: The Effects of GATT/WTO on the Formation of Preferential Trading Arrangements. *International Organization,* 57: 829.

Marks, Frederick W., III. 1973. *Independence on Trial: Foreign Affairs and the Making of the Constitution.* Baton Rouge: Louisiana State University Press.

Marshall, John. [1819] 1969. "A Friend of the Constitution" Essays. In *John Mar-*

shall's Defense of McCulloch v. Maryland, ed. Gerald Gunther, 155. Stanford: Stanford University Press.

Martin, Lisa. 1992. *Coercive Cooperation: Explaining Multilateral Economic Sanctions.* Princeton, N.J.: Princeton University Press.

———. 1993. Credibility, Costs, and Institutions: Cooperation on Economic Sanctions. *World Politics* 45: 406.

———. 2000. *Democratic Commitments: Legislatures and International Cooperation.* Princeton, N.J.: Princeton University Press.

Maxwell, Mary. 1990. *Morality among Nations: An Evolutionary View.* Albany: State University of New York Press.

McClanahan, Grant V. 1989. *Diplomatic Immunity: Principles, Practices, Problems.* New York: St Martin's.

McDermott, Rose. 1998. *Risk-Taking in International Politics: Prospect Theory in American Foreign Policy.* Ann Arbor: University of Michigan Press.

McGillivray, Fiona, and Alastair Smith. 1999. Cooperating Democrats, Defecting Autocrats. Unpublished manuscript. Yale University.

McGinnis, John O., and Mark L. Movsesian. 2000. The World Trade Constitution. *Harvard Law Review* 114: 511.

McKinley, President William. [1898] 1917. A Proclamation, Apr. 26, 1898. In *A Compilation of the Messages and Papers of the Presidents,* ed. James D. Richardson, 6474. Volume 15. New York: Bureau of National Literature.

Mearsheimer, John. 2001. *The Tragedy of Great Power Politics.* New York: Norton.

Mercer, Jonathan. 1996. *Reputation and International Politics.* Princeton, N.J.: Princeton University Press.

Military and Paramilitary Activities in and against Nicaragua (Nicar. v. U.S.). 1986. I.C.J. 14 (June 27).

Miller, David. 1995. *On Nationality.* New York: Clarendon Press.

Milner, Helen V., and B. Peter Rosendorff. 1997. Democratic Politics and International Trade Negotiations. *Journal of Conflict Resolution* 41: 117.

Moore, John Bassett. 1906. *A Digest of International Law.* Volume 7. Washington, D.C.: Government Printing Office.

Moravcsik, Andrew. 1995. Explaining International Human Rights Regimes: Liberal Theory and Western Europe. *European Journal of International Relations* 1: 157.

———. 2000. The Origins of Human Rights Regimes. *International Organization* 54: 217.

Morgenthau, Hans. 1948a. *Politics among Nations: The Struggle for Power and Peace.* New York: Knopf.

———. 1948b. The Twilight of International Morality. *Ethics* 58: 79.

———. 1951. *In Defense of the National Interest.* New York: Knopf.

Morrow, James D. 1994a. *Game Theory for Political Scientists.* Princeton, N.J.: Princeton University Press.

————. 1994b. Modeling the Forms of International Cooperation: Distribution versus Information. *International Organization* 48: 387.

Murphy, Liam B. 2000. *Moral Demands in Nonideal Theory.* New York: Oxford University Press.

Murphy, Sean D. 1996. *Humanitarian Intervention: The United Nations in an Evolving World Order.* Philadelphia: University of Pennsylvania Press.

Nagel, Thomas. 1991. *Equality and Partiality.* New York: Oxford University Press.

Niebuhr, Reinhold. 1932. *Moral Man and Immoral Society: A Study in Ethics and Politics.* New York: Scribner.

Norman, George, and Joel P. Trachtman. 2004. The Customary International Law Supergame: Order and Law. Unpublished manuscript.

Nussbaum, Martha Craven. 1996. Patriotism and Cosmoplitanism. In *For Love of Country: Debating the Limits of Patriotism,* ed. Joshua Cohen and Martha Craven Nussbaum. Boston: Beacon Press.

Ogdon, Montell. 1936. *Juridical Bases of Diplomatic Immunity: A Study in the Origin, Growth and Purpose of the Law.* Washington, D.C.: John Byrne.

Oppenheim, L. 1912. *International Law.* Volume 1. London: Longmans, Green.

O'Rourke, Sister Mary Martinice. 1963. The Diplomacy of William H. Seward during the Civil War: His Policies as Related to International Law. Unpublished Ph.D. dissertation. University of California, Berkeley.

Owlsey, Frank L. 1935. America and the Freedom of the Seas, 1861–1865. In *Essays in Honor of William E. Dodd,* ed. Avery Craven, 194. Chicago: University of Chicago Press.

Oye, Kenneth A., ed. 1986. *Cooperation under Anarchy.* Princeton, N.J.: Princeton University Press.

Page, Benjamin I., and Jason Barabas. 2000. Foreign Policy Gaps between Citizens and Leaders. *International Studies Quarterly* 44: 339.

Pahre, Robert. 2001. Agreeable Duties. In *International Trade and Political Institutions: Instituting Trade in the Long Nineteenth Century,* ed. Fiona McGillivray et al., 29. Northampton, Mass.: Edward Elgar.

————. 2003. Agreeable Customs: The Politics of Trade Cooperation. Unpublished manuscript.

Phillimore, Sir Robert. 1879. *Commentaries upon International Law.* Volume 1. 3rd edition. London: Butterworths.

Phillips, W. Alison, et al. 1936. *Neutrality: Its History, Economics, and Law,* Volume 2: *The Napoleonic Period.* New York: Columbia University Press.

Pierce, President Franklin. [1856] 1897. Fourth Annual Message (Dec. 2, 1856). In *A Compilation of the Messages and Papers of the Presidents, 1789–1897,* ed. James D. Richardson, 397. Washington, D.C.: Government Printing Office.

Piliavin, Jane Allyn, and Hong-Wen Chang. 1990. Altruism: A Review of Recent Theory and Research. *Annual Review of Sociology* 16: 27.

Poe, Steven. 2004. The Decision to Repress: An Integrative Theoretical Approach to the Research on Human Rights and Repression. In *Understanding Human Rights Violations: New Systematic Studies*, ed. Sabine C. Carey and Steven C. Poe, 16. Aldershot, England: Ashgate.

Poe, Steven C., and C. Neal Tate. 1994. Repression of Human Rights to Personal Integrity in the 1980s: A Global Analysis. *American Political Science Review* 88: 853.

Pogge, Thomas W. 1992. Cosmopolitanism and Sovereignty. *Ethics* 103: 48.

———. 2002. *World Poverty and Human Rights: Cosmopolitan Responsibilities and Reforms*. Cambridge, England: Blackwell.

Posner, Eric A. 2003. A Theory of the Laws of War. *University of Chicago Law Review* 70: 297.

———. 2004. International Law and the Disaggregated State. Unpublished manuscript.

Posner, Eric A., and John Yoo. 2004. A Theory of International Adjudication. Unpublished manuscript.

Post, Robert. 2000. Between Philosophy and Law: Sovereignty and the Design of Democratic Institutions. *Nomos* 42: 209.

Power, Samantha. 2002. *"A Problem from Hell": America and the Age of Genocide*. New York: Basic Books.

Pratt, Cranford, ed. 1990. *Middle Power Internationalism: The North-South Dimension*. Kingston, Canada: McGill-Queen's University Press.

Princz v. Federal Republic of Germany. 1994. 26 F.3d 1166 (D.C. Circuit).

Putnam, Robert D. 1988. Diplomacy and Domestic Politics: The Logic of Two-level Games. *International Organization* 42: 427.

Quigley, Harold Scott. 1917. The Immunity of Private Property from Capture at Sea. *American Journal of International Law* 11: 22.

Randall, H. J. 1908. History of Contraband of War. *Law Quarterly Review* 24: 449.

Raustiala, Kal. 2003. Form and Substance in International Agreements. Unpublished manuscript.

Raustiala, Kal, and Anne-Marie Slaughter. 2002. International Law, International Relations and Compliance. In *Handbook of International Relations*, ed. Walter Carlsnaes, Thomas Risse, and Beth A. Simmons, 538. London: Sage.

Rawls, John. 1964. Legal Obligation and the Duty of Fair Play. In *Law and Philosophy*, ed. Sidney Hook. New York: New York University Press.

———. 1971. *A Theory of Justice*. Cambridge, Mass.: Harvard University Press.

Ray, Edward John. 1991. Changing Patterns of Protectionism: The Fall in Tariffs and the Rise in Nontariff Barriers. In *International Political Economy: Perspectives on Global Power and Wealth*, ed. Jeffry A. Frieden and David A. Lake, 338. 2nd edition. New York: St. Martin's.

Raz, Joseph. 1987. Government by Consent. *Nomos* 29: 76.

Regina v. Bartle. 1999. 2 W.L.R. 827, 38 I.L.M. 581.

Reilly, John E., ed. 1999. *American Public Opinion and U.S. Foreign Policy*. Chicago: Chicago Council on Foreign Relations.

Reinhardt, Eric. 2001. Adjudication without Enforcement in GATT Disputes. *Journal of Conflict Resolution* 45: 174.

———. 2003. To GATT or Not to GATT: Which Trade Disputes Does the U.S. Litigate, 1975–1999? Unpublished manuscript.

Reservations to the Convention on the Prevention and Punishment of the Crime of Genocide, Advisory Opinion. 1951. I.C.J. 15 (May 28).

Restatement (Third) of Foreign Relations Law. 1987. Philadelphia: The American Law Institute.

Rich, Norman. 1973. *Hitler's War Aims: Ideology, the Nazi State, and the Course of Expansion*. New York: Norton.

Riesenfeld, Stefan A. 1942. *Protection of Coastal Fisheries under International Law*. Washington, D.C.: Carnegie Endowment for International Peace.

Risse, Thomas. 2000. "Let's Argue": Communicative Action in World Politics. *International Organization* 54: 1.

Risse, Thomas, and Kathryn Sikkink. 1999. The Socialization of International Human Rights Norms into Domestic Practices: Introduction. In *The Power of Human Rights: International Norms and Domestic Change*, ed. Thomas Risse, Steve Ropp, and Kathryn Sikkink, 1. Cambridge, England: Cambridge University Press.

Rogers, John. 1999. *International Law and United States Law*. Brookfield, Vt.: Dartmouth University Press.

Rogowski, Ronald. 1989. *Commerce and Coalitions: How Trade Affects Domestic Political Arrangements*. Princeton, N.J.: Princeton University Press.

RoperASW. 2002. *Americans' Attitudes toward an International Criminal Court*. New York: RoperASW.

Russett, Bruce. 1993. *Grasping the Democratic Peace: Principles for a Post–Cold War World*. Princeton, N.J.: Princeton University Press.

Sandler, Todd, and Keith Hartley. 2001. Economics of Alliances: The Lessons for Collective Action. *Journal of Economic Literature* 39: 869.

Sartori, Anne. 1999. The Might of the Pen: A Contribution to the Theory of Diplomacy. Unpublished manuscript.

Satow, Sir Ernest. 1957. *A Guide to Diplomatic Practice*. 4th edition. London: Longmans.

Savage, Carlton. 1934. *Policy of the United States toward Maritime Commerce in War*. Volume 1. Washington, D.C.: Government Printing Office.

Schachter, Oscar. 1968. Towards a Theory of International Obligation. *Virginia Journal of International Law* 8: 300.

Schelling, Thomas C. 1963. *The Strategy of Conflict*. Cambridge, Mass.: Harvard University Press.

Schmitz, Hans Peter. 1999. Transnational Activism and Political Change in Kenya and Uganda. In *The Power of Human Rights: International Norms and Domestic Change,* ed. Thomas Risse, Steve Ropp, and Kathryn Sikkink, 39. Cambridge, England: Cambridge University Press.

Schraeder, Peter J., Stephen W. Hook, and Bruce Taylor. 1998. Clarifying the Foreign Aid Puzzle: A Comparison of American, Japanese, French, and Swedish Aid Flows. *World Politics* 50: 294.

Schultz, Kenneth A. 1998. Domestic Opposition and Signaling in International Crises. *American Political Science Review* 92: 829.

Schwartz, Warren F., and Alan O. Sykes. 1997. The Economics of the Most Favored Nation Clause. In *Economic Dimensions in International Law: Comparative and Empirical Perspectives,* ed. Jagdeep S. Bandari and Alan O. Sykes, 43. New York: Cambridge University Press.

Schwarzenberger, Georg. 1955. The Standard of Civilisation in International Law. *Current Legal Problems* 8: 212.

Scott, James Brown, ed. 1921. *The Proceedings of the Hague Peace Convention of 1907.* Volume 3. New York: Oxford University Press.

Setear, John K. 1996. An Iterative Perspective on Treaties: A Synthesis of International Relations Theory and International Law. *Harvard International Law Journal* 37: 139.

Seward, William H. [1861] 1965. Correspondence Circular (Apr. 24). In *Papers Relating to Foreign Affairs, Accompanying the Annual Message of the President to the Second Session of the Thirty-Seventh Congress,* ed. U.S. Department of State, 34. Washington, D.C.: Government Printing Office.

Simmons, A. John. 1979. *Moral Principles and Political Obligations.* Princeton, N.J.: Princeton University Press.

Singer, Peter. 1972. Famine, Affluence, and Morality. *Philosophy and Public Affairs* 1: 229.

Slaughter, Anne-Marie. 1995. International Law in a World of Liberal States. *European Journal of International Law* 6: 503.

Slaughter, Anne-Marie, Andrew S. Tulumello, and Stephan Wood. 1998. International Law and International Relations Theory: A New Generation of Interdisciplinary Scholarship. *American Journal of International Law* 92: 367.

Snidal, Duncan. 1985. Coordination versus Prisoners' Dilemma: Implications for International Cooperation and Regimes. *American Political Science Review* 79: 923.

Spanish Royal Decree. [1898] 1901. (Apr. 23). In *Papers Relating to the Foreign Relations of the United States,* 774. Washington, D.C.: U.S. Government Printing Office.

Spence, A. Michael. 1973. Job Market Signalling. *Quarterly Journal of Economics* 87: 355.

Spinoza, Benedictus de. 1958. *The Political Works: The Tractatus Theologico-*

Politicus in Part, and The Tracatatus Politicus in Full. Ed. and Trans. A. G. Wernham. Oxford: Clarendon Press.

Sprout, Harold, and Margaret Sprout. 1966. *The Rise of American Naval Power 1776–1918.* Princeton, N.J.: Princeton University Press.

Srinivasan, T. N. 1998. Regionalism and the WTO: Is Nondiscrimination Passé? In *The WTO as an International Organization,* ed. Anne O. Krueger, 329. Chicago: University of Chicago Press.

Steinberg, Richard H. 2002. In the Shadow of Law or Power? Consensus-Based Bargaining and Outcomes in the GATT/WTO. *International Organization* 56: 339.

Steiner, Henry, and Philip Alston. 2000. *International Human Rights in Context: Law, Politics, and Morals.* 2nd edition. Oxford: Oxford University Press.

Stephan, Paul B. 1996. Accountability and International Lawmaking: Rules, Rents and Legitimacy. *Northwestern Journal of International Law and Business* 17: 681.

———. 2002. Courts, Tribunals, and Legal Unification: The Agency Problem. *Chicago Journal of International Law* 3: 333.

Stucky, Scott. 1985. The Paquete Habana: A Case History in the Development of International Law. *University of Baltimore Law Review* 15:1.

Swaine, Edward T. 2002. Rational Custom. *Duke Law Journal* 52: 559.

Swift v. Tyson. 1842. 42 U.S. 1.

Sykes, Alan O. 1991. Protectionism as a "Safeguard": A Positive Analysis of the GATT "Escape Clause" with Normative Speculations. *University of Chicago Law Review* 58: 255.

———. 2004. International Law. In *Handbook of Law and Economics,* ed. A. Mitchell Polinksy and Steven Shavell. Amsterdam: Elsevier.

Takahashi, Sakuye. 1908. *International Law Applied to the Russo-Japanese War.* American edition. New York: Banks Law Publishing.

Tamir, Yael. 1993. *Liberal Nationalism.* Princeton, N.J.: Princeton University Press.

Taylor, Charles. 1996. Why Democracy Needs Patriotism. In *For Love of Country: Debating the Limits of Patriotism,* ed. Joshua Cohen and Martha Craven Nussbaum, 119. Boston: Beacon Press.

Tesón, Fernando R. 1998. *A Philosophy of International Law.* Boulder, Colo.: Westview.

The Batavier II. 1917. 2 Brit. and Col. Prize Cases 432.

The Bermuda. 1865. 70 US (3 Wall) 514.

The Marie Glaeser. 1914. 1 Brit. and Col. Prize Cases 38.

The North Sea Fisheries Convention, Convention between Great Britain, Belgium, Denmark, France, Germany, and the Netherlands, for regulating the Police of the North Sea Fisheries. 1882 (In Consolidated Treaty Series 160: 219).

The Paquete Habana. 1900. 175 US 677.

The Peterhoff. 1866. 72 US (5 Wall) 28.

The Springbok. 1866. 72 US (5 Wall) 1.

The Suez Canal Convention. 1888. Convention between Great Britain, Austria-Hungary, France, Germany, Italy, the Netherlands, Russia, Spain, and Turkey, Respecting the Free Navigation of the Suez Maritime Canal (In Consolidated Treaty Series 171: 241).

The Young Jacob and Johana. 1798. 1 C. Rob. 20.

Thomas, Daniel C. 1999. The Helsinki Accords and Political Change in Eastern Europe. In *The Power of Human Rights: International Norms and Domestic Change,* ed. Thomas Risse, Steve Ropp, and Kathryn Sikkink, 205. Cambridge, England: Cambridge University Press.

Thomas, Hugh. 1997. *The Slave Trade: The Story of the Atlantic Slave Trade, 1440–1870.* New York: Simon and Schuster.

Thucydides. 1982. *The Peloponnesian War,* ed. T. E. Wick. Columbus, Ohio: McGraw-Hill.

Trask, David F. 1981. *The War with Spain in 1898.* New York: Macmillan.

Trebilcock, Clive. 1981. *The Industrialization of the Continental Powers, 1780–1914.* New York: Longman.

Trebilcock, Michael J., and Robert Howse. 1999. *The Regulation of International Trade.* 2nd edition. London: Routledge.

Turlington, Edgar. 1936. *Neutrality: Its History, Economics and Law, the World War Period.* Volume 3. New York: Columbia University Press.

United Nations Development Programme. 2002. *Human Development Report 2002: Deepening Democracy in a Fragmented World.* New York: Oxford University Press.

United Nations, Office of the High Commissioner for Human Rights. 2003. Online. Available at www.unhchr.ch/pdf/report.pdf.

United States Department of State. 1988. *Study and Report Concerning the Status of Individuals with Respect to Diplomatic Immunity in the United States, Exhibit B, prepared in pursuance of the Foreign Relations Authorization Act, Fiscal Years 1988–89, Pub L No 100-204, § 137.* Washington, D.C.: Government Printing Office.

Verzijl, J. H. W., W. P. Heere, and J. P. S. Offerhaus. 1992. *International Law in Historical Perspective.* Volume 11. Boston: M. Nijhoff.

Vienna Convention on the Law of Treaties. 1969. (May 23). Art. 56, 1155 U.N.T.S. 331, 345.

Viner, Jacob. 1950. *The Customs Union Issue.* New York: Carnegie Endowment for International Peace.

Waltz, Kenneth Neal. 1979. *Theory of International Politics.* Reading, Mass.: Addison-Wesley.

Walzer, Michael. 2000. Governing the Globe: What Is the Best We Can Do? *Dissent* fall: 44.

Weil, Prosper. 1983. Towards Relative Normativity in International Law? *American Journal of International Law 77*: 413.

Weinberg, Gerhard L. 1980. *The Foreign Policy of Hitler's Germany: Starting World War II 1937–1939*. Chicago: University of Chicago Press.

Weiss, Edith Brown. 2000. Strengthening National Compliance with Trade Law: Insights from the Environment. In *New Directions in International Economic Law: Essays in Honour of John H. Jackson*, ed. Marco Bronckers and Reinhard Quick, 457. The Hague: Kluwer Law International.

Wendt, Alexander. 1999. *Social Theory of International Politics*. New York: Cambridge University Press.

Westcott, Allan F., et al. 1947. *American Sea Power since 1775*. Chicago: J. B. Lippincott.

Westlake, John. 1910. *International Law*. Volume 1. Cambridge, England: Cambridge University Press.

Wilson, Clifton E. 1967. *Diplomatic Privileges and Immunities*. Tucson: University of Arizona Press.

Wolfke, Karol. 1964. *Custom in Present International Law*. Wroclaw, Poland: Prace.

Woolsey, Theodore Dwight. 1901. *Introduction to the Study of International Law*. 6th edition. New York: Charles Scribner's Sons.

Yoo, John C. 1996. The Continuation of Politics by Other Means: The Original Understanding of War Powers. *California Law Review 84*: 167.

———. 2000. The Dogs That Didn't Bark: Why Were International Legal Scholars MIA on Kosovo? *Chicago Journal of International Law 1*: 149.

Young, H. Peyton. 1998. *Individual Strategy and Social Structure: An Evolutionary Theory of Institutions*. Princeton, N.J.: Princeton University Press.

Young, Iris Marion. 2000. *Inclusion and Democracy*. Oxford: Oxford University Press.

INDEX

Canada, 149

cannon-shot rule, 59, 65. *See also* territorial seas doctrine

Carr, Edward Hallett, 170–71

Carter, Jimmy, 122

cheap talk. *See* international law rhetoric

China
and ambassadorial immunity, 57
Franco-Chinese conflict, 48
and human rights law, 117, 124
Sino-Japanese War of 1894, 48

Civil War (U.S.), 46–48, 52–53, 168

Clinton, Bill, 5, 214, 219

CNN, 213, 220

coercion
and bilateral prisoner's dilemma, 32
and coincidence of interest, 29
and cooperation, 117–19
and human rights law, 115–19, 134
and international agreements, 88–90
and multinational international law, 35
and the territorial seas doctrine, 60, 62, 66
and treaties, 28, 120, 133

coincidence of interest
and bilateral prisoner's dilemma, 30, 32
and coercion, 29
fishing vessel game theory, 27–28
free ships, free goods, 53–54
Genocide Convention, 111
human rights law, 111–12, 134
international agreements, 88–90
multinational international law, 35
and the territorial seas doctrine, 62, 66
and treaties, 28, 120, 133

cold war, and human rights law, 115, 121

comity, 23, 61–62, 66, 68, 183

communications, and multilateral treaties, 86–87

compliance (international law). *See also* *specific treaties*
bureaucracies for compliance, 104–6
and cooperation, 104
and coordination, 104
and customary international law, 100
and human rights, 120–21
and international law scholarship, 83–84, 100
and moral obligations, 165, 200–203
and rational choice, 9–10, 100, 102

and reputation, 100–104
and state self-interest, 104, 192
theories for, 15, 100–104

Comprehensive Test Ban Treaty, 89

consent, 189–93

consideration doctrine, 98

Constitution (U.S.), 198, 211–13

continuous voyage, 47–48, 50, 51

contraband, and the London Naval Conference, 51

Convention against Torture and Other Forms of Cruel, Inhuman, and Degrading Treatment, 108, 123

Convention on the Elimination of All Forms of Discrimination Against Women, 108, 115, 131

Convention on the Prevention and Punishment of the Crime of Genocide, 98, 108, 111, 131

Convention on the Rights of the Child, 108

Conybeare, John A. C., 143

cooperation
in bilateral prisoner's dilemma, 29–32
and coercion, 117–19
and enforcement of sanctions, 162
in European Community human rights law, 126
focal points, 41–42
and human rights law, 112–15
and international agreements, 84–85
and international law rhetoric, 176–77
multilateral, 35, 162
and multilateral prisoner's dilemmas, 36
and multilateral treaties, 86
and treaties, 97, 104, 119

coordination
and battle of the sexes games, 33–35
and bilateral prisoner's dilemma, 33
and customary international law, 85
and GATT, 144
and international agreements, 84–85
and international law rhetoric, 175
in multilateral treaties, 87–88
and multinational international law, 35
multistate coordination games, 37
and treaty compliance, 104

Corn Laws, 136

corporations, 5, 104–5, 187–88, 191, 210

the Holy See, 89
Honduras, 122
hostage crisis. *See* Iran
Hovering Acts, 63
Hughes, Charles Evans, 169
Human Rights Committee (of ICCPR),
    127
human rights law. *See also individual states*
    and Amnesty International, 120
    and coercion, 115–19, 134
    and coincidence of interest, 111–12, 134
    and the cold war, 115, 121
    and cooperation, 112–15, 117–19
    and economic sanctions, 118
    in the European Community, 126
    and the *Filartiga* decision, 132–33
    and Human Rights Watch, 120
    and international law, 111–12, 117, 134
    and international law rhetoric, 125
    and NATO, 116–17, 122
    and NGOs, 123–26
    and state self-interest, 7, 108–10, 117
    treaties. *See* treaties, human rights
human rights treaties. *See* treaties, human
    rights
Human Rights Watch, 120
Hume, David, 186
Hungary, 192

IBM, 211
ICC (International Criminal Court), 205,
    206, 215–16
ICCPR (International Covenant on Civil
    and Political Rights). *See also* human
    rights law; *individual states*
    and international law, 124
    and international law rhetoric, 169
    and NGOs, 127
    ratification of, 108
    and RUDs, 111–12
    and RUDs (table), 129
ICTY (International Criminal Tribunal for
    the Former Yugoslavia), 116
Indonesia, 124
Industrial Revolution, and tariffs, 136
innocent passage, 62
institutionalism, 16–17
intellectual property, 159–60
international agreements, 84–85, 87–90, 91–
    95, 98

International Atomic Energy Agency, 86
International Court of Justice, 96
International Covenant on Civil and
    Political Rights. *See* ICCPR
    (International Covenant on Civil and
    Political Rights)
International Covenant on Economic,
    Social, and Cultural Rights, 108
International Covenant on the Elimination
    of All Forms of Racial
    Discrimination, 108
International Criminal Court (ICC), 205,
    206, 215–16
International Criminal Tribunal for the
    Former Yugoslavia (ICTY), 116
international law. *See also* customary
    international law
    changes to, 40–43, 197–99
    and comity, 23
    compliance with. *See* compliance
    (international law)
    and consent, limits of, 189–93
    and contract law, 119
    and corporate law, 187–88
    and cosmopolitan duty, 14
    and domestic law, 195
    enforcement of. *See* enforcement
    and the European Community, 5
    and game theory, 11–12, 13
    and GATT, 157–58, 161
    human rights law. *See* human rights law
    and the ICCPR, 124
    and international trade, 135
    legal obligations. *See* legal obligations;
        opinio juris
    moral obligations. *See* moral obligations
    nature of, 3, 225–26
    and nonlegal agreements, 82
    obligations under, 186–89, 194
    pacta sunt servanda. See pacta sunt
        servanda
    and rational choice, 3–4, 7–8
    rhetoric. *See* international law rhetoric
    scholarship. *See* international law
        scholarship
    and slavery, 107
    and the standard of civilization, 128–30
    and the state, 4–5
    and state borders, 11–12
    state self-interest. *See* state self-interest

nineteenth-century trade treaties, 140, 142
special obligations, 83
treaties, 17, 21
legislative participation (treaties), 91–94
letters of intent, 90–91, 98, 203
liberal democracies. *See also* cosmopolitan duty
anticosmopolitan sentiments in, 215–19
foreign policy, 213, 222–23
and global government, 223–24
and human rights law, 109–10, 124
and human rights treaty ratification, 130–32
and the ICC, 205–6
ICCPR RUDs, 127–30
and international law, 134
and international legal obligations, 194
and treaties, 111, 127–32
Lincoln, Abraham, 47–48
Locarno Treaties, 168
London Naval Conference, 51–52
Lourenco Marques (port), 49–50
Luban, David, 214

Malta, 89
The Marbrouck (ship), 75
Médecins sans Frontières, 211
Mexican War, 70
Mexico, 149
MFN (most favored nation), 141–43, 149–50
middle powers, 222
Milosevic, Slobodan, 116, 118
Moi, Daniel arap, 123
moral obligations
and changes to international law, 197–99
and citizen well-being, 193–97
and compliance, 165, 200–203
and consent, 189–93
and domestic law, 199
and economic sanctions, 192
and international law rhetoric, 190–91
and international law scholarship, 185
and *pacta sunt servanda*, 189
of states, 14, 186–89
and treaties, 205

moralism, and international law rhetoric, 181–84
Morel, Edmund, 125
Morgenthau, Hans, 170, 186
most favored nation (MFN), 141–43, 149–50
Mozambique, 49–50
multilateral prisoner's dilemmas, 36, 87, 135, 145, 149–50. *See also* bilateral prisoner's dilemma
multilateral trade negotiations, 145–47
multilateral treaties, 85–88, 107–8, 135
multinational international law, 35–38
multistate prisoner's dilemmas. *See* multilateral prisoner's dilemmas
Munich Agreement, 179
Museveni, Yoweri, 123
Myanmar, 124, 131

NAFTA, 5, 91, 149
Nagel, Thomas, 208
Napoleonic Wars, 72, 73, 136
nationalism, 186
NATO, 86–87, 116–17, 122
natural law, 26
Nazi-Soviet pact, 168
NGOs (nongovernmental organizations), 123–27
Niebuhr, Reinhold, 170–71
nineteenth-century trade treaties, 135–43
nongovernmental organizations (NGOs), 123–27
nonlegal agreements, 81–82, 84, 94–95, 99, 115
nontariff barriers, 147–49
North American Free Trade Association. *See* NAFTA
North Atlantic Treaty Organization. *See* NATO
Norway, 61–62, 168

OAS, 122–23
OPEC, 81, 87
opinio juris, 15, 23–26, 38–39, 69, 189
Orange Free State, 49
Ottoman Empire, 111
Oxfam International, 211

Smith, Adam, 136
soft law, 81
Somalia, 110, 214
South Africa, 118
Soviet Union. *See also* Russia
 disintegration of, 4, 5
 and GATT, 149
 and the ICCPR, 131
 and international law rhetoric, 168
 Nazi-Soviet pact, 168
Spain, 60–61, 64, 114, 118. *See also* Spanish-
 American War
Spanish-American War, 48–49, 52
Sparta, 167
State Department (U.S.), 105–6
state self-interest
 as basis for international law, 3, 13–14,
 202, 225–26
 and compliance under international law,
 192
 and cooperation, 126, 203
 and cosmopolitan duty in the U.S., 205–
 6
 and customary international law, 39–40,
 42–43, 133
 defined, 6–7
 and foreign aid, 110
 and GATT, 138–39, 145, 154
 and global government, 223
 and human rights law, 7, 108–10, 117
 and ICCPR ratification, 128
 and international law rhetoric, 13–14,
 170–72, 174, 181, 184
 and international trade, 138–39
 and the *Paquete Habana* ruling, 76
 and protectionism, 162
 and the territorial seas doctrine, 66
 and treaties, 104, 138–39, 192
Sudan, 214
Sweden, 58, 112, 113, 220–23

Tanzania, 123
tariffs. *See* trade barriers
telecommunications, 100–101
terms-of-trade externalities, 138
territorial boundaries, 42, 64
territorial seas doctrine, 59–66
Test Ban Treaty, 94, 217
Thirty Years' War, 113

three-mile limit. *See* territorial seas
 doctrine
Thucydides, 167, 174
torture, 24, 108, 111, 123, 132
trade barriers, 136–40. *See also* GATT
 (General Agreement on Tariffs and
 Trade); protectionism
Transvaal, 49
treaties. *See also specific treaties*
 and ambiguity in international law, 31
 and bilateral prisoner's dilemma, 139
 bureaucracies for compliance, 104–6
 and coincidence of interest, 28
 compliance. *See* compliance
 (international law)
 and consent in international law, 190–92
 and customary international law, 23
 defined, 81
 and executive powers, 91, 94
 human rights. *See* treaties, human rights
 and international law scholarship, 83–84
 and legalization (of international
 agreements), 17, 21
 legislative participation, 91–93, 94
 MFN, 141–42
 and moral obligation, 205
 multilateral. *See* multilateral treaties
 and reputation, 101–4
 and retaliation, 100–101
 RUDs. *See* RUDs (reservations,
 understandings, and declarations)
 and state self-interest, 104, 138–39, 192
 and the territorial seas doctrine, 63–64
 Vienna Convention on Treaties, 88, 95–
 98
treaties, human rights, 28, 107, 120–21, 130–
 34
Treaties of Westphalia, 113–14, 119
Treaty of Moscow, 89, 91–93
Treaty of Rome, 149–50
Treaty of Sèvres, 103
Treaty of Versailles, 90, 94, 103, 168, 179
tribunals, 153–54, 157
Turkey, 46, 103, 110, 178

Uganda, 123–24
United Kingdom. *See* Britain
United Nations
 and cosmopolitan duty, 208
 and customary international law, 23

Lightning Source UK Ltd.
Milton Keynes UK
UKOW041216200812

197788UK00003B/1/P